Looking at disability through a sociocul[...] [...] book continues his much needed efforts to center the lives of persons with disabilities as an issue of human rights that should concern us all. He demonstrates how our communities can be both inclusive and equitable, articulating a much needed approach to Disability Studies that rests on diversity and inclusion. Urban planning, institutional design, disability rights discourse and other aspects of Disability Studies should be rooted in recognizing the non-monolithic nature of persons with disabilities (PWD). This book represents an important intervention for educators, policymakers, and activists who wish to contribute to a more just world by deepening understanding and humanizing the lived experiences of PWD.

- **Diana J Fox**
Professor of Anthropology, Founding Editor,
Journal of International Women's Studies, Bridgewater State University

An indispensable resource for scholars, activists, and anyone committed to understanding the complex landscape of disability, *The Lexicon of Disability Studies* offers a comprehensive journey into the nuanced intersections of language, culture, and identity. With meticulous scholarship and a keen eye for inclusivity, this book not only unpacks the terminology of disability but also challenges readers to critically engage with power dynamics and societal norms. A must-have addition to any library, its pages resonate with wisdom, empathy, and a profound commitment to fostering a more inclusive society.

- **Prof. Nilika Mehrotra**
The Centre for the Study of Social Systems,
Jawaharlal Nehru University, New Delhi

Going beyond, the present work is more than a mere collection of terms; it is a reflection of the dynamic and evolving nature of Disability Studies capturing the richness of the domain and encompassing medical, social, cultural, and legal perspectives. Every expression is carefully crafted to offer a clear definition, historical context, and contemporary relevance, making it an indispensable resource for students, scholars, practitioners, and others engaged in the dialogue about disability.

- **Prof. Anil Kumar Aneja**
Head, Department of English, University of Delhi

The Lexicon of Disability Studies

Vivek Singh

BLACK EAGLE BOOKS
Dublin, USA | Bhubaneswar, India

Black Eagle Books
USA address:
7464 Wisdom Lane
Dublin, OH 43016

India address:
E/312, Trident Galaxy, Kalinga Nagar,
Bhubaneswar-751003, Odisha, India

E-mail: info@blackeaglebooks.org
Website: www.blackeaglebooks.org

First International Edition Published by
Black Eagle Books, 2024

THE LEXICON OF DISABILITY STUDIES
by **Vivek Singh**

Cover & Interior Design: Ezy's Publication

ISBN- 978-1-64560-572-0 (Paperback)
Library of Congress Control Number: 2024944547

Printed in the United States of America

Acknowledgements

This book is a collective effort of mine and my dedicated research scholars, who have been instrumental in enriching the academic field. I discussed the idea for this book with Ms. Nitu Mukherjee and Mr. Harsh Prasad, whom I had the pleasure of teaching the basics of Disability Studies. This inspired me to create a book that would be beneficial for students, researchers, and teachers interested in this field. I am deeply grateful to Nitu and Harsh for their significant contributions in shaping and editing this book wherever necessary.

I would also like to extend my heartfelt thanks to my research scholar, Mr. Rishabh Kumar, who has always been ready to assist me. His meticulous editing of the bibliography and other necessary revisions have been invaluable. Additionally, I am thankful to Ms. Pallavi and Ms. Sudeshna Mukherjee, who were always available to assist with checking citations and other details. I extend my heartfelt gratitude to Ms. Neha, Mr. Atul, and Ms. Ragini for their meticulous review of the draft.

I am deeply appreciative of Prof. Nilika Mehrtotra and Diana J. Fox for taking the time from their busy schedules to write the book blurb. Your endorsement, Prof. Mehrtotra and Dr. Fox, holds significant meaning for me.

I am sincerely thankful to Prof. Anil Kumar Aneja for graciously agreeing to write the foreword despite his demanding responsibilities. Your contribution is invaluable to this work.

Special thanks to Satya Pattanaik for generously allowing me the time needed to complete the manuscript.

Thank you all for your unwavering support and encouragement throughout this journey.

This book would not have been possible without the help of many others who contributed to shaping my ideas, especially the classroom environment where these ideas often originate. I am also grateful to my friends who consistently encourage me to undertake challenging projects and support me unconditionally.

Lastly, I want to express my deepest appreciation to my family, who continuously motivate me to keep working hard. My wife, Pragya, deserves special mention for her understanding and patience, as I am often engrossed in my academic world, leaving little time for her. Thank you for your unwavering support and understanding.

Foreword

As society progresses towards an enhanced under-standing and acceptance of an inclusive worldview, the field of Disability Studies has emerged as a crucial academic and social discipline, offering insights that challenge preconceived notions and advocate for the rights and dignity of persons with disabilities. This lexicon stands as a testimony to this progress, providing a comprehensive resourceof the language and concepts that characterize our engagement with disability.

Going beyond, the present work is more than a mere collection of terms; it is a reflection of the dynamic and evolving nature of Disability Studies capturing the richness of the domain and encompassing medical, social, cultural, and legal perspectives. Every expression is carefully crafted to offer a clear definition, historical context, and contemporary relevance, making it an indispensable resource for students, scholars, practitioners, and others engaged in the dialogue about disability.

This scholarly book, meticulously crafted as an instructive resource by Dr. Vivek Singh, serves to elucidate critical terms associated with disabilities. Designed as a potential textbook, its systematic exploration of key concepts, offers substantial value to a diverse readership, including students, research scholars, and educators engaged in Cultural Studies, with a particular emphasis on Disability Studies.

While navigating the pages of this lexicon, readers will encounter terms that highlight the intersectionality of disability, recognising how it intersects with race, gender, sexuality, and other facets of identity. This comprehensive approach underscores the importance of viewing disability not as a monolithic experience, but rather, as a multifaceted aspect of human diversity.

In the Indian context, interest in Disability Studies has surged following the implementation of theRights of Persons with Disabilities Act (RPwD) 2016 and the National Education Policy (NEP) 2020, leading many universities to incorporate dedicated courses on the subject. This development has created a growing demand for comprehensive educational resources that can support both teaching and learning in this burgeoning field.

For researchers, this book offers a structured and accessible introduction to the key terms and concepts that underpin Disability Studies. It enhances understanding, fosters critical thinking, and equips readers with the knowledge necessary to engage thoughtfully with the subject matter. The systematic approach ensures that even beginners can grasp the complexities of the terminology while providing clear and comprehensive definitions, historical context, and contemporary relevance. Thus, the present work becomes an invaluable reference for scholars enabling them to navigate the academic discourse of Disability Studies with confidence.

Educators will benefit from the book's instructional design, which facilitates effective teaching and learning. The structured layout and in-depth analysis of terms make it a practical tool for designing course curricula, preparing lectures, and guiding classroom discussions. By providing a reliable and authoritative resource, this book helps educators to convey complex concepts in a lucid manner.

Further, this lexicon serves as a call to action. By fostering a deeper understanding of the language and concepts related to disability, it encourages readers to become advocates for change. It challenges us to think critically about the ways in which language informs our perceptions and interactions, as well as to use this knowledge to promote equity and inclusion.

To sum up, this book is designed to meet the needs of a diverse and growing readership. It is an essential resource for anyone engaged in the study or teaching ofDisability Studies. As interest in this area of research continues to rise, the following pages will undoubtedly become a cornerstone in the academic landscape, supporting the intellectual pursuits of students, scholars and educators alike.

Prof. Anil Kumar Aneja

Introduction

Disability has often been marginalized and overlooked. It is considered a minority issue despite its significant impact on millions of lives worldwide. Tom Shakespeare highlights that while only about fifteen percent of the population may identify as disabled, the true scope of disability reaches far beyond this statistic, encompassing over a billion people globally. Disability is a multifaceted and complex phenomenon, with many lives intersecting with it in various ways. Understanding disability requires grappling with its ontology and epistemology, which can be challenging due to its dynamic nature. Disability is not a static condition but rather a social experience in constant transition, evolving either positively or negatively over time. Many people may not be born with impairments but may acquire them through accidents, illnesses, or the aging process. Disability is closely intertwined with aging, as evidenced in the field of gerontology, where disability becomes increasingly prevalent among older people. As people age, they may experience a decline in physical or cognitive functioning, leading to various forms of impairment and disability. This highlights the pervasive nature of disability across the lifespan and underscores the need for a comprehensive understanding of its complexities. Understanding disability is crucial not only for those directly involved in Disability Studies but for everyone across various disciplines. The social model of disability broadens our understanding by highlighting that pregnancy, for instance, can be considered a form of disability due to the limitations it may impose on people. Thus, familiarity with the basics of disability is essential for comprehensively discussing and addressing other identities and social issues, such as gender, caste, class, race, ethnicity, and tribal affiliations.

By delving into the complexities of disability, people can gain insights into its intersections with other aspects of identity and society. This knowledge enables more inclusive and informed discussions and actions across various fields. This book is written with clarity and accessibility at its core, ensuring its suitability for students and scholars from various backgrounds. It aims to demystify the disocurse of disability and encourage curiosity among students, fostering a more inclusive and accepting attitude towards disability within society. By promoting understanding and reducing fear or apprehension about disability, people can engage more confidently and respectfully with people who have disabilities. This not only enhances social interactions but also contributes to building a more inclusive and equitable society where everyone's needs and experiences are valued and respected.

Throughout history, disability has often been viewed through various lenses, each shaping how society perceives and responds to it. The medical model of disability, for instance, characterizes disability as a personal deficiency or impairment that needs to be remedied or treated. Within this framework, people with disabilities are often seen as lacking full human capacity, and the focus is on finding ways to overcome or manage their impairments. Similarly, the religious model of disability attributes disabilities to divine punishment for perceived wrongdoing or moral flaws. This perspective extends beyond physical conditions to include judgments about an individual's character and worthiness. Both the medical and religious models place the burden of disability on the individual, overlooking broader social and environmental factors that contribute to disability. In contrast, disability scholars and activists advocate for a social model of disability, which posits that disability is not solely the result of individual impairments but is largely shaped by societal barriers and injustices. According to scholars like Colin Barnes, addressing disability requires challenging the social and cultural environments that perpetuate exclusion and discrimination against people with disabilities.

Disability Studies reframes the discourse around disability by examining the meanings, stigmas, and symbols associated with disabled bodies. Rather than viewing disability as a problem to be cured or fixed, Disability Studies interrogates the prejudices and stereotypes that marginalize people with disabilities. It seeks to dismantle systems of exclusion and promote a more inclusive society where all people, regardless of ability, can participate fully. As Tobin Siebers highlights, the presence of disabled people in discussions fundamentally alters the culture and nature of those discussions. Disability Studies brings new perspectives to contentious debates, such as those surrounding abortion, assisted suicide, and genetic research, by foregrounding the experiences and perspectives of disabled people. In doing so, it challenges conventional thinking and fosters greater understanding and empathy towards people with disabilities.

The aim of this book is to shed light on disability as a cultural and minority identity, offering insights for students, researchers, and educators who are interested in exploring the complexities of cultural and minority identities. It is crucial to recognize that disability is not an inherent biological or natural trait but rather a dynamic social category that has the potential to reshape societal structures. Rather than viewing disability solely through the lens of social control, it is important to acknowledge its multifaceted nature, encompassing both positive and negative dimensions. Without delving into the intricacies of disability, our understanding may be limited, leading to misconceptions and negative outcomes. By reframing our perspective, we can appreciate disability as a significant aspect of identity formation. Tobin Siebers emphasizes that disability identity should not be viewed through a solely negative lens. Instead, disability offers a unique lens through which people navigate their experiences and identities. By embracing disability as a part of human diversity, we can foster a more inclusive and understanding society that celebrates the richness of all identities. Through this exploration, we can deepen our understanding of disability and its role in shaping individual experiences and societal dynamics. In his writing, Tobin Siebers delves into the complex nature of disability, highlighting both its positive and negative aspects. He suggests that feeling comfortable in one's own skin is a desirable state, as it implies a sense of self-acceptance and confidence. However, he acknowledges that this comfort can lead people to struggle with imagining themselves in different circumstances, including those involving disability.

Siebers suggests that disability serves as a reminder of the fragility inherent in the human condition. It underscores the reality that people are susceptible to change, deterioration, and mortality over time. This notion challenges the perception of disability solely as a negative experience, instead framing it as an intrinsic part of the human experience that encompasses both vulnerability and resilience. The lives of people with disabilities have undoubtedly undergone significant transformation in recent years. While strides have been made towards inclusivity in many schools and institutions, there still exist prevalent beliefs and practices that perpetuate exclusionary principles. For instance, public transportation systems often remain inaccessible to people with disabilities, hindering their mobility and independence. Despite advancements, remnants of religious and medical paradigms persist in shaping societal attitudes towards bodies marked with differences.

This book endeavors to shed light on key concepts such as access, humanity, ethics, institutions, invisibility, and minority, etc. which are often overlooked or disconnected from the discourse of disability. By exploring these concepts through the lens of Disability Studies, the book aims to challenge prevailing assumptions and foster a deeper understanding of the complex interplay between disability and society. It seeks to bridge the gap between academic discourse and lived experiences, offering valuable insights for students, scholars, and educators engaged in Disability Studies. Moreover, the book adopts an interactive and engaging language, making it accessible to beginners and encouraging interest in the field of Disability Studies. By employing clear and relatable language, it aims to demystify complex concepts and stimulate curiosity among readers from various disciplines. In doing so, it promotes interdisciplinary dialogue and collaboration and highlights the relevance of Disability Studies across academic domains and societal contexts.

Since 2010, my engagement in this field has provided me with opportunities to interact with students and educators worldwide, fostering a deep understanding of the intricate nuances surrounding disability discourse. This journey has inspired me to pen this book, driven by a desire to illuminate several crucial points:

a)   Distinguishing between disability and disease is paramount, as they represent distinct phenomena with unique implications for people' lives and societal perceptions.

b)   Exploring the direct relationship between disability and aesthetics reveals how societal norms and perceptions shape the aesthetic value assigned to different bodies.

c)   Understanding the theory of 'affect' is essential for engaging with disability discourse, as it sheds light on the emotional and experiential dimensions of disability.

d)   While terms like 'differently abled' are often used as euphemisms, they may inadvertently reinforce the dichotomy between ability and disability, perpetuating harmful stereotypes.

e)   The interchangeable use of terms such as 'disabled,' 'crippled,' 'handicapped,' and 'impaired' overlooks their nuanced meanings and implications, contributing to societal misconceptions.

f)   Metaphors used to describe people with disabilities can exacerbate stigma and marginalization, further complicating societal perceptions of body diversity.

g)   Disability is not a monolithic identity but a diverse spectrum of experiences and realities, challenging simplistic categorizations.

h)   The notion of human perfection is a fallacy, as no

individual embodies flawless physical or cognitive attributes.

i) Different sensory impairments, such as blindness or deafness, entail distinct experiences and implications, necessitating nuanced understanding and accommodation.

j) Distinguishing between being disabled and being impaired is crucial, as each condition entails unique challenges and experiences that require holistic consideration.

k) Comprehensive understanding of disability necessitates exploration of its multifaceted nuances and complexities embedded within societal, cultural, and historical contexts.

l) Disability is dynamic and context-dependent, evolving over time and across cultures, challenging static definitions and perceptions.

m) Stigma associated with mental disabilities often goes unnoticed, highlighting the need for heightened awareness and inclusive practices.

n) Exploring the experiences of parents of disabled children is essential for a more inclusive understanding of disability, acknowledging their unique perspectives and challenges.

o) Despite inclusive principles, many educational institutions fail to translate them into practice, highlighting the persistent barriers to accessibility and inclusion.

p) Assistive technologies can both empower and disable people, underscoring the importance of critical examination and ethical considerations in their development and implementation.

q) Environmental ethics and disability ethics may not

always align, necessitating careful consideration of the intersecting ethical dimensions inherent in disability discourse.

r)   The concept of disability is inherently contextual, influenced by various factors such as cultural norms, linguistic barriers, and social environments.

s)   Representations of disability in media and literature play a significant role in shaping societal perceptions and redefining the narratives surrounding disability.

t)   The sexualization of disabled people perpetuates harmful stereotypes and misconceptions, underscoring the need for nuanced understanding and respectful portrayal.

u)   Disability is not a moral issue, and the association of moral values with disability perpetuates prejudiced beliefs and unjust treatment of people with disabilities.

v)   Aesthetic standards contribute to the discrimination and marginalization of people with disabilities, reinforcing societal norms of beauty and normalcy.

w)   Disabled people are not 'freaks,' and the construction of the 'freak' archetype is a social construct rooted in ableist ideologies and stereotypes.

x)   Capitalism and neoliberalism intersect with the discourse of ability to perpetuate exclusion and marginalization of disabled people, highlighting systemic inequalities and injustices.

Drawing from the wealth of ideas and insights discussed, *The Lexicon for Disability Studies* serves as a comprehensive exploration of disability across diverse cultures and contexts. It aims to provide readers with an introduction to the multifaceted concept of disability, inviting them to delve deeper into its complexities and implications. Through a curated selection of terms,

The Lexicon offers readers a nuanced understanding of disability, encompassing various cultural perspectives and lived experiences. Each entry in *The Lexicon* serves as a gateway to further exploration, encouraging readers to engage with a breadth of knowledge and firsthand accounts related to disability. By offering Suggested Reading and resources, the lexicon empowers readers to expand their understanding and delve into specific topics of interest. Whether exploring the social model of disability, examining the intersectionality of disability with other identities, or delving into the experiences of people living with disabilities, the lexicon provides a starting point for deeper inquiry and reflection. By fostering curiosity and interest in Disability Studies, *The Lexicon for Disability Studies* seeks to promote awareness, empathy, and inclusivity. It invites readers to interrogate prevailing narratives and challenge societal norms, ultimately contributing to a more equitable and inclusive society for people of all abilities.

Suggested Readings:

Shakespeare, Tom. *Disability: The Basics.* Routledge. London and New York. 2018.

Siebers, Tobin. *Disability Theory.* The University of Michigan Press. Ann Arbor, 2008.

Ableism

Ableism is a term that encapsulates the prejudiced attitudes and discriminatory behaviors directed towards people with disabilities by those deemed as able-bodied within society. It originates from ingrained societal norms dictating what is considered "normal" ability. This pervasive concept significantly contributes to the creation of barriers that hinder the full participation and inclusion of people with disabilities in various aspects of life. Terry defines ableism as "the collection of beliefs and behaviors that endorse unequal treatment based on observable or presumed disparities in physical, mental, or behavioral attributes" (Terry 1996:4–5). This definition highlights how ableism manifests through both conscious and subconscious actions, perpetuating unequal treatment and marginalization of people with disabilities. It is crucial to recognize that ableism not only affects people with disabilities but also extends its reach to other marginalized groups within society. By understanding and addressing ableism, we can work towards dismantling systemic barriers and fostering a more inclusive and equitable society for all.

Suggested Readings:

Bartlett, Peter. *Judging Disability: The Problem of Ableism.* Nottingham University, Student Human Rights Law Centre, 1997, http://www.nottingham.ac.uk/law/hrlc/hrnews/may97/bart.htm. Accessed 24 September 2021.

Davis, Lennard. *Enforcing Normalcy: Disability, Deafness, and the Body.* Verso, 1995.

McRuer, Robert. "Compulsory Able-Bodiedness and Queer/Disabled Existence." *Disability Studies: Enabling the Humanities*, edited by Sharon L. Snyder et al., Modern Language Association, 2002, pp. 88-99.

Access

The concept of access delineates the interaction between people with disabilities and their physical surroundings. Access, in this context, denotes the "opportunity, permission, or right" to approach people or things, encompassing the ability to acquire something. It encompasses endeavors to adapt infrastructure and technology to accommodate diverse human needs. Access also alludes to capability—the capacity to enter a university campus and operate electronic devices like laptops and mobile phones. The overarching goal of promoting access is to foster a more inclusive society, facilitating increased opportunities for social, economic, political, and cultural participation. However, people with disabilities often face barriers to access. A cursory examination of university buildings, buses, trains, banks, and stations reveals that these spaces are typically not designed with the needs of people with disabilities in mind. Consequently, disabled people encounter difficulties in navigating these environments. A significant challenge arises from the prevailing societal perception that there is nothing inherently wrong with the design or social infrastructure. This lack of acknowledgment perpetuates a cycle where people with disabilities are held responsible for their struggles, overlooking the fundamental issue—the absence of inclusive design during construction. Rather than recognizing the oversight in architectural planning, there tends to be a misguided belief that disabled people must address the problem themselves. This mindset disregards the fact that the onus should be on those responsible for constructing buildings and public facilities. Initiatives by disability movements and government awareness programs aim to bring about positive changes in infrastructure. Despite these efforts, a persistent challenge remains in altering the prevailing mindset that perpetuates discriminatory beliefs. The need for broader societal awareness and understanding is crucial to fostering genuine inclusivity in both social and architectural spheres.

The Rights of Persons with Disabilities Act of 2016 mandates strict adherence to specified rules and conditions, particularly concerning the construction of buildings. According to the Act, no establishment can obtain permission for building construction if the proposed structure does not comply with the regulations set forth by the Central Government under section 40. Additionally, no establishment is granted a certificate of completion or allowed occupancy unless it strictly adheres to these regulations. Specifically addressing access to transportation, the Act outlines that the appropriate Government must implement measures to ensure facilities for persons with disabilities at key transit points such as bus stops, railway stations, and airports. These facilities should align with accessibility standards covering parking spaces, toilets, ticketing counters, and ticketing machines. Moreover, the Act emphasizes the need for access to all modes of transport, including retrofitting older modes wherever technically feasible and safe for persons with disabilities, economically viable, and without necessitating major structural changes in design. The Act also underscores the importance of accessible roads to facilitate the mobility necessary for persons with disabilities. Despite the concerted efforts by the government and disability advocacy movements, a substantial number of people with disabilities continue to face challenges in accessing various infrastructures. Access, in this context, is not solely about physical barriers but also involves power dynamics. The inability to access social infrastructure can render people invisible, as it limits their opportunities to address concerns. Achieving access is a crucial step toward promoting equality in society.

Access becomes a pivotal concept when delving into the realms of rights and opportunities, particularly in the context of economic and social justice. Conversations surrounding these issues often center around the discourse of access, encompassing various facets such as entry to employment, the legal system, healthcare, education, and transportation. As we engage in discussions about access, it becomes evident that external obstacles hinder our ability to reach essential resources. This discourse prompts a deeper exploration of equality, where arguments sometimes arise suggesting that people with physical limitations cannot be considered equal to their able-bodied counterparts. These viewpoints prompt contemplation on whether the focus should be on eliminating external barriers or on modifying our bodies. It becomes clear that the essence of access lies not in curing disabilities but in realizing social potential through the removal of external hindrances. Importantly, the concept of access is rooted in societal concerns rather than individual ones, emphasizing the need to address external barriers rather than altering people themselves. To grant access is to empower people and redefine the very notion of citizenship. In a welfare state, the assurance is that citizens possess the right to autonomy. Conversely, in a neoliberal society, there is a shift towards valuing independence and individualism as prerequisites for good citizenship. Unfortunately, in this neoliberal framework, people with disabilities often face discrimination, perceived as burdens on society. The neoliberal society's transition from a cooperative to a competitive ideology exacerbates this marginalization of people with disabilities, challenging the inclusivity and equality that access seeks to achieve.

Accessibility is the proactive effort to create an environment that is welcoming, achievable, and available to people of diverse abilities. It involves modifying surroundings to increase the likelihood that people can actively engage in society in a meaningful way. It is crucial to distinguish accessibility from participation; while participation is the actual act of taking part, accessibility is about providing the freedom to enter and utilize a given situation. Whether one chooses to exercise that freedom is a matter of personal choice. Accessibility is not a singular action but a state of liberty—a liberty to access and utilize an environment. The level of enjoyment of this liberty depends on individual preferences and desires. It is an interactive concept, meaning that an environment might be accessible to one person and not to another. This prompts the important question of whether a given environment is accessible to people with disabilities. Thus, careful consideration is necessary to ensure that environments are inclusive and accommodating for everyone.

Suggested Readings:

Pechansky, R., and C. Thomas. "The Concept of Access: Definition and Relation to Customer Satisfaction." *Medical Care*, vol. 19, no. 2, 1981, pp. 127–140.

Steinfeld, Edward. "Major Issues in Developing Building Standards." *Barrier-Free Environments*, edited by Michael Bednars, Dowden, Hutchinson and Ross, Strouds-burg, PA, 1977.

Accident

Accidents represent a crucial aspect of the disability discourse, as they can occur unpredictably and affect people from all walks of life. In the common perception, accidents are often identified as significant contributors to the occurrence of disabilities, potentially resulting in permanent impairments. Following such incidents, people typically seek medical attention to regain their previous level of functioning. Road accidents, in particular, stand out as a leading cause of disability for a substantial number of people. An accident is essentially an unexpected event leading to physical trauma. The fact that anyone can become a victim of an accident underscores the importance of comprehending the dynamics of disability. This understanding not only adds depth to the discourse on disability but also introduces complexities, as it emphasizes the diverse and unforeseeable nature of the circumstances that can lead to impairment. Various opportunities exist for disabled people or those who have lost limbs or specific body parts. In historical contexts, such as World War II, unique abilities were recognized, like employing deaf people in noisy environments due to perceived suitability. However, societal perspectives on disability have evolved. Traditionally, disabilities were often interpreted as divine intent, carrying religious significance in ancient times. The industrialization era marked a shift, viewing non-normative bodies as accidental deviations. This perception aligns with a medicalized viewpoint, treating disabilities as anomalies requiring correction. Contrary to the medicalized perspective, Disability Studies challenge the notion that disabilities are accidental, asserting that they constitute a valuable diversity essential to society. Embracing the disability experience is crucial, as it challenges the prevailing idea of accidents and introduces tension within the field of Disability Studies. Recognizing disability as a fundamental aspect of diversity contributes to a more inclusive and enlightened societal perspective.

Suggested Readings:

Cooter, Roger, and Bill Luckin, editors. *Accidents in History: Injuries, Fatalities, and Social Relations.* Amsterdam: Rodopi, 1997.

Davis, Robert. *Death on the Streets: Cars and the Mythology of Road Safety.* Leading Hawes, UK: Leading Edge, 1993.

Monin, Lydia, and Andrew Gallimore. *The Devil's Gardens: A History of Landmines*. London: Pimlico, 2002.

Tenner, Edward. "Accidents in History: Injuries, Fatalities, and Social Relations (Review)." *Technology and Culture*, vol. 41, no. 1, Johns Hopkins University Press, 2000, pp. 117–120, https://doi.org/10.1353/tech.2000.0039.

Accommodation

In Disability Studies, the term "accommodation" holds significant importance, particularly in the context of making societal adjustments for people with disabilities. The Rights of Persons with Disabilities Act (RPWD Act) of 2016 addresses the concept of "reasonable accommodation." According to the Act, reasonable accommodation involves making necessary and appropriate modifications and adjustments to ensure that people with disabilities can equally enjoy and exercise their rights, without imposing a disproportionate or undue burden in specific cases. The Act explicitly mandates that the appropriate government must take necessary measures to guarantee reasonable accommodation for people with disabilities. This essentially means creating an environment that is conducive to the needs of people with disabilities. It is crucial to recognize that providing reasonable accommodation is not an act of charity; rather, it is a fundamental right of people with disabilities. Denying reasonable accommodation is explicitly considered an act of discrimination. Despite the clarity of the Act in emphasizing the provision of reasonable accommodation according to individual requirements, it does not explicitly define what "reasonable" means in the context of accommodation. Reasonable accommodation, in the context of supporting people with disabilities, entails ensuring that existing facilities and practices are accessible to all. Unfortunately, people with disabilities often face discrimination due to misconceptions that accommodations would be burdensome and impede productivity. However, empirical research indicates that, in the long run, accommodations are often less costly and more advantageous than initially perceived. Moreover, disability accommodations can extend benefits beyond the individual, positively impacting the broader society.

Commonly, employers may be hesitant to provide accommodations, fearing financial strain and disruptions to workflow. Nevertheless, evidence suggests that accommodating people with disabilities can be a cost-effective strategy. Creating an inclusive work environment not only fosters diversity but can also lead to increased productivity and employee satisfaction. The concept of "reasonable accommodation" is undergoing a paradigm shift, moving beyond the notion of mere concessions. Disability Studies challenges traditional definitions and advocates for a universal design approach. This approach seeks to create environments that are inherently accommodating to the widest range of users, eliminating barriers for everyone. For instance, if an employee requests the option to work from home, an employer can view this not as a singular exception but as an opportunity to implement telecommuting services. This accommodation not only supports people with disabilities but also caters to a broader audience, including those with various needs, preferences, or situations (e.g., parents, caretakers, or people with heavy responsibilities). Embracing a universal design philosophy can lead to greater overall satisfaction among employees and result in cost savings for the company.

The shift towards a universal design approach not only promotes inclusivity but also acknowledges the broader societal benefits of accommodating diverse needs. Employers stand to gain not only in terms of legal compliance but also through enhanced productivity, employee satisfaction, and a more resilient and adaptable workplace.

Suggested Readings:

Karlan, Pamela S., and George Rutherglen. 'Disabilities, Discrimination, and Reasonable Accommodation'. *Duke Law Journal*, vol. 46, no. 1, JSTOR, Oct. 1996, p. 1, https://doi.org10.2307/1372964.

Activism

Barnes and Mercer define 'Disability Activism' as the collaborative political involvement carried out by and for people with disabilities. Longmore emphasizes the crucial significance of collective political efforts in providing a platform for and influencing the futures of disabled people. In this framework, activism involves both direct and confrontational methods, exemplified by actions like obstructing traffic or entrances to draw attention to accessibility concerns. On the other hand, advocacy, often used synonymously with activism, entails less confrontational approaches, such as participating in petition signing campaigns.

Both disability activism and advocacy play crucial roles, each with its own distinct approach. Disability activism operates with a sense of urgency, employing high-confrontation tactics to attract media attention and public support. While this heightened visibility can be effective, it also carries the risk of triggering police repression and legal actions. On the other hand, advocacy takes a more cautious approach, acknowledging these potential risks and opting for a lower degree of confrontation. The aim is to navigate challenges carefully while still working towards the common goal of improving the lives of people with disabilities.

In a democratic framework, activism becomes a cornerstone, defining the active role of citizens in pursuing the common good. Citizenship, characterized by informed decision-making and collaboration for societal interests, aligns seamlessly with the concept of social activism. In the context of disability advocacy, this social activism contributes to gradual improvements in services and policy changes that protect the rights of people with disabilities. Both approaches have their merits, and their combined efforts can lead to positive societal change.

Suggested Readings:

Charlton, James. *Nothing about Us without Us: Disability, Oppression and Empowerment.* Berkeley; University of California Press, 1998.

Oliver, M. *Disability, Citizenship and Empowerment.* Milton Keynes, UK; Open University Press,1993.

Aesthetics

Aesthetic judgments can perpetuate ableism by centering around a normative concept of beauty and physical perfection. The term "aesthetics" originated in the 18th century within discussions about perception and emotion. Immanuel Kant, for instance, differentiated between judgments based on an object's conceptual aspects (such as its purposes, intentions, and utility) and aesthetic judgments. The former leans toward objectivity and is contingent on how the object serves practical needs, while the latter is more about the subjective experience of the object. Kant introduced the idea of disinterested pleasure in aesthetic judgment, contrasting it with the self-interested pleasure derived from an object's practical utility. Despite the subjectivity inherent in aesthetic judgment, there is a paradoxical desire for validation from others. People who experience disinterested pleasure hope that others will share similar perceptions and feelings about the same object. This paradox highlights the influence of collective approval in what is known as bourgeois aesthetics.

Bourgeois aesthetics, in turn, is implicated in ableism. Despite the apparent subjectivity of aesthetic judgment, it is not free from social attitudes and cultural contexts. Normative values and cultural discourses create a framework that excludes diverse views on the body, beauty, and sensory satisfaction. As an example, Diego Velazquez's 17th-century painting "Las Meninas" features a court dwarf placed beside the Infanta, creating a stark contrast that emphasizes societal norms of youthful perfection. Aesthetic judgment becomes intertwined with pre-existing normative definitions of perfection and beauty, acting as a barrier against embracing bodily diversity. The aesthetic theories surrounding the sublime in the 18th century were, in part, influenced by discourses in medical sciences, as noted by Michel Foucault in his exploration of the "politics of health." Edmund Burke, in his work, *Philosophical Enquiries into the Origin of Our Ideas of the Sublime and Beautiful (1757)*, posits that the sublime surpasses beauty, leading to heightened consciousness and action compared to the passive nature of beauty. Burke associates the sublime with the release from physical pain and the subsequent recognition of health, often overlooked in our daily lives. This release from pain transcends reason, resulting in the profound experience of the "joys of convalescence." Within the Gothic tradition in art and literature, the sublime is intricately linked to the portrayal of otherness, encompassing diverse body types, forms, and psychologies. Characters in Gothic fiction often exhibit bodily deformities, mental disabilities, or psychic distress, as seen in works like Mary Shelley's, *Frankenstein (1818)*or Edgar Allan Poe's *The Fall of the House of Usher (1839)*. Ruth Anolik suggests that while the Gothic tradition presents human differences as monstrous, it paradoxically argues for the humanity of these monstrous figures.

David Mitchell and Sharon Snyder introduce the concept of "narrative prostheses," referring to images of monstrous, diseased, or disabled bodies symbolizing a redemptive narrative of bodily renewal. This trope, rooted in Western tradition and tracing back to Oedipus's self-blinding, links a disabled body with moral corruption. The death of the monster is then portrayed as the restoration of health and moral order, serving as a form of pedagogy. This aesthetic strategy appeals to the audience's emotions, offering a model of bodily perfection and normalcy juxtaposed with the 'otherness' from which the audience may distance themselves. In the realm of modernist art, the grotesque and deformed bodies are frequently employed as metaphors for the conditions of modern life, such as alienation, fragmentation, ennui, monotony, and stress. Expressionist portraits, like those portraying demented urban denizens, or T.S. Eliot's depiction of a blind and neurasthenic figure in *The Waste Land* (1922) exemplify this trend. Even Nazi "Entartete Kunst" ("degenerate art") exhibitions in the late 1930s utilized modernism's depiction of "defective" or dysgenic people in expressionist and surrealist art as a metaphor for the perceived decline of Western culture.

Contrary to the endorsement of "Great German

Art Exhibitions" by Hitler, which idealized Aryan bodies in rural settings, modern art often utilizes disability as a symbolic representation of moral flaws. This narrative trope frequently centers around the recuperation of moral strength and philosophical wisdom by an able-bodied hero during a period of convalescence. Notable examples include the narrator of Edgar Allan Poe's *The Man of the Crowd* (1840) des Esseintes in Joris-Karl Huysman's *ARebours* (1884) and Friedrich Nietzsche's *Thus Spoke Zarathustra* (1883). These characters' recovery from illness marks the beginning of a renewed enthusiasm for life.

In the realm of modern aesthetics, theories play a taxonomic role akin to biopolitics. Biopolitics, evident in 18th and 19th-century medical discourses, rationalizes, categorizes, and demarcates bodies and cognitive registers. Similarly, aesthetic theories seek to organize, rationalize, and distribute sensory experiences. A prevalent idea in modern aesthetics is that formalist theories, such as literature's defamiliarization, reveal the devices of language, like metaphors, rhymes, and narrative frames. This mirrors the concept of disabilities unsettling the notions of bodily normalcy and averageness. AtoQuayson refers to the discomfort experienced by able-bodied people in the presence of disabilities as 'aesthetic nervousness,' acknowledging the contingency of bodies. Lennard J. Davis argues that, as disability transcends identity categories, it disrupts biopolitical and disciplinary regimes attempting to fix and categorize bodies through medical discourses, institutions, and technologies. Both aesthetic defamiliarization and disability deconstruction critique the theory of mimesis, challenging the idea of a pre-given ideal and perfect world that can be represented in art. The process of delineating and constituting what constitutes a 'normal body' results in nontraditional bodies becoming more visible in visual culture. Historically, eugenicists and race theorists used photography to catalog aberrant or dysgenic "types," while films like "The Black Stork (1917)" provided documentary evidence justifying practices such as fetal euthanasia, sterilization, and incarceration. Aesthetic values were employed to define "lives not worth living," removing these people from the public eye to prevent their appearance in public spaces. In the United States, "ugly laws" were enforced in various cities. Modern reform movements, encompassing suffragism, birth control, women's health, workplace improvements, and settlement houses, often drew inspiration from eugenicist ideas about health, genetic purity, and ability. Both high art and mass culture played a role in reinforcing the preoccupations of 18th and 19th-century medical and social sciences with enforcing normalcy. The intersection of aesthetics and biopolitics contributes to the process of human disqualification, placing nontraditional bodies at risk of discrimination, abuse, and even death.

In a paradoxical twist, contemporary aesthetics and biopolitics play a role in bringing visibility to bodies that deviate from traditional norms, such as those with disabilities. The concept of "disability aesthetics," as articulated by Siebers, underscores the shaping influence of disability on aesthetics and the artistic practices of people with disabilities. These artists engage in a critical examination of ableism embedded in modern aesthetics. For instance, when activists from the American Disabled for Accessible Public Transit (ADAPT) abandoned their wheelchairs to crawl up the U.S. Capitol stairs in support of the Americans with Disabilities Act, it constituted an act of transgression—a blend of civil disobedience and a form of performance art highlighting disability issues. This performative dimension blurs the lines between art and activism, a characteristic feature of much contemporary disability aesthetics. Consider a performance artist born without arms who poses nude, emulating classical sculpture to redefine the beauty of a disabled female body. In doing so, she challenges societal norms and places beauty at the intersection of gender and disability. Neurodiversity activist Amanda Baggs, an autistic artist, uses a software interface to translate her written text into an electronic voice, urging the audience to comprehend her language of repetitions, scratchings, and humming. The blind photographer Evgen Bavcar takes a unique approach by photographing classical sculptures and archaeological sites, physically engaging with the objects through touch rather than relying on visual perception. Similarly, deaf people reject the label of disability, considering themselves a linguistic minority. Poets like Clayton Valli, Debbie Rennie, Patrick Graybill, and Ella Mae Lentz create works in American Sign Language, directly addressing a non-hearing audience.

The diverse expressions within disability aesthetics challenge the conventional aesthetic discourse that historically marginalized people with disabilities, relegating them to dungeons, freak shows, or asylums—a darker aspect of Enlightenment thinking. This resistance and challenge to normative aesthetics highlight the rich and varied experiences of people with disabilities, breaking away from a singular, homogenous narrative.

Suggested Readings:

Armstrong, Tim. *Modernism, Technology and the Body: A Cultural Study.* Cambridge, UK: Cambridge University Press, 1998.

Blum, Virginia L. *Flesh Wounds: The Culture of Cosmetic Surgery*. Berkeley: University of California Press, 2003.

Brueggemann, Brenda Jo. *Lend Me Your Ear: Rhetorical Constructions of Deafness*. Washington, DC: Gallaudet University Press, 2002.

Davis, Kathy. *Reshaping the Female Body: The Dilemma of Cosmetic Surgery*. New York: Routledge, 1995.

Davis, Lennard. *Enforcing Normalcy: Disability, Deafness, and the Body*. New York: Verso, 1995.

Gilman, Sander L. *Creating Beauty to Cure the Soul: Race and Psychology in the Shaping of Aesthetic Surgery*. Durham, NC: Duke University Press, 1998.

Gilman, Sander L. *Making the Body Beautiful: A Cultural History of Aesthetic Surgery*. Princeton, NJ: Princeton University Press; Doubleday Select Bookclubs, 1999.

Kant, Immanuel. "What Is Enlightenment?" *On History*, edited by Lewis White Beck. Indianapolis, IN: Bobbs Merrill, 1963.

Romm, Sharon. *The Changing Face of Beauty*. St. Louis, MO: Mosby Year Book, 1992.

——— "Feminist Theory, the Body and the Disabled Figure." *The Disability Studies Reader*, edited by Lennard Davis. New York: Routledge, 1997.

Thomson, Rosemarie Garland. *Extraordinary Bodies: Figuring Physical Disability in American Culture and Literature*. New York: Columbia University Press, 1997.

Affect

Affect and effect are two distinct concepts in the realm of emotions and bodily experiences. While affect is often used interchangeably with feelings and emotions, it is associated with theories that seek to understand experiences that defy simple binary explanations.

Scholars like Eve Kosofsky Sedgwick, Adam Frank, and Brian Massumi have delved into affect theory, arguing that conventional cultural theories fall short in explaining certain bodily experiences that transcend language. According to psychoanalytic theory, language is insufficient to explain everything, especially when it comes to bodily experiences that may be expressed, shared, generated, or concealed beyond the constraints of language. This is particularly pertinent in the realm of Disability Studies, where scholars are drawn to affect theory due to its ability to account for feelings of shame that may exist outside the boundaries of language. Unlike approaches that seek to overcome shame, disability scholars view it as having transformative potential, enabling expression and shaping identity.

A significant contribution of affect theory is its impact on our understanding of power dynamics. Traditionally, affecting someone implies influencing their mental and emotional state, suggesting that the person eliciting emotions holds power over the affected individual. However, affect theory nuances this perspective by highlighting that the one feeling emotions is not necessarily passive. In saying, "I moved her," there is uncertainty and ambiguity. On the other hand, expressing, "I was moved by her," suggests a clearer attribution of affective response to an external stimulus, emphasizing the impact of the other person's outward expressions on one's feelings. When we acknowledge being affected by someone, it implies a reciprocal exchange, where our feelings are drawn by the inner emotions of the other person. For example, the sentence "I was touched by the change in his behavior" describes a positive and empathetic relationship, emphasizing the mutual influence of emotions.

From the perspective of Disability Studies, the concept of affect poses significant concerns, as it historically subjected people with disabilities to perceptions of pity, charity, and admiration. It raises the question of whether people deemed to lead tragic lives actually view their experiences in the same light. The observer often imposes their emotions onto others, and the uncontrollable nature of affect means one cannot ascertain how their emotions are being received or interpreted. Pity, ostensibly well-intentioned, may elicit anger and disgust from the person it is directed towards.

Affect is closely entwined with the issue of stigma. Consider the phrase "she spoke in an affected manner," commonly used to criticize behaviors deemed unnatural. This criticism is evident, for instance, when a gay man's behavior, commonplace among gay people, is deemed atypical for a straight man. Disabled people may adopt presumed normative gestures to navigate social interactions without being stigmatized. However, the irony lies in labeling one's mannerisms as 'affected' while deeming someone else's similar affect as normal. This reflects a paradox in the affective, social realm, assuming that natural behaviors are either spontaneous or consciously learned and assumed.

Susan Schweik argues that aesthetics and affect are inherently intertwined, projecting normative physical appearance as a standard. She further demonstrates how the public reacts with aversion to the appearance of people considered 'freaks,' driven by the discomfort of experiencing affective states such as disgust and shame. In essence, affect, in terms of emotional experience, is intricately linked to the challenging fate of bodies perceived to deviate from norms of aesthetic expression in public spaces.

Suggested Readings:

Frank, Arthur. *The Wounded Storyteller: Body, Illness, and Ethics.* Chicago: University of Chicago Press, 1995.

Clough, Patricia Ticineto, ed. *The Affective Turn: Theorizing the Social.* Durham, NC: Duke University Press. 2007.

Tomkins, Silvan S. *Affect, Imagery, Consciousness: The Complete Edition: Two Volumes.* New York: Springer, 2008.

Schweik, Susan: *The Ugly Laws: Disability in Public.* New York: NYU Press, 2009

Aging

Ageing is an ongoing and complex process characterized by age-related physiological changes, such as puberty and menopause. Conditions like hypertension and coronary artery disease often manifest as people age, impacting both physical and mental well-being. This biological perspective, however, overlooks the broader influences of economic, political, social, and cultural factors on a person's ability to fulfill social roles. It's essential to recognize that, akin to disability, ageing is not just a biological phenomenon but also a cultural one. Ageing is frequently stereotyped as a period of decline and deterioration, but it should be understood as a dynamic process with various dimensions. One notable convergence of ageing and disability occurs in the concept of frailty. The challenges associated with frailty highlight the interconnected nature of these two experiences.

Historically, cultural attitudes towards ageing have evolved. In the seventeenth century West, puritans revered the elderly, considering ageing a sacred pilgrimage to God. Religious motivations drove reformers who assisted both the elderly and people with disabilities. However, during the Victorian age, societal focus shifted towards youth as a symbol of growth and expansion. This era saw the segregation of people with disabilities into mental asylums, diminishing their autonomy. Medical interventions aimed at eradicating disability led to decreased visibility of this population. Similar to people with disabilities, older people faced ridicule and pity during certain periods. Notably, special schools were established for children with disabilities, emphasizing societal efforts to address diverse needs. The intersection of Disability Studies and gerontology highlights the shared challenges and experiences of these groups. Understanding ageing requires acknowledging its multi-faceted nature, encompassing both biological and cultural dimensions. The historical context reveals shifts in societal attitudes towards the elderly and people with disabilities, emphasizing the importance of recognizing the interconnectedness of these experiences.

Aristotle posited that the ageing process represents a phase of withdrawal and internal reflection. Conversely, Cicero and Montaigne argued that ageing serves as a period for self-discovery. Plato viewed ageing as the cultivation of wisdom and a transformation of the soul, while Leonardo da Vinci perceived it as a time of grappling with the inevitable physical decline. Charcot, in contrast, regarded ageing as a latent stage for diseases emerging in old age. Many philosophical perspectives link ageing with illness, a theme evident in early medical theories emphasizing the connection between disease and ageing. Modern medical theories, however, emphasize enhancing the functional health of older people, leading to a prevalent focus on health promotion. This emphasis has given rise to the misconception that age-related changes inherently signify illness or disease. While such changes are universal, their impact varies depending on individual circumstances.

The discourse on ageing intersects with that of disability, as ageing is an unavoidable aspect of human existence. Disability Studies scholars like Stiker argue that we are all "Temporarily Abled Bodies" (TAB), as everyone eventually confronts the consequences of ageing. Ageing brings about functional limitations, mobility restrictions, speech incoherence, and various challenges that no one can escape. Physiological changes occur at each life stage due to ageing, but individual experiences may differ, resulting in distinct issues such as heart disease, hypertension, nerve failure, and more. These factors contribute to limitations in movement and the ability to lead a normal life. Architectural obstacles and attitudinal barriers further hinder active participation in socialization for ageing people.

The Americans with Disabilities Act (ADA) of 1990 outlines specific criteria to define disability. Firstly, an individual must have a physical or cognitive impairment that significantly limits major life activities, hindering active participation in social functions and impeding the achievement of life goals. Secondly, a person with a history of impairment or thirdly, someone perceived by others as having such an impairment can be considered disabled. Disability is commonly associated with old age, whether it is a temporary or prolonged condition. Some people develop disabilities later in life, while others experience them early on and age with a disability. This duality creates varied perspectives, as some people fear the potential disabilities that may come with aging, while children with permanent disabilities may anticipate increased challenges as they grow older.

Modern technological advancements and improved medical facilities have led to a significant reduction in the overall mortality rate. However, the rising life expectancy brings concerns about an increased likelihood of experiencing disability. In the United States, there is a growing population of people aging with a disability. Unlike in the past, where disabled people often had shorter lifespans, advancements in medical care now allow those with lifelong disabilities to live longer than previously expected.

The relationship between ageing and disability is dynamic and influenced by various social factors, including religious beliefs, economic conditions, and literary representations. These factors contribute to evolving perspectives on the intersection of aging and disability over time. Religion has played a pivotal role in shaping societal attitudes towards the elderly and disabled people over the centuries. In the early 17th century, Puritan influence fostered a culture of respect for elders and a commitment to charity for those with disabilities. Ageing was viewed as a spiritual journey towards God, instilling a sense of reverence for the elderly. However, a significant shift occurred during the Victorian era, driven by Darwin's "survival of the fittest" theory from *On the Origin of Species* (1859). This theory, emphasizing the superiority of an ideal bodily structure, led to the marginalization of disabled and elderly people. Society began perceiving only the young generation with perfect physical features as fit to ensure the survival of the future race.

The 20th century witnessed advancements in medical science, aiming to eliminate genetic defects and deformities. Despite not achieving complete success, these efforts led to the confinement of disabled people in asylums and special schools, limiting their social exposure. In more recent times, a positive transformation has taken place. Aging people are now perceived as active, strong, and capable of living independently, dispelling the notion of pity associated with old age. Similarly, the perception of disabled people has undergone a positive shift. This evolving perspective has gradually unraveled the negative stereotypes and stigmas deeply ingrained in our cultural consciousness regarding ageing and disability.

Ageing can be examined from two distinct viewpoints. From a societal standpoint, ageing signifies the triumph of society in fostering a human population with extended lifespans through advancements in hygiene, improved medical facilities, and enhanced nutrition. Conversely, when viewed at the individual level, ageing encompasses biomedical, psychological, and social dimensions. Throughout the 20th century, various theories emerged to elucidate the phenomenon of ageing, falling into categories such as biological, sociological, and psychological perspectives. As people age, they naturally become more susceptible to a range of health issues, and contemporary medical practices are striving to address these challenges. The medical focus has shifted towards advocating healthy ageing and encouraging an active lifestyle. The vital organs of older people, over time, lose their efficiency, rendering them more susceptible to infections and other ailments. Similarly, disabled people may lack the same immune strength as their non-disabled counterparts due to underutilized organs.

The Disengagement Theory, posited by Cumming and Henry, supports the idea of reduced capabilities and declining health in older people. It suggests that in old age, people gradually detach emotionally and physically from others, transferring responsibilities to the younger generation. However, this perspective has faced criticism for its one-sided focus, as many older people lead active lives. Robert Havighurst's Developmental Theory proposes that older people must accept new roles, acknowledging the loss of their earlier vibrant lifestyle and confronting the inevitability of death. This includes transitioning into roles such as grandparent and widow, necessitating coping with loneliness. Paul Baltes, in 1980, viewed ageing as an ongoing process intertwined with social dynamics, emphasizing individual variations in perspectives on ageing. Elderly people encounter various losses, both psychological and physical, and must adapt to these changes as they age. Rowe and Kahn introduced the concept of "successful ageing," distinguishing between "usual ageing" and a state where elderly people, despite physiological limitations, lead healthy and content lives, actively participating in social activities and maintaining relationships. This perspective underscores the potential prevention of age-related disabilities and diseases through timely measures, attributing many issues to unhealthy lifestyles. However, it does not address disabilities faced in early life.

People with disabilities can age successfully too, challenging stereotypes and highlighting the unique aspects of their aging experience. Unlike the typical challenges faced by older people, disabled people require an environment that accommodates their needs, fostering growth and opportunities. The ageing process for them is intricately linked to societal attitudes, environmental adaptations, and policy changes that can either facilitate or hinder their well-being. In contrast to the general population, disabled people often encounter lower employment rates, leading to a financially strained lifestyle and suboptimal diet. Addressing these issues requires the implementation of policies and measures aimed at improving their overall quality of life.

Ageing is a universal process, but its impact varies based on factors such as financial, physical, and psychological well-being. The Baltimore Longitudinal Study has identified common changes associated with aging, such as reduced height and weight, decreased cerebral blood flow, diminished eyesight, and lower immunity. However, for disabled people, the consequences of aging are more pronounced, manifesting in premature medical, functional, and psychological challenges. Furthermore, disabled people face a higher mortality rate during the aging process compared to the general population. Their increased vulnerability to chronic diseases at younger ages is attributed to barriers in accessing healthcare, developmental disabilities, and environmental factors. Addressing these disparities requires a comprehensive approach encompassing healthcare accessibility, social attitudes, and policies to ensure that disabled people can age with dignity and well-being.

Suggested Readings:

Birren, J., &Schaie, K., eds. *Handbook of the Psychology of Aging*. 5th ed., San Diego: CA, Academic Press, 2001.

Herr, S., & Weber, G., eds. *Ageing, Rights, and Quality of Life*. Baltimore: Paul H. Brookes, 1998.

Janicki, M. P., & Dalton, A. J., eds. *Dementia and Aging Adults with Intellectual Disabilities: A Handbook*. Philedelphia: Francis and Taylor, 1998.

Alienation

Alienation refers to the deliberate withdrawal of affection from someone, often accompanied by indifference or aversion. This phenomenon can extend to people or groups feeling estranged from a society that was once attractive or welcoming. The deprivation of participation in societal activities can contribute to a sense of alienation, and historically, people with disabilities have faced barriers that restricted their full engagement in social life, perpetuated by those in positions of power. Philosophers like Hegel and Marx have explored the concept of alienation in different contexts. Hegel viewed alienation as a fundamental aspect of consciousness throughout history, considering it a necessary precondition for people to discover their true selves. Marx, on the other hand, extensively discussed alienation as the separation of labor from its products.

In the realm of Disability Studies, understanding alienation is crucial, particularly concerning how people with disabilities may feel marginalized due to societal stigma related to their physical conditions. Alienation can also manifest when people with disabilities disconnect their bodies from their personal identities. For instance, someone who was once athletic but loses a limb may feel betrayed by their own body, leading to a withdrawal from society and a struggle to accept the altered physical condition as an integral part of their identity. Interestingly, while there is ample discourse on alienation concerning physical disabilities, there is a noticeable gap in research regarding alienation and its relation to mental illness or cognitive impairment. Exploring this intersection could provide valuable insights into the experiences of people facing these challenges and the societal factors contributing to their sense of alienation.

Suggested Readings:
Jaegi, Rahel: *Alienation.* Columbia University Press, New York, 2014.

Alzheimer's disease

It typically manifests in the later stages of life and falls under the category of conditions known as 'dementias.' As dementia advances, people experience a decline in their ability to independently care for themselves. Moreover, the disease leads to notable alterations in behavior and personality. Despite extensive research, the precise cause of Alzheimer's disease remains elusive.

Suggested Readings:

Alzheimer's Disease International. "Factsheet 3. The Prevalence of Dementia." Alzheimer's Disease International, 1999, www.alz.co.uk.

American Psychiatric Association. Diagnostic and Statistical Manual of Mental Disorders, 4th ed.—text revision. Washington, D.C., 2000.

Audism

In 1975, Tom Humphries introduced the term "audism" to describe the discrimination faced by people who are deaf. Audism, as conceptualized by Humphries, involves the belief in the superiority of people based on their ability to hear or mimic the behaviors associated with hearing. A key aspect of audism is evident in the persistent judgment of deaf people' intelligence and success, often measured against the standards of the hearing culture's language proficiency. Furthermore, audism is not only perpetuated by those outside the deaf community but can also be internalized, with deaf people imposing the same set of standards, behaviors, and values on each other as those demanded by the hearing population. This internalized audism contributes to the oppression of fellow deaf people.The core idea of audism is the privileging of hearing abilities over deafness, and people adhering to these beliefs are referred to as "audists." The prevailing system, where hearing people receive preferential treatment, is termed "institutional audism." This system systematically promotes hearing as the norm, creating an environment that inherently disadvantages deaf people.

In the context of Disability Studies, which challenges assumptions about language being exclusively spoken, audism raises questions about the societal preference for spoken language and the associated biases against non-hearing forms of communication.

Suggested Readings:

Amman, Johann Conrad. *A Dissertation on Speech.* London: S. Low, Marston, Low and Searle, 1873.

Bahan, Ben, and H-Dirksen L. Bauman. *Audism: Toward a Postmodern Theory of Deaf Studies.*Conference presentation at Deaf Studies VI, Orlando, FL, March 2000.

Bauman, H-Dirksen L. "Audism: Understanding the Metaphysics of Oppression." *Journal of Deaf Studies and Deaf Education*, vol. 9, no. 2, 2004, pp. 239-246.

Baynton, Douglas. *Forbidden Signs: American Culture and the Campaign against Sign Language.* Chicago: University of Chicago Press, 1996.

Brueggemann, Brenda Jo. *Lend Me Your Ear: Rhetorical Constructions of Deafness.* Washington, DC: Gallaudet University Press, 1999.

Derrida, Jacques. *Of Grammatology.* Translated by Gayatri Spivak, Johns Hopkins University Press, 1974.

Lane, Harlan. *Masks of Benevolence: Disabling the Deaf Community.* New York: Alfred Knopf, 1992.

Wellman, David. *Portraits of White Racism.* Cambridge, UK: Cambridge University Press, 1993.

Begging

Throughout history and across the globe, people with disabilities have often been unfairly associated with begging, highlighting their marginalized status in society. This phenomenon has persisted for thousands of years, with biblical references recounting instances of Jesus encountering blind people who were begging. In ancient Greece, the harsh practice of killing babies born with disabilities further underscores the historical mistreatment of those with impairments. The Middle Ages witnessed widespread begging by people with disabilities, and even in artistic representations, begging became intertwined with disability. Regrettably, this trend continues today, as people with disabilities often resort to begging due to the limited availability of livelihood opportunities. For many, begging becomes a means of survival, albeit an unfortunate one. It has become a pervasive form of employment worldwide, reflecting the systemic challenges that people with disabilities face in accessing other avenues for income and self-sufficiency.

Exploring the dynamics between people without disabilities and those with disabilities through the lens of begging reveals a complex interplay. The act of begging and the subsequent act of donating unveil inherent inequalities within this relationship. While people who beg assert themselves by making their presence visible, it is crucial to recognize that begging is often a response to a society that professes justice and equal treatment for all. Paradoxically, the practice of begging not only perpetuates the subordinate position of those who beg but also exposes the inadequacies in the discourse surrounding equal opportunities for everyone. It serves as a poignant critique of a society that claims justice and equality while marginalizing a significant portion of its population.

Suggested Readings:

Buck, Dennis S. *Deaf Peddler: Confessions of an Inside Man.* Washington, DC: Gallaudet University Press, 2000.

Covey, Herbert C. *Social Perceptions of People with Disabilities in History.* Springfield, Charles C. Thomas Publisher, 1998.

Monbeck, Michael E. *The Meaning of Blindness: Attitudes toward Blindness and Blind People.* Bloomington Indiana University Press, 1973.

Blindness

Blindness, typically defined as the loss of vision, encompasses both a physical condition and a symbolic operation, as suggested by Paulson. The term takes on varied meanings depending on the context. When someone asks, 'Are you blind?' the inquiry doesn't necessarily question one's literal eyesight but serves as a symbolic operation, implying a lack of perception or understanding. Paulson notes that blindness is often employed metaphorically, acting as a figurative marker for other diminished capacities. For example, stating, 'You are blind when it comes to literature,' uses blindness as a metaphor to convey a deficiency in understanding or appreciation.

In Sophocles' play *Oedipus Rex*, the character Tiresias, a blind prophet, meets Oedipus, the king. Tiresias, despite his physical blindness, possesses the ability to see into the future, while Oedipus, who is not physically blind, remains ignorant of his actions. It is only when Oedipus gains figurative sight and comprehends the truth that he blinds himself. The concept of blindness underwent varying interpretations over different historical periods. In the

Enlightenment era, it became a subject of debate between rationalists and sensualists. In contrast, Mitchell and Snyder argue that during the Middle Ages, blindness transformed into a narrative prosthesis, serving as a storytelling device rather than a debated concept.

Diderot's "Letter on the Blind for the Use of Those Who See" provides a compelling exploration of blindness as a subject in its own right. In medieval times, a prevailing belief held that blindness was a consequence of sin, suggesting that people with disabilities were being punished for past wrongdoing. This perception persisted into the age of industry, where disability became associated with sloth. James Gall, a Scottish educator, declared that a blind person's 'condition is a state of continuous childhood. . . . He can produce for himself neither food nor clothing; and without the unceasing assistance of his friends he would of necessity perish' (1834, 13).

As societal values underwent a transformation in the neoliberal era, the narrative surrounding disability also evolved. The emphasis on collaboration and dependence diminished, giving way to a celebration of independence as a virtue. The ethos of self-reliance became a societal ideal, reinforcing the concept of sighted normalcy and casting aside the earlier notion that disability equated to inherent moral failings or perpetual dependence.

Blind people are often unfairly subjected to negative stereotypes, portraying them as helpless, foolish, or even as beggars. Unfortunately, medical organizations sometimes contribute to this issue by describing blindness as a tragedy or an unfortunate circumstance. Thérèse-Adèle Husson sheds light on the challenging experiences faced by blind people, emphasizing the harsh societal judgment they endure. When these people venture into public spaces, they become the focal point of curious stares, accompanied by hurtful comments such as "What a shame!" or "How unfortunate!" These comments not only perpetuate harmful stereotypes but also contribute to the emotional burden faced by the blind. Astonishingly, some people actively seek out blind people to deliver these disparaging remarks, subjecting them to a barrage of sad exclamations that only serve to intensify the difficulties they already face.

In *Sight Unseen* (1999) by Georgina Kleege, the author shares her personal journey of growing up with progressive vision loss and explores the concept of blindness within a cultural framework. Kleege challenges the prevailing notion presented by Michalko, who views blindness as a deficiency threatening sighted culture. According to Michalko, blind people are compelled to either conform to societal norms by adopting practices that mimic sightedness or risk facing societal rejection. However, Disability Studies' scholars, in contrast, don't perceive blindness as a problem but rather as a facet of human diversity that can be considered an asset. They advocate for a shift in focus from medical practitioners, urging them to move away from defining blindness and instead concentrate on improving the social conditions for blind people. This perspective aligns with Robert McRuer's idea that blindness disrupts conventional sighted culture, challenging its norms.

Rosemarie Garland Thomson also contributes to this discourse by challenging the dominance of visual-centric perspectives, a concept she terms "ocular centrism." The study of blindness, therefore, emerges as a valuable avenue within Disability Studies, offering fresh insights and prompting a reevaluation of research methodologies. Many existing disciplinary practices rely on visually oriented approaches to studying the human body, and blindness prompts a necessary reconsideration of these methods.

Importantly, the exploration of blindness raises critical questions about how sight-centric perspectives contribute to the negative construction of the identities of women, queer people, and people of color. By shedding light on these issues, the study of blindness advocates for a reexamination of the foundational assumptions of modernity to foster better inclusivity. It encourages a broader societal interrogation into prevailing norms, urging a shift towards a more inclusive understanding of human diversity.

Suggested Readings:

Barasch, Moshe. *Blindness: The History of a Mental Image in Western Thought*. New York: Routledge, 2013.

Gleeson, Brendan. *Geographies of Disability*. London: Routledge, 2002.

Kleege, Georgina. *Sight Unseen*. New Haven, CT: Yale University Press, 1999.

Michalko, Rod. *The Mystery of the Eye and the Shadow of Blindness*. Toronto: University of Toronto Press, 1998.

Monbeck, Michael. *The Meaning of Blindness: Attitudes toward Blindness and Blind People*. Bloomington: Indiana University Press, 1973.

Oliver, Michael Henry. *The Politics of Disablement*. London: Macmillan, 1990.

French, Sally. 'Can You See the Rainbow? The Roots of Denial'. *Disability Barriers, Enabling Environments*, edited by J. Swain et al., UK: Open University Press, 1993.

Charity

The term "charity" finds its roots in Christianity, originating from the Latin word "caritas," which embodies the selfless love for fellow human beings. Initially, "charity" encompassed the concept of providing aid and support to the impoverished and needy. Within the Christian framework, the terms "love" and "charity" are often used interchangeably, reflecting the notion that if God loves humanity, humans should reciprocate by loving both God and one another. In the Bible, particularly in Matthew's Gospel, there's a profound emphasis on the equivalence of loving God and loving one's neighbor. This equivalence is highlighted in passages where it's asserted that loving God with all one's heart is tantamount to loving one's neighbor, as both are recipients of God's love. This sentiment is captured in the teachings of Stiker, who references Matthew's Gospel and elaborates on the six "acts of mercy" outlined within it: providing food, offering drink, welcoming strangers, clothing the naked, visiting the sick, and attending to the imprisoned.

Throughout the Middle Ages, these acts of charity were not only integral to Christian doctrine but also became prevalent themes in artistic representations and religious teachings. Iconographical depictions of these acts flourished, serving as visual reminders of the Christian duty to extend compassion and assistance to those in need. Moreover, homilies delivered during this period frequently reinforced the importance of practicing these acts of mercy, underscoring the Christian belief in the interconnectedness of love for God and love for one's fellow human beings.

In the evolution of charity within society, alms emerged as a primary means of demonstrating compassion towards fellow human beings, particularly the impoverished. This transition reflects a movement of resources from the affluent to those in need. Saint John elaborates on this concept by emphasizing that since God is not visibly present, believers must manifest their faith through tangible actions, as prescribed by Matthew's Gospel. During this period, societal expectations placed a burden on the wealthy to contribute significantly to the alleviation of sickness and poverty through monetary donations or material goods. Consequently, institutions dedicated to charitable endeavors proliferated, leading to the establishment of leper houses across Europe. Notably, these efforts extended beyond mere philanthropy; they laid the groundwork for the eventual medicalization of institutions like hospitals, which originally served charitable purposes. However, as societal perspectives evolved, charity began to face criticism. Within the disability movement, activists rejected the notion of charity, advocating instead for their rights. This sentiment was encapsulated in the slogan, "We don't want charity—we want our rights." While acknowledging the aid provided to the sick and impoverished, activists emphasized the necessity of addressing systemic issues rather than relying solely on charitable gestures. Central to their argument was the call for equal civic rights and opportunities for people with disabilities.

It's crucial to recognize that charity and rights are not mutually exclusive concepts but rather interconnected aspects of social justice. Historically, the discourse surrounding rights emerged from critiques of charitable practices, highlighting the need for systemic changes to address underlying inequalities and promote inclusivity within society.

Suggested Readings:

Forrest, Alan I. *The French Revolution and the Poor*. New York: St. Martin's Press, 1981.

Stiker, Henri-Jacques. 'The System(s) of Charity'. *A History of Disability*, edited by Henri-Jacques Stiker and William Translated, University of Michigan Press, 1999.

Communication

According to the Oxford English Dictionary, communication originally referred to interpersonal contact, social interaction, and association. By the 16th century, its meaning expanded to encompass the transmission or exchange of information, knowledge, or ideas. This evolution reflects the pivotal role communication plays in human interaction and the dissemination of knowledge. A comprehensive definition of communication involves any action through which one individual imparts or receives information about another person's needs, desires, perceptions, or knowledge. It is fundamentally a dynamic process of exchanging information, facilitating understanding, and fostering connections between people. Moreover, communication serves as a mechanism for fulfilling social needs, enabling people to establish and maintain relationships within their social spheres.

Beyond its functional aspects, communication also plays a profound role in shaping personal identity and fostering a sense of self. Through communication, people express their thoughts, feelings, and beliefs, contributing to the development and maintenance of their unique identities. Additionally, communication facilitates affiliation with various social groups, providing people with a sense of belonging and connection to broader communities. The debate surrounding whether animals possess language capabilities has persisted, with many arguing that while animals communicate, only humans utilize language. This distinction is often drawn by highlighting examples such as bees' intricate dances to convey information about pollen locations. While such behaviors demonstrate complex communication systems in animals, they fall short of the linguistic complexity observed in human language.

Human language uniquely allows for the conveyance of abstract ideas and concepts through words and sentences. Unlike animals, humans possess the ability to articulate and interpret symbolic representations, enabling the exchange of sophisticated thoughts and expressions. Additionally, humans have the capacity for metacognition, reflecting on and manipulating language itself, a feature not observed in animal communication systems. Various forms of animal communication may indeed substitute for speech, but they lack the comprehensive linguistic structure found in human languages. Sign languages, however, present an interesting parallel to spoken languages. Like spoken languages, sign languages exhibit phonological features, although they differ in their modalities of expression. Sign languages are composed of movements, locations, and hand shapes rather than vowels and consonants, yet they share fundamental linguistic properties with spoken languages. The acquisition of sign language by deaf children from signing parents mirrors the process of spoken language acquisition in hearing children. This similarity underscores the linguistic nature of sign languages and challenges the notion that they are merely gestural or inferior forms of communication.

Despite their linguistic complexity, sign languages have historically been marginalized, particularly in comparison to spoken languages. This bias often stems from misconceptions about the nature of sign languages and the communities that use them. However, growing recognition of the linguistic richness and cultural significance of sign languages is gradually challenging these misconceptions and promoting greater appreciation for their unique expressive capabilities. Imagine a scenario where deaf children are seamlessly integrated into the spoken community, leading to a natural adaptation of communication methods among hearing residents. As more deaf children join this community, sign language gradually becomes prevalent alongside spoken language. This development highlights the community's embrace of linguistic diversity, cherishing both spoken and sign languages as integral modes of communication.

This shift challenges traditional views of communication as a mere transmission of information and instead emphasizes its role in representing shared beliefs and cultural practices. Communication is recognized as a dynamic process that involves not only the exchange of information but also the performance of social and cultural activities. Just as human actions are influenced by their context, language is constantly shaped and reshaped within social and cultural frameworks. Moreover, communication is understood as inherently multimodal, extending beyond verbal expression to encompass gestures, facial expressions, and other forms of bodily interaction. People with disabilities, far from being limited in their ability to communicate, actively engage with a range of material and communicative resources to navigate their environment and interact with others.

Bigelow's work underscores this point by highlighting how parents of blind children achieve intersubjectivity and shared intentionality through coordinated actions rather than shared eye gaze. By aligning their movements with their child's hand gestures, parents establish a rich communicative bond that transcends traditional notions of language and communication. This illustrates the dynamic and adaptive nature of human interaction, where people creatively employ various modalities to engage with the world and connect with others. 'Autistic children are said to lack shared intentionality because they do not track the eye movement of others, but as recent research has shown, their sociality and interest in others are simply achieved by other means, such as physical proximity and verbal engagement' (Akhtar and Gernsbacher 2007:23).

In the realm of Disability Studies, the interaction between people and technology takes on a profound significance, fundamentally reshaping our understanding of communication and human experience. Unlike traditional perspectives that often view technology as a secondary or compensatory aid, Disability Studies acknowledges technology as integral to the human experience—an extension of both the body and the mind. From this perspective, technology is not merely an external tool but an intrinsic aspect of human behavior and cognition. It serves as an extension of the body and mind, amplifying and augmenting human capabilities. This perspective challenges conventional views that segregate technology from human activity, instead recognizing that human activity unfolds within the framework of technology. This holistic understanding of technology's role transforms the very notion of personhood, emphasizing the symbiotic relationship between people and their technological environment. Rather than viewing technology as separate or supplementary, Disability Studies acknowledges its seamless integration into everyday life, shaping and facilitating human interactions and experiences. Furthermore, this perspective highlights the performative nature of human activity within the context of technology. As people engage with various technological tools and platforms, they not only utilize these resources but also contribute to their ongoing evolution and adaptation. In this way, technology becomes an active participant in shaping human behavior and societal norms, blurring the boundaries between the physical and digital realms.

Disability Studies offers a nuanced understanding of the relationship between people and technology, recognizing the interconnectedness and mutual influence between the two. By embracing technology as an extension of the body and mind, Disability Studies expands our conception of human potential and redefines the very essence of personhood in the modern age.

Suggested Readings:

Baynton, Douglas C. *Forbidden Signs: American Culture and the Campaign Against Sign Language*. University of Chicago Press, 1996.

Braithwaite, Dawn O., and Teresa L. Thompson. "Handbook of Communication and People With Disabilities." *Routledge eBooks*, 1999,https://doi.org/10.4324/9781410603647.

Gannon, Jack R. *Deaf Heritage: A Narrative History of Deaf America*.National Association of the Deaf, 1981.

O'Neill, Ynez Viote. *Speech and Speech Disorders in Western Thought before 1600*. Praeger, 1980

Cripple

In the early twentieth century, the term "crip," derived from "cripple," was commonly used as informal slang, particularly to describe people with mobility impairments. However, its usage carried a negative connotation, often serving as a derogatory label intended to shame and stigmatize people based on their physical condition. Journalists frequently employed "cripple" or "crip" as a metaphor, further perpetuating its negative associations. Despite its historical usage as a pejorative term, "crip" has undergone a significant transformation within disability communities. Rather than symbolizing shame or stigma, "crip" has been reclaimed and embraced as a source of pride and cultural identity. People with disabilities advocate for "crip culture" and "crip pride," recognizing the term as a symbol of cultural empowerment and transformation.

In Disability Studies, "crip" is utilized to assert a disability identity and claim space within crip culture. Unlike its previous usage, "crip" no longer categorizes people based on specific impairments; instead, it represents a broader sense of disability identity and solidarity. Some people within disability communities prefer the term "crip" over other labels like "handicapped" or "disabled," viewing it as a more empowering and inclusive descriptor. The embrace of "crip" reflects a shift in societal attitudes towards disability, highlighting the importance of reclaiming language and challenging traditional narratives of disability. By reclaiming and redefining terms like "crip," people with disabilities assert their agency and assertiveness in shaping their own identities and experiences. This linguistic empowerment is an integral aspect of the broader movement towards disability pride and cultural acceptance. Nancy Mairs writes, 'As a lover of words, I like the accuracy with which it describes my condition: I have lost the full use of my limbs'. Another benefit for Mairs is the reaction the word receives:

People—crippled or not—wince at the word cripple, as they do not at handicapped or disabled. Perhaps I want them to wince. I want them to see me as a tough customer, one to whom the fates/ gods/viruses have not been kind but who can face the brutal truth of her existence squarely. As a cripple, I swagger (p. 9).

In the twenty-first century, the term clipping critiques the dominant culture's norms. Carrie Sandhal writes,

Cripping spins mainstream representations or practices to reveal able-bodied assumptions and exclusionary effects. Cripping exposes the arbitrary delineation between normal and defective and the negative social ramifications of attempts to homogenise humanity(2003: 37).

The term "cripple" historically referred to people with locomotor disabilities or those who exhibited a limp while walking. Specifically, it denoted people whose physical impairments predominantly affected their ability to walk, thereby restricting their mobility and often impeding their social interactions. However, its usage has evolved over time and has become widely regarded as offensive and derogatory, particularly within disabled communities and among scholars in Disability Studies.

The term "cripple" is deemed unacceptable due to its negative connotations and its tendency to reduce people to their physical limitations. By labeling someone as a "cripple," focus is shifted solely to their physical appearance and limitations in mobility, disregarding their multifaceted identity and capabilities. This narrow focus perpetuates stereotypes and undermines the diverse talents and contributions of people with disabilities. Furthermore, the term "cripple" is criticized for its narrow scope, as it primarily addresses locomotor disabilities while overlooking other types of impairments present in society. This narrow categorization reinforces a limited understanding of disability and fails to acknowledge the diverse experiences and challenges faced by people with varying types of impairments.

Although "cripple" was once favored by journalists and newspaper editors, its usage has significantly declined as society has become more attuned to the need for respectful and inclusive language. However, with the emergence of Disability Studies and increased awareness surrounding the nuances of language used to describe disabled people, the term has garnered renewed attention and scrutiny. This renewed consideration reflects a broader societal shift towards greater sensitivity and inclusivity in language usage, particularly concerning issues related to disability.

In Simi Linton's essay "Reassigning Meaning," she explores the reclamation and reassignment of terminology used to refer to disabled people. Over time, the term "crippled" underwent a transformation, becoming abbreviated and more commonly known as "crip." Disability Studies scholars, along with the disabled population, began to advocate for themselves, sparking a movement towards embracing crip culture and taking pride in their crip identity. For many, identifying as "crip" became a powerful assertion of existence rather than a mere acknowledgment of impairment. The term shifted focus away from physical limitations, instead emphasizing the assertion of identity and the demand for recognition within society. As a result, many writers and people with disabilities today prefer to be addressed as "crip" rather than using terms like "handicap" or "disabled."

More recently, some people with disabilities have reclaimed the term "cripple," using it as a form of self-identification and as a means of challenging the stigma associated with disability. In academic and activist circles within the field of Disability Studies, the term "cripple" is sometimes used to refer to people who embrace their disability and reject the notion that they need to be "fixed" or "cured" to conform to mainstream societal norms. This perspective has come to be known as the "crip" or "cripple" movement. It is crucial to recognize, however, that the use of the term "cripple" remains contentious and can be deemed offensive by many people with disabilities. Therefore, it is imperative to prioritize the preferences of people when selecting language to describe their disability, ensuring that respect and dignity are maintained. Ultimately, the evolution and acceptance of terminology within the disability community reflect broader shifts in societal attitudes towards disability and the ongoing struggle for recognition, inclusion, and empowerment.

Suggested Readings:

Sandahl, Carrie."Queering the Crip or Cripping the Queer? Intersections of Queer and Crip Identities in Solo Autobiographical Performance." *GLQ: A Journal of Lesbian and Gay Studies*, vol. 9, no. 1–2, Duke UP, Apr. 2003, pp. 25–56. https://doi.org/10.1215/10642684-9-1-2-25.

Zola, I. K. 'Self, Identity, and the Naming Question: Reflections on the Language of Disability'. *Social Science and Medicine*, vol. 36, 1993, pp. 167–173.

Cyborg

The term "cyborg" typically refers to a person who has undergone physiological, electronic, and biochemical modifications, resulting in an altered or augmented state. Originally rooted in science fiction, the concept of the cyborg has expanded to encompass real-world applications, particularly in the context of artificial limbs and prosthetics. However, its usage extends beyond mere technological enhancements; within Disability Studies, the notion of the cyborg serves as a tool to challenge ableist assumptions and explore diverse embodied experiences. Drawing on Donna Haraway's influential work, the cyborg is conceptualized as a figure that transcends traditional boundaries, embodying potent fusions of human and machine. In this sense, the cyborg represents a departure from fixed notions of identity and offers a framework for understanding the complexities of human embodiment. While technology often intersects with notions of normalization, rehabilitation, and cure, scholars within Disability Studies argue that cyborg theory can offer a means to disrupt the rigid boundary between disabled and non-disabled people. By embracing the potential of bionic technologies and other forms of augmentation, the cyborg challenges traditional stereotypes and fosters a more inclusive understanding of disability. The increasing proliferation of bionic technologies holds promise for transforming societal attitudes towards people with physical disabilities. By showcasing the capabilities and possibilities afforded by these advancements, the cyborg serves as a catalyst for reimagining disability and advocating for greater acceptance and integration within society.

Cyborg theory extends its relevance beyond the realm of theoretical discourse, offering valuable insights into the lived experiences of people with disabilities who navigate intimate relationships with technology. This includes people who rely on assistive devices such as wheelchairs, prosthetics, and implants to enhance their mobility and functionality. By examining the intersection of disability and technology through a cyborg lens, researchers aim to unravel the complexities of being a disabled subject within the context of post-industrial power dynamics. The intimate relationship between disabled people and technology underscores the profound impact of technological advancements on shaping disability experiences. Assistive devices serve not only as functional aids but also as integral components of people' identities and lived realities. Through the lens of cyborg theory, researchers delve into the multifaceted interactions between human bodies and technological artifacts, exploring how these relationships influence perceptions of disability and embodiment. Moreover, cyborg theory provides a framework for analyzing disability within the broader context of post-industrial power structures. In an era characterized by technological advancements and shifting socio-political landscapes, understanding the experiences of disabled people requires a nuanced exploration of power dynamics and societal norms. By interrogating the intersections of disability, technology, and power, researchers seek to illuminate the ways in which disabled subjects navigate and negotiate their identities within contemporary society.

The term "cyborg" denotes an individual who has integrated with technology to enhance or extend their abilities. This concept challenges conventional perspectives on disability, which often view it as a fixed and static condition requiring "cure." Instead, the cyborg perspective posits disability as a fluid and socially constructed experience that can be altered and redefined through technological interventions. Although commonly associated with science fiction, the notion of the cyborg also intersects with real-world applications, particularly in the realms of artificial limbs and rehabilitation. Throughout literary history, disabled characters have been depicted utilizing artificial limbs or assistive devices, serving as potent symbols of loss, trauma, and sacrifice.

In literary narratives, artificial limbs often serve as poignant metaphors, reflecting the profound impact of disability on the human experience. For instance, Captain Ahab in Herman Melville's *Moby Dick* loses his leg to a giant whale, with his prosthetic limb symbolizing both physical and emotional loss. Similarly, in Mahesh

Dattani's play *Tara*, the character Tara's artificial leg serves as a stark reminder of the sacrifices she has made in her life. By incorporating artificial devices into storytelling, authors convey the depth of loss and the intensity of emotion experienced by their characters. These literary representations highlight the complexities of disability and challenge societal perceptions of physical difference. In the realm of science fiction, the representation of cyborgs often carries dual meanings, reflecting both the extraordinary superhuman capabilities of the character and the darker implications of technology. On one hand, cyborgs are depicted as possessing enhanced abilities that surpass those of ordinary humans, showcasing feats of strength, agility, and resilience. However, this portrayal also unveils the unsettling reality of how technology can dehumanize people, reducing them to mere mechanical objects and alienating them from society. The centrality of a character with an artificial limb or other technological enhancements can accentuate their perceived otherness, leading to further isolation and marginalization. While they may possess superhuman qualities, they are often objectified and treated as anomalies, perpetuating their sense of detachment from the rest of humanity.

In the context of Disability Studies, cyborgs are people who integrate technologies such as prosthetics, implants, and assistive devices into their bodies to overcome limitations and achieve greater independence. Rather than viewing these technologies as separate objects compensating for deficits, they are seen as extensions of the body that can enhance and transform the individual's abilities. By embracing technology as a means of empowerment, cyborgs challenge traditional notions of disability and redefine what it means to live with physical limitations.

They demonstrate the potential of technological integration to break down barriers and enable people to lead fulfilling and autonomous lives. However, they also raise important ethical questions about the implications of merging human biology with artificial enhancements, prompting critical reflection on the intersection of technology, identity, and humanity.

Suggested Readings:

Donna Haraway, "A Cyborg Manifesto: Science, Technology, and Socialist-Feminism in the Late Twentieth Century," in *Simians, Cyborgs and Women: The Reinvention of Nature* (New York; Routledge, 1991), pp.149-181.

Telotte, J. P. *Replications: A Robotic History of the Science Fiction Film.* University of Illinois Press, 1995.

Warrick, Patricia S. *The Cybernetic Imagination in Science Fiction.* MIT Press, 1980.

Deafness

The term "deafness" encompasses a spectrum of conditions wherein people have difficulty understanding speech solely through auditory means. It encompasses any degree of hearing impairment, ranging from mild to profound. Beyond its literal definition, "deafness" is also employed metaphorically to denote a refusal to listen or learn, reflecting a broader societal perception. Deafness is not solely a medical condition but also a state of being and becoming, shaping people' identities and experiences. Schools designed for deaf students have played a crucial role in fostering a sense of shared identity and culture among deaf communities. These institutions provide a supportive environment where people can communicate and connect with others who share similar experiences.

In Disability Studies, the discourse surrounding

deafness challenges the prevailing pathological model, which views deafness as a deficiency or impairment to be remedied. Instead, Disability Studies scholars focus on exploring the cultural attributes of deafness, recognizing it as a rich and diverse cultural identity. They delve into various aspects of deaf culture, including linguistic practices such as sign language, literature, values, marriage patterns, and community institutions. By studying deaf cultural attributes, Disability Studies' scholars aim to highlight the strengths and resilience of deaf communities while challenging societal norms and attitudes towards deafness. This approach promotes a more inclusive understanding of disability, one that celebrates diversity and recognizes the unique contributions of deaf people to society. Through their research and advocacy, scholars strive to create a world where deafness is not viewed as a deficit, but rather as a vibrant and integral part of human diversity.

Suggested Readings:

Baker, C., and R. Battison, editors. *Sign Language and the Deaf Community.* Silver Spring, MD: National Association of the Deaf. 1980.

Colson, Elizabeth, and Clifford Geertz. 'The Interpretation of Cultures: Selected Essays'. *Contemporary Sociology*, vol. 4, no. 6, SAGE Publications, Nov. 1975, p. 637, https://doi.org10.2307/2064031.

Ladd, Paddy. *Understanding Deaf Culture.* Multilingual Matters, 2003.

Wilbur, Ronnie. "The Deaf Experience: Classics in Language and Education. Harlan Lane (Ed.), Franklin Philip (Trans.). Cambridge, Mass.: Harvard University Press, 1984. Pp. 221." Applied Psycholinguistics, vol. 6, no. 2, 1985, pp. 198–202., doi:10.1017/S0142716400006135.

Deformity

The term "deformity" refers to a significant deviation in the shape, color, or other aspects of the body's appearance from what is considered the community's preconceived norm. The Oxford English Dictionary (OED) defines deformity as "the quality or condition of being marred or disfigured in appearance; disfigurement, unsightliness, ugliness." Deformities can arise from various factors such as accidents, genetic mutations, birth complications, or hormonal anomalies. However, the concept of deformity is highly subjective and context-dependent. It hinges on two presumptions: first, the existence of a standard "normal" body from which deviations are judged, and second, the establishment of societal consensus regarding attributes that constitute deformity. This understanding underscores the influence of social norms and power dynamics in shaping perceptions of bodily appearance.

The perception of deformity varies across cultures and historical periods, reflecting diverse beliefs and value systems. In ancient times, deformity was often associated with ominous signs, demonic influence, or supernatural forces. Some cultures resorted to extreme measures, such as ritualistic killings of deformed infants, based on superstitions and fears. Conversely, certain cultures revered people with deformities, viewing them as possessing special powers or connections to the divine. Deformed people were sometimes elevated to positions of authority, such as shamans or priests, symbolizing a shift in societal attitudes towards deformity.

In contemporary society, attitudes towards deformity continue to evolve, albeit with lingering stigmas and prejudices. Disability rights movements and advocacy efforts have challenged negative perceptions of deformity, advocating for greater acceptance and inclusion of people with diverse physical appearances. Throughout history, attitudes towards deformity have been diverse and often shaped by cultural, religious, and societal beliefs. In Leviticus, for example, participation in religious rituals was prohibited for those deemed as deformed, reflecting a perception of physical imperfection as impurity. Similarly, in ancient Greek culture, deformity was sometimes associated with moral corruption, as seen in Homer's portrayal of the Therapists in the Iliad. However, Greek society was relatively tolerant towards people with disabilities, exemplified by the revered figure of the god Hephaestos, who was himself deformed.

In contrast, the Romans linked deformity to magical power, viewing it as a potential source of supernatural abilities. During the Medieval period, deformity was often interpreted as a manifestation of God's wrath or punishment for sin. Despite this, there were instances where people with deformities were respected and revered, particularly in Christian contexts. Figures like Gregory of Tours and Teresa of Avila were treated as saints, with their deformities seen as marks of divine favor or opportunities for Christian charity and mercy.

In modern times, with the rise of biomedicine and eugenics, deformity has increasingly been viewed through a medical lens, often seen as a marker of disease or genetic abnormality. This shift in perspective has led to the pathologization of deformity and the medicalization of its treatment, emphasizing interventions aimed at "fixing" or eradicating physical differences.

Suggested Readings:

Davis, Lennard J., editor *The Disability Studies Reader*. 5th ed., Routledge, 2016, https://doi.org10.4324/9781315680668.

Longmore, Paul K., and Lauri Umansky. *The New Disability History: American Perspectives*. NYU Press, 2001.

Garland-Thomson, Rosemarie. *Extraordinary Bodies: Figuring Physical Disability in American Culture and Literature*. Columbia UP, 1997.

Dependency

Why do we call a dependent person a parasite? Why do we hate dependency? To live a human life, don't we need knowledge, care, culture, technology, and social and economic goods? Negative perception of dependency is deeply ingrained in societal attitudes, driven by a desire for self-reliance and autonomy. However, it is essential to recognize that dependency is an inherent aspect of the human condition. To lead a fulfilling human life, people require access to knowledge, care, culture, technology, and social and economic resources, all of which necessitate some level of dependency. Dependency is pervasive in modern life, from reliance on government services to the utilization of natural resources for sustenance. Yet, societal norms often stigmatize dependency, particularly when it is associated with specific groups such as people with disabilities. This stigma contributes to the perception of disability as a social problem, reinforcing stereotypes and marginalizing people based on their level of dependence.

The emphasis on self-reliance and independence stems from cultural ideals that prioritize individual autonomy and agency. In societies shaped by wage labor and economic independence, there is an expectation for people to support themselves and their families financially. However, this expectation often excludes marginalized groups, such as women, from economic independence due to systemic barriers and discriminatory practices. Furthermore, societal attitudes towards dependency are often steeped in moral judgments, equating welfare dependence with laziness, emotional dependence with weakness, and chemical dependence with a lack of willpower. These perceptions perpetuate stigma and discrimination, further marginalizing people who rely on assistance or support.

In response to these societal attitudes, people with disabilities have challenged the notion of dependence inherent in disability. Instead, they have advocated for a redefinition of independence that encompasses the vast networks of assistance and provision necessary for human flourishing. By reframing dependency as a natural and necessary aspect of human interdependence, people with disabilities seek to challenge stigma, promote inclusion, and advocate for a more equitable society.

The literary and disability scholar Lennard J. Davis argues, 'The seeming state of exception of disability turns out to be the unexceptional state of existence" (2007, 4). The perspective of people with disabilities challenges the notion that dependence is solely an internal characteristic of the individual. They reject being treated as objects of paternalistic concern and assert that societal structures play a significant role in creating dependency among people with impairments. Society is often designed in a way that reinforces dependency for people with disabilities, making them reliant on others for support and accommodation. Furthermore, the concept of independence is not solely about self-sufficiency but also about self-determination. People with disabilities emphasize the importance of having agency and control over their own lives, including the ability to make choices and pursue goals according to their own preferences and values. This understanding of independence prioritizes autonomy and empowerment, rather than mere self-reliance.

By challenging the traditional understanding of dependence and independence, people with disabilities advocate for a more inclusive and equitable society that recognizes and respects the rights and autonomy of all its members. They assert their right to participate fully in society on their own terms, free from paternalistic attitudes and structural barriers that perpetuate dependency. Through this lens, independence is redefined as the ability to exercise self-determination and live a life of dignity and fulfillment, regardless of one's physical or cognitive abilities. As medical sociologist and disability rights activist Irving Zola writes: "The important thing was that I got there under my own steam, physically independent and mainstream. But the price I paid was a high one . . . I, for far too long, contributed to the demise of my own social and psychological independence" (1988, 24). The independence to which he aspired was, he discovered, "the quality of life that [he] . . . could live with help" (De Jong 1983, cited in Zola 1988, 24).

Suggested Readings:

Barton, Len. *Disability and Dependency.* London: Falmer Press, 1989.

Oliver, Michael. *The Politics of Disablement.* London: Macmillan, 1990.

Disability Studies

The emergence of the Disability Studies movement represents a significant shift in societal attitudes towards physically impaired people. This movement seeks to enhance the quality of life for people with disabilities by advocating for policies, legislation, and societal changes that promote inclusion and equality. At its core, Disability Studies aims to challenge and dismantle the stigma and negative stereotypes that have long been associated with disability. Central to the efforts of Disability Studies activists is a focus on the status of disabled people within society. This involves identifying and addressing the various barriers—societal, architectural, and infrastructural—that hinder their full participation in social activities. These barriers can range from physical obstacles like inaccessible buildings to attitudinal barriers rooted in prejudice and discrimination.

Moreover, Disability Studies sheds light on the privileges afforded to those who conform to society's prescribed norms and standards. By examining historical and contemporary contexts, Disability Studies activists uncover the genealogical histories of disabled people, revealing the systemic exclusion and isolation they have endured across centuries. This critical analysis serves to challenge the status quo and advocate for systemic changes that promote equity and justice for all people, regardless of ability. Traditional approaches to disability are re-examined and condemned for their exclusionary practices. Disability Studies critiques the medical model of disability, which pathologizes impairment and places the burden of adaptation solely on the individual. Instead, it advocates for a social model of disability, which recognizes disability as a product of societal barriers and calls for collective action to remove these barriers and promote inclusivity.

In the past, disabled people faced severe discrimination and marginalization, often sanctioned by laws rooted in eugenic ideals. Eugenics, a belief system that aimed to create a genetically "improved" human race by eliminating perceived flaws, led to the sterilization and isolation of disabled people. These practices were considered legitimate under the law, reflecting a societal preference for an idealized concept of humanity devoid of disability. Despite these historical injustices, disability has been largely overlooked as an academic discipline, mirroring the exclusion experienced by disabled people in mainstream society. Many universities have failed to incorporate Disability Studies into their curricula, neglecting the rich history and perspectives of disabled communities. This omission perpetuates biases and reinforces the marginalization of disabled voices within academic discourse. Moreover, Disability Studies itself faces biases and prejudices within academia. The field challenges ableist notions of superiority and highlights the importance of addressing negative stereotypes associated with disability. However, these challenges are often met with resistance, further hindering efforts to promote inclusivity and equity.

In the early twentieth century, there was a concerted effort to eradicate disability from society through various means, including medical interventions aimed at curing or managing impairments. However, this approach reduced disabled people to objects of scrutiny and treatment, overlooking their humanity and agency. Addressing the needs of the disabled population goes beyond simply enhancing the physical accessibility of society; it requires confronting and dismantling negative stereotypes and systemic barriers. This necessitates a comprehensive study of the discourses and history of disability, uncovering the root causes of exclusion and isolation experienced by disabled people. By challenging ableism and advocating for social and systemic change, Disability Studies seeks to create a more inclusive and equitable society for all. In the evolution of Disability Studies, a shift has occurred from older perspectives that primarily focused on acknowledging the exclusionary practices that segregated disabled people from mainstream society to newer approaches that prioritize disciplinary practices aimed at advancing progressive disability goals.

One of the key developments in this transition has been a heightened awareness of ethical issues surrounding the treatment of disabled persons, particularly in the context of scientific and medical experimentation. Critical Disability Studies endeavors to explore the mental anguish experienced by disabled people who internalize societal norms and expectations imposed upon them.

Historically, during the 1980s, approaches to disability were predominantly rooted in the medical field, which often adopted an individualistic approach centered solely on the body. In this paradigm, disabled bodies were viewed as subjects requiring medical intervention to remedy perceived abnormalities and bring them closer to a standard of normalcy. This approach positioned disability as a medical problem to be cured through surgical procedures and other interventions. First-generation Disability Studies scholars critiqued this medicalized perspective, arguing that it failed to address broader societal responsibilities for providing access and accommodations for disabled people. Instead, it placed undue emphasis on "fixing" the disabled person themselves, treating them as objects in need of correction rather than recognizing the systemic barriers that contributed to their marginalization.

In contrast to this medical model, Critical Disability Studies approaches advocate for a more holistic understanding of disability that considers social, cultural, and environmental factors. These approaches seek to challenge ableism and promote inclusivity by addressing systemic inequalities and advocating for structural changes that enable full participation and empowerment for disabled people. In the realms of insurance decisions regarding disability, differing approaches have been observed across various countries. While the American Medical Association (AMA) resisted the notion of assigning insurance decisions solely to clinical assessments, in both Germany and the United States, doctors have been granted a supreme role in evaluating and determining the validity of disability claims. This practice has faced significant criticism from scholars in the field of Disability Studies. According to scholars, such practices objectify disabled people, reducing them to mere objects of scrutiny and judgment. In this paradigm, the disabled person's body becomes the subject of examination and assessment, with doctors wielding the authority to determine the extent of disability and allocate necessary resources and facilities accordingly. This approach has been heavily scrutinized for perpetuating ableist ideologies that prioritize certain forms of human existence over others. scholars like Len Barton argue that such practices reinforce societal norms and standards that exclude those who deviate from the perceived norm of "normal" human stature.

In response, Disability Studies seeks to challenge and modify existing notions of supremacy attributed to certain human forms. By advocating for a more inclusive and equitable approach to disability, Disability Studies aims to prevent the exclusion and marginalization of people who do not conform to traditional notions of ability and normalcy. This involves recognizing the diversity of human experiences and identities, and promoting social structures and policies that accommodate and empower all people, regardless of their physical or cognitive differences. In earlier times, disabled people were often viewed through the lens of charity and pity, relegated to a life of dependency on others for basic sustenance. This approach perpetuated a narrative of helplessness and inadequacy, positioning disabled people as passive recipients of mercy rather than active participants in society. Institutions established in the mid-nineteenth century further reinforced this perspective by admitting only those disabled people deemed to have a chance of being cured, thereby bolstering the belief in the medical model of disability—that medical interventions could effectively eliminate disability. Conversely, disabilities perceived as incurable or difficult to remedy were often left unaddressed, their existence hidden away to avoid acknowledging the limitations of medical professionals in curing disability. This selective approach to providing care and support marginalized people whose disabilities did not conform to the narrow parameters of curability.

In the 1920s, there emerged a shift towards promoting personal adaptation techniques and adjustment skills among disabled people. This ableist perspective emphasized the need for disabled people to adapt to a society fraught with barriers and limitations, placing the burden of accommodation solely on the individual rather than addressing systemic barriers to inclusion. The emergence of special schools in contrast to the eugenics era represented a step towards providing formal education and services to disabled children. These schools aimed to enhance the quality of life for disabled people through education and rehabilitation, challenging the prevailing medical model of disability. Disability activists and advocates criticized the medical model for its narrow focus on cure and instead advocated for holistic approaches that prioritized education, empowerment, and social inclusion as means to improve the lives of disabled people. Disability Studies activists emphasize the importance of challenging normative expectations placed upon bodies and addressing societal exclusions of those who deviate from the perceived norm. Rather than placing the burden of adjustment solely on the individual in a disabling society, the focus should be on understanding and addressing the perspectives and experiences of disabled people. However, the closure of rehabilitation centers and institutions that confine socially misfit disabled people presents complex challenges. While it may signify progress towards inclusion and deinstitutionalization, there are concerns about the safety and well-being of both disabled people and the broader society. For instance, releasing aggressive people with disabilities into the community without adequate support and supervision could potentially pose risks to public safety, particularly if they are not in a stable mental state.

Disability Studies also critique the insufficient environmental accommodations and the unwelcoming nature of societal structures, which further marginalize disabled people. Additionally, issues such as poverty, unemployment, and restrictions on disability insurance exacerbate the dependence of disabled people on the ableist majority. These systemic barriers perpetuate inequality and hinder the full participation and empowerment of disabled people in society. In addressing these challenges, Disability Studies advocates for systemic changes that prioritize the needs and rights of disabled people. This includes improving environmental accessibility, addressing economic disparities, and promoting policies that support the autonomy and inclusion of disabled people. By centering the perspectives and experiences of disabled people, Disability Studies seeks to create a more equitable and inclusive society for all.

Disabled people often find themselves trapped in a cycle of dependency and poverty within capitalist societies, where human worth is often measured by one's ability to contribute to the workforce and generate profits for society. In response to this unequal power dynamic prevalent in ableist societies, the 'person first' movement emerged in the 1960s. This movement aimed to challenge the prevailing narrative that prioritized disability as a defining characteristic over the individual's identity. The 'person first' approach advocated for using the term "person with a disability" instead of "disabled person," emphasizing the personhood of people before their disability. By placing the emphasis on the person rather than their disability, this approach sought to empower disabled people and recognize their inherent value beyond their bodily structure or abilities. It aimed to counteract the stigma and devaluation that often accompany labels and designations used to describe disabled people.

In Britain, the formation of the Union of Physically Impaired Against Segregation marked a significant turning point in the disability rights movement. This organization challenged the prevailing medical model of disability, which confined disabled people to nursing homes and rehabilitation centers. Instead, they advocated for a social model of disability, which posited that the root cause of disability lies within society itself rather than within the individual.

According to the social model of disability, societal barriers and systemic discrimination are responsible for the marginalization and suffering experienced by disabled people, rather than any inherent flaw or deficiency within the individual. By shifting the focus from individual deficits to societal shortcomings, the social model of disability seeks to promote inclusivity, accessibility, and equality for disabled people. It aims to empower disabled people to participate fully in society and advocate for their rights and dignity. Disability is not an inherent condition of people but rather a construct imposed upon them by society, resulting in limitations to their mobility and active engagement in social life. This societal imposition leads to the exclusion of disabled people from various facets of society, including employment opportunities, social interactions, and educational environments. Discrimination based on physical differences and the lack of accommodations further exacerbate the challenges faced by disabled people, despite legal mandates such as the Americans with Disabilities Act of 1990 aimed at fostering their social inclusion.

Even with legislative measures in place, barriers persist within institutional structures, including universities, that hinder the full participation of disabled people. These barriers range from physical obstacles within infrastructure to attitudinal barriers that perpetuate stigma and discrimination. Disability Studies has played a crucial role in raising awareness about these barriers and advocating for accessible environments, including classrooms and educational facilities, to ensure the active involvement of disabled students.

At its core, Disability Studies seeks to deconstruct the normalized exclusion of bodies deemed deviant by societal standards. It challenges the notion that disability is a deficiency or aberration, asserting instead that disabled bodies are simply variations within the spectrum of human diversity. By highlighting the social construction of disability, Disability Studies emphasizes the importance of recognizing and valuing the experiences and perspectives of disabled people.

In many ways, Disability Studies aligns with other fields of identity studies, such as gender or queer studies, which similarly seek to deconstruct societal norms and challenge systems of oppression. By examining the intersections of disability with other forms of identity and oppression, Disability Studies contributes to broader conversations about social justice and equity for marginalized communities.

The legacy of the traditional charity model in Disability Studies continues to exert influence on contemporary understandings of disability. This model often depicts disabled people as inherently needy and lacking in efficiency, perpetuating stereotypes that justify their exclusion from employment opportunities and societal participation. Such portrayals of disability as inherently limiting and dependent contribute to the marginalization of disabled people, reinforcing barriers to their full integration into society. However, advancements in science, technology, and shifting societal attitudes have begun to challenge these entrenched perceptions. The development of innovative technologies, such as digital media, keyboard, and voice recognition software, has greatly enhanced accessibility for disabled people, allowing them to navigate and engage with various social and cultural spheres previously inaccessible to them. These technological innovations have played a crucial role in breaking down physical and communication barriers, enabling disabled people to participate more fully in educational, professional, and social activities.

Moreover, evolving societal attitudes towards

disability have contributed to greater recognition of the capabilities and contributions of disabled people. Increasing awareness of the social model of disability, which posits that societal barriers rather than individual impairments are the primary source of disability, has led to calls for greater inclusivity and accessibility in all aspects of society.

Suggested Readings:

Albrecht, Gary L., et al. *Handbook of Disability Studies*. SAGE, 2001.

Barnes, Colin, et al. *Disability Studies Today*. Polity, 2002.

Davis, Lennard J., editor. *The Disability Studies Reader*. 5th ed., Routledge, 2016, https://doi.org10.4324/9781315680668.

Oliver, Michael. *Understanding Disability: From Theory to Practice*. Palgrave Macmillan, 1996.

Snyder, Sharon, et al. *Disability Studies: Enabling the Humanities*. Modern Language Association, 2002.

Barnes, Colin. 'Disability Studies: New or Not so New Directions?' *Disability &Society*, vol. 14, no. 4, Informa UK Limited, July 1999, pp. 577–580, https://doi.org10.1080/09687599926136.

Shakespeare, Tom. *Disability Reader: Social Science Perspectives*. A&C Black, 1998.

Diversity

Diversity is a fundamental characteristic of human society, manifesting in myriad forms across the globe. From linguistic variations and cultural customs to racial identities and religious beliefs, diversity permeates every aspect of human existence. This diversity encompasses differences in language, skin color, caste, socioeconomic class, customs, cuisines, traditions, habits, religions, nationalities, and more. Despite the rich tapestry of diversity, there exists a universal desire among all people to be treated with equality and fairness. Disability, too, is an integral aspect of diversity. Just as people vary in their languages, cultures, and beliefs, they also differ in their physical and cognitive abilities. Disability represents a spectrum of conditions and impairments that influence how people interact with the world around them. However, despite these differences, people with disabilities share the same fundamental humanity as their non-disabled counterparts. In embracing diversity, it is essential to recognize that no particular group should be privileged or considered superior to others. Every individual, regardless of their abilities or background, deserves equal respect, dignity, and opportunities. Disability inclusion falls within the broader framework of promoting diversity and ensuring that all members of society are valued and included. By acknowledging and celebrating diversity in all its forms, societies can foster greater understanding, empathy, and solidarity among people. Embracing diversity enriches the fabric of human experience, allowing for the recognition and appreciation of the unique contributions and perspectives of every individual, including those with disabilities.

The Eugenics movement, which gained traction in the late nineteenth and early twentieth centuries, was rooted in the belief in a scientifically determined notion of normality that disregarded the value of diversity. Proponents of eugenics sought to categorize people into groups based on various criteria such as health, age, strength, and intelligence, in order to delineate those considered normal from those deemed abnormal. Notably, people belonging to white, middle-class European populations were typically classified as more normal, while groups from Asian and African countries were often relegated to the category of abnormal. Central to the eugenics agenda was the endeavor to ascertain the degree of normality or abnormality within populations. Social policy and public health initiatives of the time were directed towards reducing the number of people deemed abnormal, often labeled as feeble-minded, while simultaneously increasing the number of those considered fit.

The core objective of eugenics was to eliminate or minimize diversity within human populations. This pursuit of a homogeneous, purportedly superior genetic makeup was driven by the belief that it would lead to societal progress and advancement. Tragically, the eugenic principles espoused by proponents were co-opted by the Nazi regime in Germany, leading to horrific atrocities during the Holocaust. Nazis employed eugenic theories of normality to justify the systematic extermination of various groups, including Jews, homosexuals, and people with disabilities or deafness. These marginalized groups were targeted for eradication based on their perceived deviation from the eugenic ideal of normality, further highlighting the dangers inherent in the eugenics movement's disregard for diversity and its catastrophic consequences for humanity. Unfortunately, discussions surrounding diversity often neglect to include disability as a dimension worth considering. While conversations about diversity frequently address factors such as race, caste, and gender, differences related to the body are frequently omitted from the discourse. According to Davis, this omission may stem from a collective reluctance to confront the inherent frailty of the human condition. Moreover, it may serve as a reminder that disability challenges the neoliberal ideal of the autonomous individual who can shape their own destiny and wield consumerist power.

In the neoliberal framework, individuality and the ability to dictate one's fate are highly valued, but disability disrupts this narrative by highlighting the role of fate and powerlessness. Consequently, disability is often marginalized and stigmatized within neoliberal societies. This marginalization extends even to university campuses, which often uphold neoliberal ideologies. While universities may promote diversity, they frequently fail to adequately address the needs and perspectives of people with disabilities. Davis suggests that university courses should actively engage with bodily differences and celebrate diverse identities, including disability. However, despite the rhetoric of diversity and inclusivity, the reality is often different. Disability identity is often treated as inferior or undesirable, and people with disabilities may feel compelled to suppress or conceal their identity to conform to societal norms. In this context, the notion of diversity is called into question. While diversity implies the ability to choose and embrace various identities, disability is often excluded from this framework. Instead, disability is viewed as an undesirable characteristic that challenges societal norms and expectations. This highlights the need for a more inclusive understanding of diversity that encompasses all facets of human experience, including disability.

The influence of medicine in shaping societal norms of human existence cannot be overstated. Medical standards often dictate what is considered "normal" or "abnormal" in terms of physical and cognitive functioning. While diversity advocates for the acceptance of differences, there is often reluctance to embrace abnormalities as celebrated aspects of human diversity, particularly when it comes to medical conditions or birth defects. In the medical context, abnormalities or birth defects are typically viewed as undesirable and may evoke feelings of fear, discomfort, or even rejection. Parents, for example, may feel distressed upon learning that their child has a condition that deviates from the perceived norm. As a result, there is a societal inclination to conceal or mitigate these differences rather than celebrate them.

Disability Studies challenges this prevailing mindset by advocating for the inclusion of disability within the discourse of diversity. Despite the discomfort or unease associated with deviations from the norm, Disability Studies argues that disability is an inherent aspect of human diversity and should be acknowledged and celebrated as such. Instead of viewing disability as a deviation to be corrected or concealed, Disability Studies encourages society to recognize it as a natural variation of the human experience. While the integration of disability into the discourse of diversity may pose challenges and discomfort, Disability Studies maintains that it is essential for fostering a more inclusive and equitable society. By embracing disability as a legitimate dimension of diversity, society can move towards greater acceptance, understanding, and support for people with disabilities.

Suggested Readings:

Butler, Judith. *Undoing gender*. Routledge, 2004.

Hardt, Michael, and Antonio Negri. *Multitide: War and Democracy in the Age of Empire*. Penguin, 2004.

Laclau, Ernesto and Chantal Mouffe. *Hegemony and Socialist Strategy: Towards a Radical Democratic Politics*. Verso. 1988.

Mitchell, David T., and Sharon L. Snyder. *The Body and Physical Difference: Discourses of Disability*. University of Michigan Press.1997.

Snyder, Sharon L., and David T. Mitchell. *Cultural Locations of Disability*. University of Chicago Press, 2006.

Divyang

The process of labeling people with disabilities has significant implications for the construction of their identities. Throughout history, disabled people have been subjected to various labels, many of which carry negative connotations and contribute to the stigma surrounding disability. These labels not only perpetuate harmful stereotypes but also exert power dynamics, with those doing the labeling assuming authority over the lives of disabled people. Furthermore, the act of labeling strips disabled people of their agency and autonomy, as they are often assigned labels without their input or consent. This lack of control over their own identities can have profound psychological effects on disabled people, further marginalizing them within society.

The Disability Rights Movement, which originated primarily in the Western world, has been instrumental in challenging these harmful labeling practices and advocating for the rights and dignity of disabled people. However, it was not until the 1990s that India began to witness the emergence of disability rights activists and the advancement of the disability rights movement within the country. These activists have worked tirelessly to challenge discriminatory practices, promote inclusivity, and empower disabled people to assert control over their own identities. Through advocacy, education, and policy reform, they have sought to dismantle the barriers that prevent disabled people from fully participating in society and exercising their rights.

In India, the terminology used to refer to disabled people often reflects a reliance on borrowed words from

English, leading to a scarcity of indigenous terms for disability. This reliance on English terminology can result in crude translations in Indian languages, further complicating the understanding of disability from an Indian perspective and perpetuating stereotypes associated with the label of disability. For example, the English term "disabled" is commonly translated into Hindi as "aksham," which directly conveys the idea of incapability or inability. Similarly, the translation of "impairment" as "vikalangata" can carry negative connotations, as it refers to a deformed limb or physical deformity in many Indian languages. In contrast, there is growing recognition and acceptance of the term "vikalangata" within the Indian context, as it is an indigenously developed designation that acknowledges the diverse experiences and capabilities of disabled people. Similarly, in the Western context, the term "impairment" is often preferred as a more neutral and respectful way to empathize with disabled people. Disability Studies scholars draw a clear distinction between the terms "disability" and "impairment," highlighting the nuanced differences in their meanings and implications.

"Impairment" typically refers to any bodily deformity, cognitive deficiency, or intellectual retardation that deviates from accepted norms and significantly restricts an individual's physical movement or functioning. These impairments can pose challenges and limitations, hindering people from leading fulfilling lives and achieving their goals to varying degrees. On the other hand, "disability" is regarded as a social construct rather than an inherent characteristic of an individual. It emphasizes the role of society in creating barriers that disable people with impairments. These barriers include infrastructural obstacles, lack of accessibility in education and employment, and the perpetuation of stereotypical attitudes by the ableist majority. Translating the word "disabled" directly into Hindi as "aksham" and substituting the existing Hindi term "viklang" without proper contextual groundwork would be both misleading and inappropriate. The evolution of terminology used to refer to disabled people reflects shifting societal attitudes and efforts to convey more respectful and empowering language.

Initially, the term "handicapped" was commonly used, but its association with begging, derived from "hand-in-cap," was deemed demeaning. As a result, alternative terms such as "cripple," "physically challenged," and "person with disability" emerged in an attempt to uplift the dignity and value of disabled people. While terms like "differently abled" may sound politically correct, they often fail to capture the discrimination and oppression experienced by disabled people. Additionally, they do not effectively shift the focus from the individual to society, as the term "disability" does. Disability Studies scholars advocate for the use of the term "disabled" because it emphasizes societal responsibility for the discrimination and marginalization faced by disabled people. By attributing disability to societal barriers rather than individual deficits, this terminology promotes a more inclusive and equitable understanding of disability.

On the occasion of World Disability Day on December 3, 2015, Prime Minister Narendra Modi Ji launched the Accessible India campaign with the intent of addressing the needs and challenges faced by persons with disabilities. During this initiative, he introduced the term 'divyang' as a replacement for the prevailing term 'viklang'. This terminology shift was aimed at imbuing a sense of empowerment and dignity into the discourse surrounding disability. Drawing parallels with Mahatma Gandhi's use of the term 'harijan' to uplift the Dalit communities, Prime Minister Modi Ji sought to convey a similar sentiment of reverence and inclusivity towards people with disabilities. 'Harijan', meaning 'children of god', carried profound religious connotations, aligning with Gandhi's vision of integrating marginalized groups into the societal mainstream. Likewise, 'divyang', translating to 'divine body part', was intended to evoke a sense of divine blessing associated with people facing physical or cognitive challenges. However, while both terms sought to instill a sense of respect and acknowledgment, the usage of religious symbolism in describing marginalized communities raises concerns about its adequacy in addressing their needs comprehensively. Critics argue that the term 'divyang' may inadvertently reinforce a hierarchical distinction between persons with disabilities and those without, suggesting a divine favoritism towards the former. Such implications risk overshadowing the fundamental principles of social justice, equality, and accessibility that people with disabilities rightfully deserve. Instead of relying on euphemistic labels, the focus should be on addressing systemic barriers and promoting genuine inclusion. Persons with disabilities require tangible support mechanisms, such as accessible infrastructure, equitable opportunities, and inclusive policies, to fully participate in society on equal terms.

The term 'divyang', when translated into English, does not neatly correspond to terms like 'impairment' or 'disability'. In adopting 'divyang', there's a risk of overlooking the socially constructed nature of disability. Rather than recognizing disability as a multifaceted issue shaped by societal attitudes and structures, 'divyang' tends to view it as a purely personal and individual tragedy.

Prime Minister Narendra Modi's endorsement of 'divyang' suggests a belief in divine blessing, wherein people with disabilities are perceived as specially favored by God. This notion implies that any loss of bodily function is compensated by the granting of additional sensory abilities, making them more attuned to their surroundings. However, this perspective draws on age-old myths that attribute superhuman powers or a heightened sixth sense to disabled people. By perpetuating such ideas, Modi ji inadvertently reinforces superstitions rather than confronting them with evidence-based reasoning. The media serves as a primary conduit for shaping societal attitudes, and within Indian culture, its influence is particularly significant. Therefore, when leaders like Modi Ji endorse terms like 'divyang', it not only reflects their individual perspectives but also has the potential to shape broader societal perceptions. In this case, the uncritical adoption of 'divyang' risks reinforcing outdated and unsubstantiated beliefs about disability, rather than fostering a more informed and inclusive understanding. Disability often finds its way into language and culture as a metaphor, with expressions like "ignorance is blindness," "fear as crippling," or "short intellect as dumb." Such linguistic constructs shape societal perceptions of disability, often inadvertently reinforcing stereotypes and diminishing the humanity of people with disabilities. The introduction of the term 'divyang' by Prime Minister Modi Ji further adds to this complex narrative.

In his speech, Prime Minister Modi Ji highlighted the unique abilities possessed by people with disabilities, framing them as possessing extraordinary qualities akin to superhuman attributes. For instance, he referred to how a person with visual impairment reads Braille with their fingers, attributing exceptional qualities to their sense of touch. While seemingly positive, this narrative risks perpetuating a negative discourse surrounding disability. By emphasizing the extraordinary abilities of people with disabilities, there's a subtle implication that their worth and acceptance in society are contingent upon their ability to "overcome" their disabilities and excel despite societal barriers. This narrative places undue pressure on people with disabilities to conform to societal standards of success, often at the expense of their well-being and dignity. Moreover, by framing disability as something to be overcome or compensated for with extraordinary abilities, there is a danger of overlooking the systemic barriers and discrimination that people with disabilities face on a daily basis. This approach may inadvertently reinforce the notion that disabilities are solely individual challenges rather than societal issues that require broader structural changes to address effectively. Simi Linton, a prominent Disability Studies scholar, critiques the concept of 'overcoming' within the discourse surrounding disability. She argues that this notion inadequately addresses the systemic barriers and societal responsibilities for the inaccessibility faced by disabled people. Instead, it places the burden of overcoming these obstacles solely on the shoulders of the disabled themselves. By framing disability as something to be overcome, society implicitly places the onus on disabled people to prove their worth and capabilities. This perpetuates a harmful narrative that suggests disabled people must constantly strive to surpass the limitations imposed by their impairments in order to be recognized and lead fulfilling lives. In essence, it places the responsibility for achieving inclusion and acceptance squarely on the individual, rather than acknowledging the broader societal structures that contribute to exclusion and discrimination. Furthermore, this emphasis on 'overcoming' can inadvertently reinforce negative stereotypes about disability, portraying disabled people as inherently disadvantaged and in need of overcoming their circumstances to be considered valuable members of society. This narrative not only undermines the diverse experiences and contributions of disabled people but also reinforces the notion of their 'otherness' within society. While the intention behind using terms like 'overcoming' may be to inspire and applaud the resilience of disabled people, it ultimately fails to address the root causes of discrimination and exclusion. Instead, efforts should focus on challenging societal attitudes and dismantling barriers to accessibility and inclusion, thereby creating a more equitable and supportive environment for all people, regardless of ability.

In Indian mythology, the concept of God holds immense significance as the supreme being, existing beyond human comprehension and accessible primarily through faith and prayer. However, the inherent mystery surrounding God's existence means that true access to the divine remains elusive, and belief becomes the cornerstone of this enduring concept. By drawing parallels between disabled people and deities, there's a risk of disconnecting them from the realities of their lived experiences. When disabled people are associated with divine entities, it can create a perception that they exist on a plane separate from everyday human existence. This abstraction can hinder the understanding of their challenges and needs by those without disabilities, as they may view disability through a lens of reverence or exceptionalism akin to the divine. In effect, the term 'divyang' may inadvertently reinforce a dichotomy between 'normal' people and those with disabilities, further marginalizing the latter by positioning them as 'different' or 'other'. Furthermore, by elevating disabled people to a status of exceptionality or superiority through the use of terms like 'divyang', there is a risk of perpetuating harmful stereotypes and misconceptions. Such language may imply that disability confers special privileges or blessings, further distancing disabled people from the realities of societal barriers and discrimination they often face.

In the realm of political rhetoric and speeches, labels and metaphors are frequently wielded as potent tools to evoke emotions and shape perceptions. However, employing such language hastily and without due consideration can have detrimental effects, particularly when it comes to characterizing people with disabilities.

People with disabilities are not mere embodiments of physical or cognitive differences; they possess multifaceted identities that extend far beyond their impairments. It's crucial to recognize and respect their inherent complexity and agency. No one, regardless of their position or intentions, has the right to reduce people with disabilities to objects of inspiration or pity without their explicit consent. Empowering people with disabilities means recognizing their autonomy and granting them full authority over their own existence. This includes the right to determine how they wish to be addressed and identified. Rather than imposing labels or narratives upon them, it is imperative to prioritize their voices and preferences in shaping their own identities.

By allowing people with disabilities to assert control over their own narratives and self-definitions, we affirm their dignity and agency as equal members of society. It is through respecting their autonomy and granting them the freedom to define themselves on their own terms that true empowerment and inclusivity can be achieved. Therefore, any discourse surrounding disability must center on the principles of autonomy, consent, and self-determination, ensuring that people with disabilities are active participants in shaping their own destinies.

Suggested Readings:

Panicker, Mahesh S. "Disability and the Politics of Nomenclature." *Asian Journal of Multidisciplinary Studies,* vol. 7, 2019, p. 5.

Mendiratta, Archana, and Asha Sharma. "An Insight into the Quality of Life of Parents of Divyang (disabled) Developmental Disabilities." *Towards Excellence* 14.4 (2022).

Embodiment

Embodiment encompasses the intricate interplay between our bodily experiences and the socio-cultural contexts in which they occur. For people with disabilities, embodiment extends beyond the quest for rectifying historical injustices; it encapsulates a spectrum of sensations, from suffering and pain to pleasure and vulnerability, within specific temporal and spatial dimensions. Disability Studies scholars delve into the mechanisms by which certain bodies are deemed deviant while others are upheld as normative. Disability Studies scholarship scrutinizes institutionalization, medicalization, segregation, and even genocide to dissect the operationalization of normalization and deviance within society. Moreover, scholars endeavor to unravel the intricate relationship between disability and embodiment. Central to this exploration is the concept of corporeality, which denotes the state of inhabiting, experiencing, and being a body.

Phenomenology, coupled with philosophical inquiries into conscious experience, provides a lens through which Disability Studies scholars investigate corporeality. This approach challenges Cartesian dualism, which rigidly dichotomizes the mind and body. In Cartesian philosophy, the mind is often associated with rationality and control, while the body is relegated to a realm of irrationality and subservience. However, by embracing phenomenological perspectives, Disability Studies scholars seek to dismantle this hierarchical framework, emphasizing the inseparability of mind and body and advocating for a more holistic understanding of human experience.

Feminist perspectives delve into the intricate dynamics between rationality and the body, aiming to unravel the nuanced ways in which embodiment unfolds as a gendered experience. Within feminist discourse, there's an exploration of how societal norms often encode bodily normativity with masculine traits. This perspective sheds light on how bodily changes, such as ageing, menstruation, and menopause, are frequently stigmatized and marginalized, portraying them as forms of irrationality. Feminist phenomenology offers a unique lens through which to understand embodiment, emphasizing the significance of bodily experiences in shaping self-understanding and identity. "Embodiment frames bodily change as a horizon for self-understanding and self-definition, and the body as an agent interacting with others and with the world more generally" (Weiss: 25: 1999). Moreover, perspectives from embodied Disability Studies provide a critical lens through which to critique various philosophical inquiries, including ontology, aesthetics, epistemology, and political economy. Departing from traditional notions of personhood as rational and disembodied, disability scholars advocate for a more fluid and porous understanding of embodiment. Many Disability scholars advocate for a pluralistic approach to understanding embodiments, recognizing the intersectionality of various identity markers and asserting the independence of bodily experiences from normative standards. This perspective highlights the need to embrace diverse and multifaceted understandings of embodiment, acknowledging the complex interplay of factors that shape people' lived experiences.

Embodiment serves as a powerful lens through which to analyze both cultural and material dimensions, shedding light on the intricate political economy of difference. Disability Studies scholars have embarked on a wide array of inquiries within this realm, ranging from critiques of "disembodied citizenship" to examinations of global phenomena such as the organ trade, political subjecthood in late capitalism, the agro-industrial food system, and the neoliberal demand for flexible bodies. For instance, Davidson's work (2008) delves into the concept of "disembodied citizenship," highlighting how certain bodies are marginalized or excluded from full participation in civic life due to societal norms and structures. Meanwhile, Erevelles (2001) explores the complexities of political subjecthood within the context of late capitalism, examining how power dynamics intersect with bodily experiences and identities. Wilkerson's research (2011) delves into the global agro-industrial food system, particularly in relation to claims of an obesity pandemic, revealing how societal norms and economic forces shape perceptions of health and bodies. Additionally, McRuer (2006) delves into the neoliberal demand for flexible bodies, analyzing how capitalism's emphasis on productivity and efficiency influences perceptions of disability and embodiment.

Collectively, these studies underscore the importance of situating embodiment within specific socio-cultural and economic contexts, emphasizing the need to closely examine material circumstances and power dynamics. By interrogating the intersections of embodiment with broader societal structures, Disability Studies scholars contribute to a deeper understanding of how difference is constructed, experienced, and negotiated within diverse environments.

Suggested Readings:

Weiss, Gail. *Body Images: Embodiment as Intercorporeality.* London: Routledge. 1999.

Kittay, Eva Feder, and Licia Carlson, editors. *Cognitive Disability and Its Challenge to Moral Philosophy.* Wiley-Blackwell, 2013. Metaphilosophy, 18.

Ethics

Ethics, as a branch of philosophical inquiry, delves into fundamental questions concerning justice, morality, and the nature of a good life. It grapples with the complexities of determining what actions are just and unjust, and what constitutes a life worth living. Moreover, ethics navigates the terrain of social responsibility and justice, probing into how people and societies ought to behave towards one another. Central to ethical inquiry are considerations of moral actions, which are often evaluated against established norms and standards. In establishing ethical principles for society, it becomes necessary to draw generalizations about what is deemed right and wrong, seeking to guide human behavior towards ideals of fairness, compassion, and integrity. Disability Studies takes a critical stance towards conventional standards of moral philosophy, challenging normative actions that perpetuate the exclusion of people with disabilities. Disability Studies scholars scrutinize the very foundations of moral norms, interrogating the implicit biases and assumptions that underlie societal attitudes towards disability. In doing so, Disability Studies delves into existential questions concerning the right to inclusion and belonging within society. It interrogates the norms that dictate who is deemed "normal" and who is marginalized as "other," advocating for a more inclusive and equitable understanding of humanity.

By challenging normative frameworks and advocating for the rights and inclusion of people with disabilities, Disability Studies contributes to broader ethical discussions about justice, fairness, and social responsibility. It prompts us to reevaluate our assumptions and biases, fostering a more inclusive and compassionate society for all. The ethical frameworks within the field of medicine often fail to fully consider the diverse experiences and values of people with disabilities, leading to the exclusion of certain ways of life. Disability ethics critically examines the socio-cultural practices and norms that marginalize and devalue disabled lives.

Lennard J. Davis, in his work, scrutinizes the historical development of scientific and statistical methodologies, which have contributed to the construction of the "average" body as the normative standard. This process has marginalized bodies marked by differences, relegating them to the periphery of societal acceptance. Davis further explores how nineteenth-century notions, particularly those influenced by the science of eugenics, pathologized human variation, framing it as inherently abnormal or pathological. This perspective has had profound implications for the lived experiences of people with disabilities, shaping societal attitudes and practices.

Rosemarie Garland-Thomson's analysis focuses on the ways in which anomalous bodies are subjected to practices aimed at conformity with normative standards.

These practices, such as aesthetic surgery and gene therapy, exert pressure on people with disabilities to conform to societal ideals of bodily normality, often at the expense of their autonomy and well-being.

Similarly, Shelley Tremain delves into the ethical dimensions of disability within medical and institutional contexts, highlighting how bodies deemed anomalous are often viewed as problematic and in need of correction or elimination. This perspective underscores the pervasive ableism inherent within medical discourse and the exercise of authority over disabled bodies.

Collectively, these scholars illuminate the complex intersections of ethics, medicine, and disability, prompting critical reflection on the ways in which societal norms and practices perpetuate marginalization and exclusion. Their work underscores the importance of centering disabled voices and experiences within ethical conversations, challenging ableist assumptions and advocating for greater inclusivity and equity within medical and societal frameworks.

Disability Studies is deeply committed to reshaping ethical discourse to effectively critique the systems of oppression that perpetuate disability marginalization. Within medical communities and broader non-disabled society, there persists a prevailing narrative that frames children with disabilities as tragedies or disasters. Disability Studies seeks to dismantle these entrenched structures by offering critical insights from disability perspectives, fostering a more meaningful discourse. One of the primary tenets of Disability Studies is its rejection of the medical model of disability, which pathologizes bodily differences and frames disability solely within a medical framework. Disability scholars argue that disability is not merely a medical condition but a social and political category imbued with its own unique identity and experiences.

Simi Linton, in her seminal work *Claiming Disability* (1998), challenges the dominance of medical discourse in defining disability. She asserts that disability is fundamentally a social construct, shaped by societal attitudes, norms, and systems of power. Linton's analysis underscores the importance of recognizing disability as a multifaceted phenomenon that transcends medical definitions. Furthermore, Linton's work highlights the rejection of medical language within disability movements. Disability activists and advocates assert their autonomy and agency in defining and articulating their experiences, rejecting the notion that disability must be understood solely through medical terminology.

By centering the voices and perspectives of people with disabilities, Disability Studies endeavors to challenge ableism and promote a more inclusive understanding of disability within ethical discourse. This involves not only critiquing existing structures of oppression but also advocating for social and political change to advance the rights and dignity of people with disabilities. While Disability Studies emphasizes the rejection of medical language in defining disability, it's essential to recognize that this stance does not imply a dismissal of the importance of healthcare and medical treatment for people with disabilities. Indeed, access to healthcare services is crucial for addressing chronic conditions and ensuring the overall well-being of people with disabilities.

Susan Wendell, in her exploration of this ethical complexity, distinguishes between what she terms the "healthy disabled" and the "unhealthy disabled." She underscores the necessity of acknowledging that while some people with disabilities may not require medical intervention for their condition, others may require ongoing medical care to manage chronic illnesses or other health issues. For example, someone with cerebral palsy may not necessarily view their condition as a medical problem requiring treatment, while people with other health conditions may rely on medical interventions to maintain their health and quality of life. Wendell's analysis highlights the potential pitfalls of exclusively adhering to the social model of disability, which places emphasis on addressing systemic barriers and social structures. While these efforts are crucial for promoting inclusivity and accessibility, they must not overlook the healthcare needs of people with disabilities who require medical treatment.

Indeed, neglecting the healthcare needs of people with disabilities could have serious consequences, jeopardizing their health and well-being. Therefore, it's imperative to strike a balance between recognizing the social and environmental factors that contribute to disability and ensuring that people with disabilities have access to the medical care and support they require to live full and healthy lives.

Disability Studies serves as a critical lens through which ethical issues related to disability are reexamined, particularly within the framework of the social model of disability. This model shifts the focus from viewing disability as an individual medical problem to understanding it as a result of societal barriers and attitudes. In addition to reevaluating ethical concerns within the context of the social model, Disability Studies also delves into a range of other intersecting issues, including those related to fatness, madness, and cognitive disability. By examining these diverse dimensions of disability, Disability Studies sheds light on the complex intersections of identity, stigma, and oppression. Furthermore, Disability Studies acknowledges the diversity within the disability community and the importance of recognizing the unique experiences and needs of different groups. For example, the deaf community may assert that their experiences are not synonymous with disability, highlighting the distinct cultural and linguistic aspects of deafness. Similarly, Disability Studies recognizes that cognitive disability and physical disability may require distinct ethical frameworks for understanding and addressing their respective challenges. However, while acknowledging these distinctions, Disability Studies emphasizes the importance of avoiding hierarchies or value judgments between different disability categories. Instead, it advocates for a more inclusive and intersectional approach that recognizes the inherent dignity and worth of all people, regardless of their specific abilities or identities.

Suggested Readings:

Aristotle. *Nicomachean Ethics*. Translated by W. D. Ross, The Works of Aristotle, vol. 9, Oxford University Press, 1925.

Bentham, J. *An introduction to the principles of morals and legislation: Printed in the year 1780 (ed.1789) an introduction to the principles of morals and legislation: Printed in the year 1780 (ed.1789)*. 1789th ed., Hachette Livre - BNF, 2022. Sciences Sociales.

Blackburn, Simon. *Ethics: A Very Short Introduction*. 2nd ed., Oxford University Press, 2021,https://doi.org10.1093/actrade/9780198868101.001.0001.

Byrne, P. *Philosophical and Ethical Problems in Mental Handicap*. Palgrave Macmillan, 2000.

Mill, John Stuart. *Utilitarianism*. Cambridge University Press, 2014.

Nussbaum, Martha Craven. "Human Functioning and Social Justice." *Political Theory*,vol. 20, no. 2, SAGE Publishing, May 1992, pp. 202–46. https://doi.org/10.1177/0090591792020002002.

Nussbaum, Martha, and Amartya Sen. *The Quality of Life*. Oxford UP, 1993.

Singer, Peter. *Practical Ethics*. 3rd ed., Cambridge University Press, 2011.

Eugenics

The term "eugenics" was coined by Sir Francis Galton in 1883, marking the inception of a movement aimed at improving human genetic stock, particularly through selective breeding. However, the application of eugenics principles soon led to grave social injustices, particularly affecting people with cognitive disabilities.

Eugenicists, operating under the assumption that social problems such as crime and poverty could be controlled through genetic means, advocated for restrictive social policies and the prohibition of unions among people deemed "insane" or "feeble-minded." These terms, including "idiots," "imbeciles," and "morons," were medically defined by eugenicists to categorize people with cognitive disabilities. The eugenics movement propagated the belief that human society could be enhanced by selectively breeding people with desirable traits, while discouraging reproduction among those deemed undesirable. This notion gained traction, particularly in the industrial age, where the promise of creating a more capable and productive population held significant appeal. However, the practice of controlling reproduction and determining societal value based on genetic characteristics predates the industrial age. Some communities have long held beliefs about the value of certain members of their population, promoting those people who possess traits deemed beneficial to the community's well-being.

Despite its initial promises, the eugenics movement ultimately led to widespread human rights abuses, including forced sterilizations and discriminatory policies targeting marginalized groups. While eugenics has largely fallen out of favor as a scientific and social ideology, its legacy continues to shape debates surrounding genetics, disability rights, and social justice. Social groups throughout history have regulated their populations through various means, often involving practices of exclusion and violence. However, with the rise of modernity, the concept of eugenics emerged as a seemingly rationalized approach to population management, cloaking violence in the guise of scientific and technological progress. At the turn of the twentieth century, Europe was grappling with mass migration and growing concerns about population dynamics. In response, eugenics gained traction as a means to eliminate what was perceived as "polluted" and "weak" races, thereby safeguarding the purported purity and strength of the population. Within the framework of eugenics, certain bodies came to be stigmatized as manifestations of biological inferiority. This included people with chronic illnesses, as well as those who deviated from societal norms in terms of race, ethnicity, or sexual orientation. Such bodies were deemed undesirable and targeted for elimination or restriction through eugenic policies.

Under the guise of modern progress, eugenics was institutionalized as state policies, endorsed by governments and supported by scientific discourse. This alignment between eugenic science and state power enabled the implementation of coercive measures aimed at controlling reproduction and shaping the genetic makeup of the population. However, the rationalized veneer of eugenics served to obscure the violence inherent in its practices, which often involved forced sterilizations, institutionalization, and other forms of state-sanctioned discrimination and violence against marginalized groups. Despite its purported goals of promoting health and genetic purity, eugenics ultimately perpetuated systemic inequalities and injustices, perpetuating harmful hierarchies based on notions of biological superiority and inferiority. The legacy of eugenics serves as a stark reminder of the dangers of using science and technology as tools of social control, highlighting the need for critical examination and ethical scrutiny of practices that purport to improve the human condition through genetic manipulation and population management.

The implementation of eugenic policies throughout history involved a range of coercive measures aimed at controlling the genetic makeup of populations and promoting what was perceived as "genetically superior" traits. These policies included the compilation of records documenting so-called genetically inferior family lines, the development of intellectual categories and measurements such as IQ and hereditary genius, and the imposition of labels such as "feebleminded." Additionally, antimiscegenation laws were enacted, selective reproduction counseling was encouraged, and rewards were offered for what was deemed "good breeding" and fitness. Moreover, institutionalization and forced sterilization were utilized as means to eliminate those considered inferior.

The horrors of the Holocaust and the atrocities committed by the Nazis, who were proponents of eugenic philosophy, led to the discrediting of eugenics as a social movement. Similar to the way slavery is now viewed as a historical stain, eugenics has become a dark chapter in history. However, despite the discrediting of traditional eugenics, new forms of genetic engineering and reproductive technologies have emerged. These technologies aim to eliminate diseases and allow for control over the health and appearance of offspring. This phenomenon has been termed the "new eugenics" by scholars such as Daniel Kevles. This new iteration of eugenics is characterized by the increasing commodification of products and processes aimed at normalization, such as cosmetic surgery. In this context, disability scholars view eugenics as one of the most significant ethical issues of our time. The continued pursuit of genetic enhancement and normalization raises profound questions about the value placed on human diversity and the potential consequences for marginalized communities, particularly those with disabilities. Disability Studies thus interrogates the implications of these developments within the broader historical and social context, advocating for ethical and inclusive approaches to genetic technologies and reproductive practices.

Suggested Readings:

Snyder, Sharon, and David T. Mitchell. *Eugenics in America, 1848-1935: A Primary Sourcebook in Disability Studies.* University of Michigan Press, 2003.

Trent, James W., Jr. *Inventing the Feeble Mind: A History of Mental Retardation in the United States.* Univ of California Press, 1994.

Euthanasia

The term "euthanasia" finds its roots in the Greek language, where it translates to "good death." This linguistic juxtaposition often perplexes people, as the notion of death being inherently "good" seems contradictory. However, throughout history, the meaning and interpretation of euthanasia have evolved significantly. In Western societies, euthanasia was historically perceived as a death blessed by God, often associated with peaceful and painless passing. The concept gained traction in modern discourse when medical authorities began considering euthanasia as an option for people experiencing unbearable pain and suffering due to incurable illnesses. Scholars such as Killick Millard and Ann Mitchell have engaged in debates surrounding euthanasia, arguing that providing a humane death for those who are terminally ill and express a desire to end their suffering could lead to a more equitable distribution of resources and wealth within society. However, it is essential to note that euthanasia proponents have adamantly distanced themselves from associations with Nazism, particularly due to the regime's endorsement of involuntary euthanasia practices.

The historical context of euthanasia underscores the complex ethical considerations surrounding end-of-life care and the autonomy of people to make decisions about their own death. Discussions surrounding euthanasia continue to provoke intense debates within medical, legal, and ethical spheres, with proponents advocating for the right to die with dignity and opponents raising concerns about potential abuses and ethical implications. As such, the discourse surrounding euthanasia remains multifaceted and highly contested, reflecting the intricate intersections of morality, law, and societal values. Euthanasia encompasses various forms, each presenting unique ethical and practical considerations. In voluntary euthanasia, a deliberate action is taken to administer a life-ending substance directly to the patient's body, typically at their explicit request. This form of euthanasia is characterized by the voluntary consent of the individual involved.

Voluntary passive euthanasia, on the other hand, involves the withholding or withdrawal of medical technology or treatment that is keeping the patient alive. In this scenario, the decision is often made by medical professionals or the patient's designated decision-maker, based on the patient's wishes or the futility of further treatment. Physician-assisted suicide represents another form of euthanasia, where a medical provider supplies life-ending narcotics or substances to a patient who wishes to end their own life. In this case, the patient actively participates in their own death, with the assistance of medical professionals. Despite the availability of these different forms of euthanasia, numerous questions and debates persist within society and the medical community. Key issues include determining who has the authority to decide whether a life should be terminated, distinguishing between terminally ill and severely ill people, and establishing criteria for approving euthanasia requests.

Disability Studies scholars offer a critical perspective on these debates, arguing that people who opt for euthanasia often do so as a result of social discrimination rather than solely due to their biological condition. They contend that people with disabilities may experience suffering not because of their intrinsic medical condition, but because of societal attitudes and barriers that limit their opportunities and quality of life. In light of these considerations, discussions surrounding euthanasia must take into account broader social and structural factors that influence people' decisions. Disability Studies scholars advocate for approaches that prioritize addressing social inequalities and providing adequate support and resources to people with disabilities, rather than resorting to euthanasia as a solution to their suffering. Disability Studies scholars offer a nuanced perspective on euthanasia, challenging the notion that it represents a purely autonomous choice. Instead, they argue that euthanasia can be influenced by disability oppression, whereby societal discrimination and stigma contribute to people feeling that death is their only option to escape suffering and discrimination. While some argue that terminal illness should be distinguished from disability, asserting that active euthanasia for terminally ill people promotes autonomy, Disability Studies scholars like Batavia counter this argument. They contend that terminal illness cannot be divorced from the broader context of disability oppression and stigmatization. Additionally, they caution against the risk of perpetuating ableist assumptions by separating the experiences of terminally ill people from those with disabilities.

Felicia Ackerman further complicates the distinction between disability and terminal illness, emphasizing the interconnectedness of these experiences and the potential for stigmatization. Ackerman's argument highlights the importance of recognizing the ways in which societal attitudes towards disability can influence perceptions of terminal illness and end-of-life decision-making. Within the context of euthanasia, Disability Studies scholars express concerns that passive euthanasia may inadvertently reinforce the notion that disability is inherently burdensome or undesirable. They suggest that the availability of passive euthanasia options may contribute to a sense of hopelessness among people with disabilities, potentially leading them to consider ending their lives prematurely.

Suggested Readings:
　　Brockopp, Jonathan E. *Islamic Ethics of Life: Abortion,*

War, and Euthanasia. Columbia: University Of. South Carolina Press, 2003.

Dowbiggin, Ian Robert. *A Merciful End: The Euthanasia Movement in Modern America*. Oxford UP, USA, 2003.

Dworkin, Ronald. *Life's Dominion: An Argument About Abortion, Euthanasia, and Individual Freedom*. Alfred A. Knopf, 1993.

Gallagher, Hugh Gregory. *By Trust Betrayed: Patients, Physicians, and the License to Kill in the Third Reich*. Vandemere Pr. 1995.

Glover, Jonathan. *Causing Death and Saving Lives: The Moral Problems of Abortion, Infanticide, Suicide, Euthanasia, Capital Punishment, War and Other Life-or-death Choices*. Penguin UK, 1990.

Gormally, Luke. *Euthanasia, Clinical Practice and the Law*. Linacre Centre for Health Care Ethics. 1994.

Coward, Harold G., et al. *Hindu Ethics: Purity, Abortion, and Euthanasia*. SUNY Press, 1989.

Freak

Freak shows have historically served as platforms where people with disabilities or unique physical characteristics are put on display for an able-bodied audience, transforming them into objects of spectacle. In this theatrical setting, the "freak" becomes a focal point, representing the perceived divide between the able-bodied "us" and the disabled "them" or "other." The contemporary study of freaks and freak shows has emerged from a scholarly debate between two prominent figures: Leslie Fiedler and Robert Bogdan. Fiedler approaches the concept of the freak from an essentialist perspective, viewing otherness as an inherent trait of the individual. According to Fiedler, a "true freak" is someone who is born with a disability or distinct physical characteristic that sets them apart from the norm.

Contrastingly, Robert Bogdan challenges this essentialist viewpoint by proposing that it is the performance itself that produces the freak. In Bogdan's perspective, it is the act of display and the theatrical presentation that transforms an individual with a difference or peculiarity into a freak. Thus, he argues that being a freak is not an inherent characteristic of the individual but rather a product of societal perceptions, practices, and institutionalized norms surrounding disability and difference. Bogdan's argument suggests that the concept of the freak is not fixed or inherent but rather fluid and contingent upon social and cultural contexts. It is shaped by the ways in which people are presented and perceived within specific socio-historical frameworks, emphasizing the role of performance, display, and societal attitudes in constructing notions of freakishness.

By examining the divergent perspectives of Fiedler and Bogdan, scholars and researchers gain insight into the complex dynamics at play within freak shows and the broader societal attitudes towards disability and difference. This nuanced understanding underscores the importance of critically examining the ways in which people with disabilities are portrayed and treated within cultural and historical contexts, challenging stereotypes and advocating for greater inclusivity and respect for diversity. The constructivist perspective, advocated by scholars such as Robert Bogdan, emerged as a dominant framework in the study of freaks, coinciding with the rise of Disability Studies within the humanities. This perspective challenged essentialist notions of freakishness, asserting that the concept of the freak is socially constructed rather than inherent to the individual.

Freak shows, as a phenomenon, have a long history dating back to the beginning of recorded human civilization. Throughout history, people with unique physical characteristics or disabilities—referred to as human oddities—have been forcibly confined, categorized, and theatrically displayed for public consumption. The 18th century saw the emergence of entrepreneurial freak shows, which capitalized on public curiosity and fascination with the unusual. One notable example is Saartjie Baartman, also known as the "Hottentot Venus," who gained widespread fame as a featured exhibit in freak shows during the early 19th century. Baartman, originally from South Africa, was exhibited in England and France in the 1810s, where she was displayed as a symbol of sexual deviance and racial inferiority. Baartman's large breasts and buttocks, characteristic of the Khoikhoi tribe she belonged to, were sensationalized and exploited for entertainment purposes. Her exhibition perpetuated harmful stereotypes about race and sexuality, reinforcing colonial narratives of African inferiority and exoticism. The exploitation of Baartman serves as a stark example of the dehumanizing treatment endured by people featured in freak shows. Their bodies were commodified and objectified for profit, while they themselves were denied agency and subjected to ridicule and exploitation.

The study of freak shows, as illuminated by scholars like Rosemarie Garland-Thomson and Rachel Adams, provides valuable insights into the historical and cultural dimensions of disability and difference. By interrogating the societal attitudes and power dynamics that underpin the spectacle of freak shows, these scholars shed light on broader issues of social marginalization, ableism, and the construction of normalcy. Freak shows thrived in the

United States from approximately 1835 to 1940, coinciding with the growth of museums and circuses during this period. P.T. Barnum, a prominent figure in show business, capitalized on the popularity of freak shows by featuring famous attractions such as Tom Thumb and Chang and Eng Bunker, conjoined twins. These exhibitions contributed significantly to Barnum's commercial success. Among the notable figures showcased in freak shows was William Henry Johnson, an African American man known by the stage name "What Is It?" Johnson was exhibited as an evolutionary "missing link," adding to the spectacle and intrigue of the shows. In freak shows, bodies were meticulously arranged, posed, and displayed theatrically to maximize audience engagement. Written materials were often prepared to enhance the sense of wonder and mystery surrounding the exhibits, while also evoking feelings of fear and horror in the viewers.

The ambiguous nature of the bodies and human anomalies presented in freak shows challenged conventional understandings of what it means to be "human." By blurring the boundaries between normalcy and abnormality, the freak unsettled established notions of humanity, prompting audiences to reconsider their preconceived notions about human identity and difference. The presence of freaks in these exhibitions posed a fundamental threat to the categorical definition of "human," forcing spectators to confront the complexities and contradictions inherent in their understanding of humanity. The freak show thus served as a provocative cultural phenomenon, raising profound questions about identity, belonging, and the limits of human variation.

Freak shows served as a mechanism through which able-bodied white audiences could assert the perceived superiority of their race, bodies, and personhood. By showcasing people with unique physical characteristics or disabilities, the freak provided a contrast against which the normative standards of "normalcy" could be defined. In this way, the freak embodied the "not normal," serving as a living tool through which the able-bodied spectators could reaffirm their own normalcy in terms of their bodies and identities. Rosemarie Garland-Thomson's concept of the "normate" sheds light on this dynamic, referring to an idealized social identity based on dominant identity categories. The display of freaks in shows curated by figures like P.T. Barnum reinforced the normate by presenting a stark contrast to it, thereby reinforcing societal norms and ideals.

One particularly egregious example is the case of Joice Heth, an elderly African American woman whom Barnum exhibited as the purported 161-year-old nurse of George Washington. Her exhibition not only served to entertain audiences but also to perpetuate harmful stereotypes and validate white supremacy. Even in death, Heth was subjected to exploitation, as Barnum staged a public autopsy following her demise, further reinforcing the inferiority of the black body and affirming the supposed superiority of whiteness. Moreover, post-Civil War freak shows often featured people from exotic lands against crudely rendered backdrops meant to evoke their supposed natural habitats. This practice served to exoticize and objectify these people, reinforcing colonialist ideologies and perpetuating notions of racial and cultural superiority.

The phenomenon of "racial freaks" in freak shows depicted people whose sole "disability" was perceived as their adherence to traditional cultural practices. These people were often portrayed as non-white, regressive, and antiquated, thereby reinforcing racial hierarchies prevalent in the United States during that time. By exoticizing and dehumanizing these people, freak shows perpetuated harmful stereotypes and contributed to the marginalization of non-white communities.

The ascendancy of the medical profession eventually led to the decline of traditional freak shows. Human oddities, once objects of spectacle and curiosity, became subjects of medical scrutiny, rationalization, and explanation. Disabilities, rather than being sensationalized for entertainment purposes, were now medicalized, viewed through the lens of pathology and scientific inquiry. Although traditional freak shows waned in popularity by the mid-19th century, they underwent a transformation and found new expression in the emerging medium of television. While no longer displayed in public squares, the themes and spectacles of freak shows persisted in a changed and more refined form on television screens. One notable example of this transformation was the portrayal of overweight contestants in weight-loss contests, presented in a manner that suggested their bodies were grotesque and in need of correction.

In this modern iteration, the themes of spectacle, othering, and voyeurism remained prevalent, albeit under the guise of reality television entertainment. Audiences were invited to observe and judge people with disabilities or physical differences, perpetuating societal norms and stigmas surrounding body image and health.

Abigail and Brittany Hensel, conjoined twins sharing one body, made headlines when they signed on to do a reality show in 2012. While traditional freak shows may no longer exist as formal entertainment ventures, the underlying dynamic of able-bodied people observing and scrutinizing bodies with disabilities or unique differences persists in everyday interactions.

The field of Freak studies has played a significant role in shaping the discourse surrounding Disability Studies. It has been instrumental in examining societal attitudes towards people with disabilities or physical differences, shedding light on the ways in which these people have been historically marginalized and objectified for public consumption. Despite its historical significance, Freak Studies have somewhat receded from the forefront of scholarly inquiry in recent years, finding itself relegated to the margins of academic discourse. However, its insights remain valuable and relevant, not only within the realm of Disability Studies but also in other fields of study. Garland-Thomson explores the dynamics of visual engagement and the social rules that govern how people look at each other. By examining the gaze and its implications for both the observer and the observed, Garland-Thomson offers profound insights into the ways in which societal norms and expectations shape our interactions with people who deviate from the perceived norm.

In his poignant reflection, James Baldwin articulates a profound truth about the perception of "freaks" in society. He suggests that these people are labeled as such precisely because they are human beings who evoke a complex interplay of emotions within us, including our deepest fears and desires. Baldwin's assertion that "we are a part of each other" speaks to the intrinsic interconnectedness of humanity, wherein the experiences of others, including those deemed as "freaks," resonate deeply with our own. This sentiment can be interpreted as encapsulating a core principle within Disability Studies — the recognition of the inherent humanity and interconnectedness of all people, regardless of ability or appearance. The figure of the "freak" serves as a poignant reminder within Disability Studies of the ongoing pursuit of this goal. The anomalous body of the "freak" challenges societal norms and perceptions, prompting critical reflection on the nature of embodiment, difference, and belonging. Through the lens of Disability Studies, the "freak" emerges as a symbol of the broader human experience, inviting us to confront our own biases, prejudices, and preconceptions.

Suggested Readings:

Adams, Rachel. '*Sideshow USA: Freaks and the American Cultural Imagination*'. University of Chicago Press, 2001.

Thomson, Rosemarie Garland. *Freakery: Cultural Spectacles of the Extraordinary Body.* NYU Press, 1996.

——.*Extraordinary Bodies: Figuring Physical Disability in American Culture and Literature.* Columbia University Press, 1997.

Gender

Gender, disability, race, class, nationality, and sexuality are all constitutive agents of our Identity and living experience. The focus of attention of the Disability Studies scholars are the 'bodies', and no 'body' is capable of existing without being attributed to the category of destined gender based on its functioning and physical features and gender is assigned according to the accepted norms of a society. Both the fields, feminism as well as Disability Studies, are structured on the basis of binary, sex/gender, and impairment/disability. While sex is biological, it is predestined and inevitable but gender is a culturally constructed idea; it depends on societal views and norms and is acquired through one's behaviour, choices, and physiological structure. This stark binary between masculine and feminine poses a problem for those who stand in between the two, who, despite having the bodies of males but possessing the urges and desires of females or vice versa, can't be identified as either male or female.

Thus, gender and disability are both culturally constructed notions of society, which are produced to regulate and govern deviant, non-normative bodies. Such markers of identities objectify the material body and devalue them. Both Feminist and Disability Studies deal with the material essences of the bodies; in a way, they question the validity of the interconnection between sex and the impairment of the body.

According to Gayle Salamon and Alison Kafer, the meaning of sex and impairment is hard to define without relating it to the socio-cultural context where the bodies exist. This sex-gender binary compels us to view transgender people as physically lacking or unfit and thus in need of health care. From the perspective of the medical model, disability, gender fluidity, intersex are all pathological defects and which need to be fixed or cured by medical professionals. It cures the sexual deviants by bringing them as close as possible to the normative gender identity through surgery or medications. However, transgender people who are willing to reassign their sexual Identity by surgery are first needed to submit to the Gender Identity Disorder (GID) to be granted permission. They have no authority over their bodies. Recently the Diagnostic and Statistical Manual of Mental Disorders (DSM-5) have replaced GID with gender dysphoria. Although trans activists want to abolish this marking of transgender identities as a disorder, they are also worried about its impact on legal proceedings since GID used to fight against gender discrimination in its own way. Trans people, like the social model of disability, see the problem within the society; they focus on the unwelcoming nature of the society; environmental barriers hinder the growth of trans people rather than on their bodily difference. The mainstream society have marginalised and isolated both the disabled and trans people. To solve this problem, not the deviant bodies but the group in majority need to change their dominat beliefs and stereotypical attitudes. The oppression against the non-normative gender and the disabled bodies are heavily dependent upon one's race, class, social status, and sexual identity. Disabled people are viewed as second-class citizens of society and thus are excluded from society not much because of their disability but rather because of the dominant stigma that prevails in society. Gender plays a significant role in this, just as disabled men are considered to be less masculine. Similarly, disability makes a woman more vulnerable to society's eye. Women with disabilities are doubly marginalised; on the one hand, their disabled bodies limit their mobility, restricting their potential and achievements. On the other hand, their gender marks them as socially inferior and they are at risk of being oppressed by the patriarchal society. This sex-gender dichotomy plays a significant role in marking identities.

According to, the World Health Organization, sex is a biological factor; it depends on one's hormonal functions, body structures, chromosomal complement etc.; sex is predetermined, but gender is an acquired identity. It is a cultural and social construct which is decided by one's behaviour and sexual preferences/ choices. This creates a problem for those who fall in the middle position, those with ambiguous sexual identities, who do conform to this stark gender binary paradox. Thus, both sex and gender should be given equal value while addressing this health and disability problem. In most cases, literary works featuring prominent disabled figures or centring around the issue of disability do not focus much on gender concerns. However, in recent times many investigations have been performed on the status of disabled women as compared to disabled men, and the study reports are

1. Disabled women are financially weaker than disabled men since they do not get the opportunity to earn, being doubly marginalised by the patriarchal society and the limitation imposed upon them on top of their disability.

2. Even if they get the chance to earn, they are paid less than men.

3. They are more vulnerable to domination, being physically weak, they are at higher risk of being sexually abused than able bodied women.

4. Disabled women, due to their grotesque body structures, are often considered sexually unattractive or even "asexual".

5. Disabled women, compared to disabled men or even non-disabled women, get fewer educational opportunities.

6. Disabled women barely have access to "rehabilitation" services to the disabled men.

Disability is a dynamic process; its impact varies on the basis of culture, society, economic conditions, political circumstances etc.; this is why there is an increasing focus on gender differences among the disabled population. Compared to disabled men, disabled women are more hindered from participating in social activities or availing of education and employment opportunities. Thus, they are confined within their own bodies as well as isolated from the larger world. In the context of social relationships, disabled women are most often compelled to live a solitary life since men with physically fit bodies rarely choose such a woman to be their life partner; even if she gets married, she is more likely to get divorced or separated being unable to fulfill the demands of her in-law's house. Disabled women also face problems while bearing a child due to their physical limitations. These are the reasons why disabled women fail to have meaningful, healthy relationships and thus are forced to live in isolation from society. They have lesser self-esteem and suffer from an inferiority complex as compared to disabled men, which may be the result of her family's stigmatised attitudes towards her, be it their overprotective nature which prevents the disabled daughter from engaging in household activities or their feeling of burden at the inconveniences caused by the disabled member of the family. From the perspective of socio-cultural factors, disabled women are the subject of society's stigmatisation and discrimination. Generally, women are considered as passive, vulnerable, innocent and dependent on the male members of the family both financially and physically; on top of that, those women with disabilities are considered to be unfit to fulfill society's demands to be qualified for the social roles, such as mother, wife, sexual partners and so on. Moreover, disabled women of black identity experience a third layer of bias. They internalise society's stigmatised notions of their incompetence. So, the focus of Disability Studies, along with the endeavour to improve the living conditions and legal rights of disabled people, must also focus attention on gender bias and discrimination. If one investigates the trajectory of Disability Studies, disability has primarily been viewed as a medical issue which needs medical intervention to get closer to the norms. However, such a notion has been questioned by recent scholars and activists. Thus, the marginalised, excluded status of disabled people has been seen as the result of social oppression and discrimination for which their physical impairment or disability is not to be blamed. They become disabled because of society's inability to provide them with better, accessible infrastructure and obtainable government facilities, which prevents them from merging into mainstream social activities and living fulfilling lives. Disability is thus a social construct. On the other hand, gender though historically associated with sex, during the 1970s, feminist analysis distinguished these two terms, sex and gender, where sex is the biological, chromosomal and physiological factor like 'impairment' but gender is the result of socio-cultural impact of one's behaviour or sexual choices. Sex is natural, inborn and predetermined, but gender is an acquired identity. Femininity and masculinity came to be understood as acquired characteristics with social significance. This distinction between sex and gender highlights the latent issue of women being regarded as passive and submissive for being the 'weaker sex' as they were subjugated by the male-dominated society, but their sex was natural; it is gender which is man-made, and social product used to subjugate women and confine them within the rigid boundaries of society. Feminist activists thus disclosed the hidden agenda of the patriarchal society, their creation of gender distinction to dominate women by rendering them inferior beings. However, mainstream feminist scholars believed that all women, irrespective of their class, caste, and race, were subjected to equal discrimination and unequal treatment, but this belief was contested, as for the black women , this experience was entirely different because they were doubly marginalised, due to their race and gender, similarly, disabled women also face the same issue, since they are considered inferior not only because of their sex but also because of their deformed bodies. Both gender and disability are the social construction which imposes cultural consciousness on biological sex and impairment. Disabled people become the victim of discrimination from their very birth; some are even considered better to be dead or killed deliberately to remove the burden from the family.

Like the Eugenics sterilisation that originated in the West, in India, also with the innovation of technology, sex detection of the fetus results in much untimely death of defective or female embryos within the mother's womb itself. Due to this, the female ratio has significantly decreased compared to the male. Surprisingly, although there have been many protests and arguments being circulated by feminist critiques regarding the ethical value of the prenatal killing of female fetuses, rarely has anybody ever questioned the same crime done against defective fetuses. However, even if the fetus of a disabled girl survives, life for her, in the long run, does not seem to be an easy path. The disabled girl child sometimes do not even get proper inclusion in the family. Many a times, they cannot avail the basic necessities which are essential for survival and a healthy living, such as food, health care facilities, employment opportunities, education etc. However, during the 1980s, feminists raised the problem of addressing disabled women's experiences to the same extent that a non-disabled woman faces. They argued that the experiences of oppression for disabled women are not similar to that of other women since the disabled women are not bound by many social claims and expectations, which the feminists have challenged since disabled women were not regarded to be qualifying enough to fit in the social roles designed for women such as wife, mother etc. As a result of which, non-disabled women were subjected to patriarchal oppression and domination. If they failed to fulfill the demands and expectations of their social roles then they were physically abused. Women are generally imagined to be best suited for traditional roles; they are used for motherly metaphors and the epitome of care and affection, and disabled women, being not perfect physically or mentally, are thought not to be capable of fulfilling traditional roles. Disabled women are not considered to be 'marriage material' since their imperfect genes can pass on to the future generations or even because they may not be able to raise their children as efficiently as a non-disabled woman can. Thus, in addition to their social isolation and exclusion, they are deprived of traditional roles, which leads them to live a life devoid of happiness or meaning. Society does not provide enough opportunities or employment facilities to disabled women rendering them dependent on someone, and this view of disabled women as dependent beings prevents them from achieving the status of motherhood and being the caretaker. She, who is not able to take care of herself, how can she take care of her child, is the question raised by the society. Thus, their claim is to first achieve their identity, their 'personhood', then be recognised as women. In many societies, women, particularly those with intellectual disability, are forcefully sterilised, which is even considered to be a boon for them since they no longer have to maintain menstrual hygiene or unwanted pregnancies with defective genes. This process of sterilisation stands paradoxical to the dominant view that disabled women are 'asexual' or less attractive, which reduces their chances of being sexually active or sexually molested. Disabled women, due to their physical incapacity, can't adhere to accepted norms of beauty and perfection which fills them with an inferiority complex while getting the chance to be sexually intimate. These standards of beauty are prescribed to control women's bodies, especially those with disabilities, rather than addressing the problem of social discrimination. Disabled women, who are fully dependent upon their caregivers, are sometimes subjected to sexual abuse since they neither have a voice nor any authority over their own lives. Disabled women should raise their voice to protest against the injustices done towards them and to claim their own identities, which is not addressed in the feminist discourse. Even the mothers of disabled women are perceived to be cursed or sinners, being impregnated with such a child. There have been several instances of divorce because the mother has given birth to a disabled child, especially a disabled girl child. There is a popular slogan that "being a woman is the biggest form of disability"; until such belief is erased from society, women's empowerment is hard to achieve.

Gender and disability, along with race, class, nationality, and sexuality, are constitutive features of the ways in which our fully integrated selves—what Margaret Price (2011) calls "bodymind"—are lived and known. Universally evidence suggests that a person with a disability is stigmatised and discriminated against in society as a second-class citizen, thus placing this group at risk of alienation. Gender is one among many social divisions on which they are discriminated against and excluded from voting rights and others. Men with disabilities are thought to be less masculine and weaker than non-disabled men, and similarly, women are considered less feminine. Analysing both these dichotomies (disabled/non-disabled and man/female) is important because evidence suggests that women face "double jeopardy" due to sexism and disability bias and are at increased risk of poor health and social outcomes. Gender is seen as the same as sex differentiation, which suggests that biologically and physiologically, there are only two sexes, male and female. Gender refers to a set of social norms, rules and behaviour that can be ascribed to an individual. It refers to what is meant to be considered masculine and feminine in a given time and place.

Most of the literature on gender and disability does not focus on women and men, but rather, the focus is on people with disability compared with people without disability. The social stigma attached to disability is abnormal, and this deviance is a concern of most work of disability and not the gender or other barriers, like feminisation of poverty, abuse, violence, and sexual and reproductive rights. Recent year's research examining the impact of gender points out the decreased status of women. Women with disability face marginalization on multifarious levels. Their income, potential and decision-making power are even considered less than men with disability. They are more prone to sexual abuse and are sometimes viewed as asexual. They even have less access to rehabilitation services as compared to disabled men.

But since disability is a dynamic process, change in gender differences can occur with increasing worldwide focus on women's rights. Literature suggests that women with disabilities are at a double disadvantage as they have a lower level of participation in social activities and a lower level of self-respect and self-concept. To add to their sigma are sexism and ableism. Sexism refers to the devalued status of women in comparison with men in society. Women are seen as childlike, passive and dependent. Women with disability are often perceived as not being able to fulfill the variety of roles the society places on women in general as mother, wife and sexual partner. Society sees them as not being physically attractive and relatively passive, uninteresting, unsociable and unintelligent. Women of colour who have disabilities have to face a third layer of biases. They have lower 'self-concepts' and lower self-esteem, which come from family members as causing inconvenience or, conversely, have an overprotective attitude towards disabled women.

Gender, which was considered synonymous with sex, got challenged in the 1970s with its appearance in feminist discourse. Since then, sex refers to the biological characteristics of men/women and gender as social and psychological characteristics of feminine/masculine. Sex is related to what was bestowed by nature, and gender is related to what was a result of nature. Despite a clear enunciation of the gendered character of societal parameters, mainstream feminism went on to replicate the inequities of the patriarchal society by leaving out of its ambit many categories of women who are marked by a given system as "different" and are oppressed due to factors such as class, ethnicity, caste and physical or mental diversity. Implicit was the idea of 'Universal sisterhood'. However, this idea was contested by those who felt that their unique life conditions were not reflected in the collective experience. The process of discrimination with disabled people starts at birth. Some young disabled infants are killed or are left to die. In India, technological advances that allowed the determination of sex in the foetus have created a eugenics movement that might be unheard of in the West. But the use of technology for pre-birth genetic screening to predict disability has not been addressed. Coupled with the predominant negative assumption held about impairment and disability, it is not surprising that abortion for the impaired was not even mentioned. Even the survival to the birth of a disabled girl child, however, does not guarantee her struggle for a free existence. Despite swift social, cultural and economic changes and the current drive towards a global society, women are still defined in terms of their traditional social roles. For instance, in India, throughout her life, a woman is defined by her role as a daughter, a wife and as a mother. However, disabled women are considered unmarriable because of their "imperfections" that could be passed on to their children, and also their suitability for the role of motherhood and physical capacity to carry a pregnancy is also questioned. In many societies, intellectually disabled women are forced to have sterilisation, which is said to relax them as they no longer have to manage menstrual hygiene or deal with pregnancy or the risk of bearing a disabled child. The feminist discourse in India has paid scant attention to the issues faced by women who are the mothers of disabled children, especially girls. Women cannot validate their social status as mothers if they have given birth to disabled children and are condemned to live in shame.

Thus, disabled women must struggle not only to assert their own identities but also to assert their difference and to account for the injustices done to women that have not found expression in the language of feminism. For disabled women to resist the normality hegemony, advocacy and research are essential. Within India, what is perhaps needed is an interrogation of the normative standards that construct disabled women as passive and dependent. Researchers need to resist the tendency to borrow from the Western understanding, as the local reality is extremely important. The cause of disabled women in India would be greatly supported by cross-cultural research that listens to diverse voices and recognises that there is no single grand narrative of "the disabled woman."

Suggested Readings:

Butler, Judith. *Gender Trouble: Feminism and the Subversion of Identity.* London: Routledge1990.

Butler, Judith. *"Bodies that matter." Feminist theory and the body. Routledge,* 2017. 235-245.

Thomson, Rosemarie Garland. *Extraordinary bodies: Figuring physical disability in American culture and literature.* Columbia University Press, 2017.

Corker, Mairian, and Sally French. *Disability discourse.* McGraw-Hill Education (UK), 1999.

Gerschick, Thomas J. "Toward a theory of disability and gender." *Signs: Journal of women in culture and society* 25.4 (2000): 1263-1268.

Gerschick, Thomas J., and Adam Stephen Miller. "Gender identities at the crossroads of masculinity and physical disability." *Toward a new psychology of gender.* Routledge, 2013. 455-475.

Meekosha, Helen, and Leanne Dowse. "Enabling citizenship: Gender, disability and citizenship in Australia." Feminist review 57.1 (1997): 49-72.

Handicap

The term "handicap" has evolved over time, undergoing several etymological changes that have shaped its present-day connotations. In contemporary usage, "handicap" carries a dual meaning, reflecting both its association with physical or cognitive impairment and its application in the context of sports. On one hand, "handicap" refers to people with certain types of physical or cognitive impairments that limit their ability to achieve their life goals or hinder their growth due to various obstacles. This interpretation highlights the challenges and barriers faced by people with disabilities in navigating the world around them, underscoring the need for accessibility, inclusion, and support to ensure their full participation in society.

On the other hand, "handicap" also holds relevance in the realm of sports, where it denotes a system of providing advantages or disadvantages to athletes based on their skill levels, experience, or other factors. In this context, less experienced athletes may be given certain advantages to level the playing field and enhance the competitiveness of sporting events. However, scholars in the field of Disability Studies critique the term "handicap" as highly inappropriate and degrading, primarily due to its authoritative and paternalistic connotations. Historically, policies and legislation concerning people with disabilities have often been formulated and implemented by non-disabled people in positions of power, without meaningful input or representation from the disabled community themselves. This lack of agency and autonomy undermines the voices and experiences of disabled people, perpetuating a system of marginalization and discrimination. In light of these concerns, Disability Studies scholars advocate for the use of more respectful and empowering language that recognizes the agency, dignity, and rights of people with disabilities. This includes embracing person-first language that prioritizes the individual over their disability and acknowledges their inherent worth and humanity. By challenging outdated and stigmatizing terminology like "handicap," Disability Studies seeks to promote greater inclusivity, equality, and social justice for all members of society.

The slogan "Nothing about us, without us" encapsulates the fundamental principle of civil rights for people with disabilities, emphasizing their right to self-determination and autonomy in shaping their own destinies. To comprehend the origins of the stigma attached to disability, it is essential to delve into the etymological history of the term "handicap." The term "handicap" has multiple potential etymologies, each shedding light on its evolving meanings and societal implications. One theory traces its roots to a medieval European game known as "hand-in-cap." In this game, two participants would place their hands in a cap and wager on whose hand was stronger. Over time, "hand-in-cap" was shortened to "handicap" and began to be applied more broadly to situations where one party held an advantage over another. Another theory suggests that "handicap" originated from the phrase "cap-in-hand," which described an individual begging for alms. In this context, a "handicap" denoted a physical or mental condition that hindered a person's ability to earn a livelihood, forcing them into a position of dependency and reliance on charity.

Both etymological origins underscore the negative connotations associated with the term "handicap," portraying people with disabilities as disadvantaged and marginalized members of society. This linguistic framing perpetuated stereotypes and contributed to the systemic discrimination and social exclusion faced by people with disabilities. The evolution of the term "handicap" reflects broader societal attitudes towards disability, highlighting the historical tendency to view people with disabilities through a lens of deficiency and inferiority. By interrogating the etymology of "handicap," we can gain insights into the roots of ableism and the importance of challenging stigmatizing language in promoting inclusivity, equality, and respect for people of all abilities.

The term "handicap" acquired a more specific usage over time, particularly in the context of competitive sports. This evolution is believed to have originated from the practice of horse racing, where a faster horse would be assigned a certain disadvantage to level the playing field against a slower competitor. This measure aimed to ensure fairness and competitiveness in the race. As this practice became more common, the term "handicap" came to be associated with any disadvantage imposed on a person or team in competition, extending beyond horse racing to various other sports and areas of endeavor. In horse racing, for example, a swifter horse might carry additional weight or start further back from the finishing line, balancing the odds against its slower counterpart.

Similarly, in the sport of golf, the concept of a handicap is prevalent. Here, less skilled players are granted certain advantages, such as extra strokes or a higher par score, to compensate for their lower level of proficiency compared to more experienced players. This adjustment aims to create a more equitable playing field and enhance the overall competitiveness of the game. However, it's worth noting that while the term "handicap" in the context of sports may imply a form of advantage for less able contestants, its broader usage can still carry negative connotations, particularly when applied to people with disabilities in other aspects of life. The term's association with disadvantage and impediment underscores the importance of promoting inclusive language and attitudes that recognize the diverse abilities and contributions of all people, regardless of any perceived limitations or challenges they may face. In the late nineteenth century, the term "handicap" encompassed obstacles and challenges that hindered people from flourishing in various aspects of life. This broad usage reflected the pervasive notion of impediments or disadvantages faced by people in their pursuit of success and fulfillment.

By the 20th century, the term "handicap" began to be associated more specifically with people who had impairments or disabilities. This usage retained its earlier connotations, particularly in the realm of sports where it denoted a disadvantage given to certain competitors to ensure fairness and equal opportunities for all participants.

In the 1980s, the World Health Organization provided a formal definition of "handicap" as the physical barriers encountered by disabled people in their daily lives. These barriers, ranging from architectural obstacles to societal attitudes and stereotypes, restricted disabled people from leading lives considered "normal" by societal standards. Instead, they were confined within narrow boundaries imposed by their impairments and the societal perceptions surrounding disability.

Despite attempts to redefine "handicap" in terms of the challenges faced by disabled people, the negative connotations associated with the term persisted. Many viewed it as offensive and derogatory, undermining the self-esteem and dignity of disabled people. As a result, there was a widespread rejection of the term in favor of more respectful and inclusive language that acknowledges the agency, capabilities, and inherent worth of people with disabilities.

British activists widely embrace the definition of disability provided by the World Health Organization (WHO), which draws a clear distinction between the terms "impairment" and "disability." According to this framework, an impairment refers to a physical or cognitive defect that deviates from the societal norm of human physiology. This could include conditions such as visual or hearing impairments, mobility limitations, or cognitive disabilities. In contrast, disability is understood as the societal response to people with impairments. It encompasses the barriers, prejudices, and discrimination that people may encounter due to their impairments. Disability is not inherent to the individual's condition but is instead a product of societal attitudes, policies, and structures that marginalize and exclude people with impairments. It is important to recognize that having an impairment does not automatically equate to being disabled. Many people with impairments are able to navigate their daily lives successfully with the support of accessible environments, inclusive policies, and societal acceptance. Disability arises when societal barriers prevent people from fully participating in society on an equal basis with others.

Conversely, people who experience disability may indeed have impairments, but the disabling aspect of their experience stems from societal attitudes and barriers rather than their intrinsic abilities or limitations. By recognizing this distinction, activists seek to challenge the notion that disability is solely a consequence of individual impairments and instead advocate for social change to dismantle barriers and promote inclusivity and accessibility for all members of society.

Suggested Readings:

Ingstad, Benedicte. 'Disability in the Developing World'. *Handbook of Disability Studies*, SAGE Publications, Inc., 2001, pp. 772–792, https://doi.org10.4135/9781412976251.n35.

Human

In Disability Studies, the term "human" holds significant importance as it sheds light on the historical marginalization of people living with physical, sensory, intellectual, or psychological impairments. Throughout history, these people have often been excluded from the category of "human," alongside other marginalized groups facing discrimination in different historical contexts. This exclusionary practice extends to various groups labeled as "blind," "idiots," "mad," or "leprous," as well as to enslaved women, colonized populations, and people of color whose humanity has been systematically denied. By examining the construction of humanity through literature, Disability Studies offers valuable insights into the societal forces that shape perceptions of human worth and dignity.

Literature serves as a potent platform for exploring the complexities of human identity and the ways in which it has been constructed and contested over time. Characters such as Shakespeare's Caliban, Swift's Yahoos, Wordsworth's Idiot Boy, Faulkner's Benjy, and Shelley's monster in Frankenstein embody the paradoxical nature of humanity, challenging conventional notions of what it means to be human. Through these literary figures, Disability Studies interrogates the boundaries of human existence and exposes the arbitrary criteria used to determine who is considered fully human. By engaging with these representations, scholars and activists seek to dismantle stereotypes, challenge prejudices, and advocate for the recognition of the inherent humanity and dignity of all people, regardless of their physical or cognitive differences.

In recent scholarly discourse, there has been a growing recognition of characters in literature who exhibit traits or experiences associated with disability. These characters, traditionally viewed as embodiments of a non-human Other, can be traced back through the lineage of literary figures, finding parallels in narratives such as Oedipus from ancient Greek mythology. Throughout Western cultural history, disabled characters have often served as symbolic representations at the intersection between humanity and non-humanity, reflecting societal attitudes and perceptions towards disability. One notable example is found in Charlotte Brönte's novel *Jane Eyre,* where the protagonist Jane reunites with Mr. Rochester, a character who has become physically impaired due to blindness and injury. In this poignant moment, Jane expresses a desire to "rehumanize" Mr. Rochester, implying that his disability has somehow dehumanized him in the eyes of society. This sentiment encapsulates the societal perception that disability can strip people of their humanity, reducing them to mere objects or symbols of pity or fear. Through Jane's statement, Brönte highlights the inherent dignity and worth of people with disabilities, challenging prevailing stereotypes and prejudices that devalue their humanity. By advocating for the rehumanization of Mr. Rochester, Jane asserts the importance of recognizing and honoring the full humanity of people with disabilities, affirming their agency, dignity, and capacity for meaningful relationships and contributions to society.

In his essay "Of Deformity," Francis Bacon delves into the societal perception of people with physical deformities, arguing that their perceived inhumanity stems not from their physical condition but from the negative social responses they evoke. Bacon contends that the lack of natural affection towards deformed people is a product of societal prejudices rather than any inherent deficiency in the people themselves.

William Hay, a hunchbacked British Parliamentarian, challenged Bacon's assertions in his groundbreaking work, "Deformity, An Essay" (1754), considered the first disability memoir. Through his personal experiences and reflections, Hay provided a compelling counterpoint to Bacon's claims, shedding light on the lived realities of people with disabilities and advocating for their recognition as fully human beings deserving of respect and dignity.

The Enlightenment era, characterized by intellectual curiosity and rational inquiry, also grappled with fundamental questions about human nature and identity. Emmanuel Kant's famous query, "What is man?" epitomizes this period of philosophical introspection, highlighting the ongoing quest to understand the essence of humanity. Despite centuries of philosophical discourse, the question of what it truly means to be human remains elusive, with no objective definition to encapsulate its complexity. However, the historical record of this ongoing dialogue provides invaluable insights into the evolving perceptions and interpretations of human identity.

In recent years, there has been a growing recognition of the need to include the voices and perspectives of the disabled community in discussions about humanity. This shift reflects a broader societal acknowledgment of the importance of diversity and inclusivity in shaping our understanding of human experience.

To truly grasp the concept of humanity, it is essential to revisit and reevaluate the historical discourse surrounding the idea of humans, taking into account the diverse perspectives and lived experiences of all people, including those with disabilities. Through this comprehensive review, we can strive towards a more nuanced and inclusive understanding of what it means to be human in all its complexity.

Throughout history, various philosophers have grappled with defining the essence of humanity, each offering unique perspectives that have shaped our understanding of human identity. Plato's descriptive definition famously characterized humans as "featherless bipeds," highlighting the significance of human morphology and parentage in defining human status. In contrast, Aristotle provided a prescriptive definition, asserting that "Man is an animal rationale," emphasizing the rational capacity as the defining characteristic of humanity.

Augustine of Hippo, Albertus Magnus, and Thomas Aquinas adopted a descriptive approach, contending that any body possessing human shape and parentage inherently possesses a human essence, regardless of cognitive or physical impairments. This perspective emphasized the sanctity and value of human life, irrespective of perceived deficiencies in the mind or body. However, the conceptualization of human identity underwent a significant shift in the early seventeenth century with the emergence of mind-body dualism, championed by philosophers like René Descartes. This philosophical framework introduced the notion of a distinct separation between the mind (or soul) and the body, allowing for the possibility of a human body lacking a functioning rational mind. Descartes' view equated such ostensibly mindless human bodies with animals, which he regarded as soulless machines.

This shift in perspective challenged traditional understandings of human identity, opening up new avenues for conceptualizing the relationship between the mind and the body. Descartes' dualistic approach paved the way for further philosophical inquiry into the nature of consciousness, cognition, and the self, ultimately influencing subsequent debates surrounding the definition of humanity and the ethical implications of these conceptual frameworks.

John Locke, a prominent Enlightenment thinker, introduced a transformative shift in defining humanity, transitioning from a descriptive to a prescriptive understanding by emphasizing intellectual resemblance. He challenged conventional notions by distinguishing between the concepts of "person" and "man," employing the example of the "changeling" to illustrate this distinction. While a "man" represented an entity of human shape and parentage without necessarily possessing rational capacity, a "person" was characterized by autonomy and the ability to act independently of parental influence. Locke's conceptual framework positioned persons as central figures within classical liberalism, emphasizing traits such as independence, self-sufficiency, and property ownership. According to Locke, these liberal subjects, by virtue of their humanity, were entitled to assert political claims of justice. This perspective exerted significant influence over the development of Western liberal democracies in subsequent centuries. However, in the latter half of the twentieth century, Locke's model of the liberal subject faced criticism from feminist, postcolonial, and queer theorists. These critics highlighted the inherent biases within the model, noting its presumptive alignment with traits such as maleness, whiteness, Anglo-Europeanness, and heterosexuality. By foregrounding these biases, theorists challenged the universality and inclusivity of Locke's framework, advocating for more nuanced and intersectional understandings of human identity and political subjectivity.

This critique prompted a reevaluation of traditional liberal theories, fostering greater recognition of diverse experiences and perspectives within political discourse. As a result, contemporary discussions surrounding human rights, justice, and citizenship have become increasingly attuned to issues of gender, race, sexuality, and colonial legacies, reflecting a broader commitment to equity, inclusivity, and social justice.

A Disability Studies perspective raises important considerations for people with disabilities, particularly regarding their relationship with Locke's liberalism. For disabled people, Locke's liberalism presents a nuanced landscape. On one hand, it offers them the opportunity to forge their own identities, establish personal meanings, and determine values that transcend societal norms and expectations. This aspect of liberalism allows disabled people to articulate their humanity in terms of rights, freedoms, and dignity.

Locke's liberalism also serves as a foundational framework for advocating justice and equality for people with disabilities. It provides a platform for asserting civil rights, exemplified by legislative milestones such as the Americans with Disabilities Act (ADA) of 1990. This landmark legislation stands as a cornerstone of disability rights, offering protections and provisions that are crucial for the empowerment and inclusion of disabled people within society.

Liberalism's emphasis on rights-based discourse and historical precedent aligns with the demand for equal treatment and justice for people with disabilities. By leveraging the principles of liberalism, disabled people and their allies can advance a compelling argument for societal recognition, accommodation, and respect, thereby challenging systemic barriers and fostering a more equitable and inclusive social landscape. However,

Disability Studies sheds light on inherent issues within the tradition from which classical liberalism originated. John Locke's philosophical framework emerged in response to patriarchalism, an ideology that justified the seventeenth-century English absolutist monarchy on the basis of the divine right of kings. Central to patriarchalism was a familial metaphor, wherein God the Father governed the world, mirroring the king's paternal rule over his subjects, who were perceived as his children.

Locke sought to challenge this metaphor by exposing its fundamental flaw: the inherent inequality and lack of autonomy it imposed on people. He argued that just as children eventually mature and assert independence from their parents, so too should citizens from their rulers. However, contemporary critics have identified a contradiction in Locke's approach, noting that while he acknowledged the maturation of children into independent adults, his conception of the liberal subject resembled more of an adolescent seeking liberation from parental authority. This critique suggests that Locke's liberalism falls short in envisioning a society where people fully attain autonomy and agency. Instead, it portrays citizens as perpetually dependent on a paternalistic state, undermining the principles of equality and self-determination. From a Disability Studies perspective, this analysis underscores the need to reevaluate traditional frameworks of governance and advocate for systems that prioritize the empowerment and inclusion of all people, regardless of ability or status. Members of the disabled community contribute a crucial perspective to the discourse on the concept of the human by highlighting the inherent vulnerability of the body to age, infirmity, and unforeseen circumstances. They offer a critical assessment of John Locke's model of the liberal subject, which presupposes a state of perpetual health, wholeness, and able-bodiedness. Classical liberalism, influenced by Locke's ideals, tends to idealize a singular standard of humanity wherein every citizen is expected to possess strength, vigor, and full physical and mental capacity.

From a Disability Studies viewpoint, this alignment of classical liberalism with ableism becomes evident. Ableism, characterized by the belief in the superiority of people with typical physical and cognitive abilities, reinforces the exclusion and marginalization of those with impairments. Consequently, measures such as the Americans with Disabilities Act (ADA), which advocate for "reasonable accommodation" to be provided, become points of contention within liberal frameworks. The debates surrounding liberal conceptions of humanity are further complicated by the presence of people with intellectual and developmental disabilities. These people challenge the notion of a uniform and homogeneous citizenry envisioned by classical liberalism, prompting a reassessment of societal norms and values to accommodate diverse experiences and capabilities.

Locke and his philosophical successors have propagated the notion that people with cognitive disabilities lack the capacity for reasoning, thereby disqualifying them from being recognized as full persons. Scholars such as Georges Canguilhem and Martha Nussbaum have observed that disabled people, particularly those with cognitive impairments, are often relegated to a legal status akin to that of children. This diminished personhood has historically provided a pretext for eugenic practices, especially during the first half of the twentieth century, when forced sterilization was justified as a means of preventing the reproduction of people deemed "defective."

In contemporary contexts, advancements in prenatal screening and genetic testing have facilitated what some scholars refer to as "new eugenics." This involves the detection of genetic disorders in fetuses, leading to the selective abortion of those deemed to be "defective." For instance, upon learning that a child may be born with Down syndrome, some parents contemplate abortion as their first recourse. The prevalence of selective abortion raises ethical questions and is perceived by some as a direct challenge to the right of disabled people to exist.

The historical and ongoing practices of eugenics underscore the pervasive ableism embedded within societal attitudes towards disability, wherein people with disabilities are often viewed as inferior or unworthy of full recognition and inclusion. Contemporary philosopher Peter Singer has sparked significant debate with his assertion that people with intellectual and developmental disabilities, such as those with Down syndrome, as well as those afflicted with conditions like traumatic brain injury, dementia, or Alzheimer's disease, should be classified as non-persons. He contends that the distinction between abortion and infanticide lacks logical coherence, thus advocating that parents of newborns whom they find dissatisfactory, for any reason, should have the option of terminating their lives.

In response, philosophers like Eva Feder Kittay and Licia Carlson have undertaken the task of providing comprehensive and compelling counterarguments from the perspective of Disability Studies. They assert that denying full human dignity to people with intellectual and developmental disabilities poses a fundamental question: Why should human status be determined solely by a performance criterion such as reasoning ability? Kittay and Carlson's critiques delve deep into the ethical and philosophical implications of Singer's stance, highlighting the inherent flaws in equating personhood with cognitive function alone. They argue that such a perspective overlooks the richness and diversity of human experience, dismissing the intrinsic worth and inherent dignity of people regardless of their cognitive abilities.

By challenging Singer's premise and advocating for a broader understanding of humanity that transcends cognitive metrics, Kittay and Carlson shed light on the importance of embracing inclusivity and diversity in our conceptualization of personhood. Their arguments serve as a powerful reminder of the need to recognize and uphold the rights and dignity of all people, irrespective of their cognitive or developmental capabilities.

The elevation of characteristics like intelligence and rationality as defining traits of humanity prompts critical inquiry into the basis upon which these attributes are enshrined as essential. Disability critique offers a penetrating examination, highlighting the shifting landscape of impairment. No longer confined to a marginalized segment of society, impairment now encompasses a broader spectrum due to advancements in medical, technological, and pharmaceutical interventions.

In the contemporary context, people who would have previously succumbed to injuries, illnesses, or congenital disabilities now not only survive but thrive. This evolution challenges conventional notions of impairment and calls into question traditional understandings of human identity and capability. Donna Haraway's conceptualization of the cyborg, a posthuman hybrid traversing boundaries between human, animal, and machine, resonates deeply in this discourse. It underscores the fluidity and complexity of human embodiment in an era characterized by unprecedented technological integration. Furthermore, postmodern critics have played a pivotal role in expanding our perception of humanity beyond the confines of Enlightenment-era constructs. They have urged us to scrutinize and deconstruct established paradigms, fostering a more nuanced understanding of what it means to be human. This evolution demands a reevaluation of outdated definitions and the adoption of a more inclusive framework that transcends traditional boundaries.

The discourse surrounding disability critique prompts a reimagining of human identity—one that embraces diversity, challenges normative conceptions, and acknowledges the dynamic interplay between human, animal, and machine. By broadening the dimensions of the human experience, we can better appreciate the intricacies of embodiment and foster a more inclusive society that celebrates the richness of human variation.

Suggested Readings:

Berube, Michael. "Equality, Freedom, And/or Justice for all: A Response to Martha Nussabaum." *Metaphilosophy*, vol. 40, no. 3/4, 2009, pp. 352–65. *JSTOR*, http://www.jstor.org/stable/24439789. Accessed 8 July 2023.

Berube, Michael. *Life as We Know It: A Father, a Family, and an Exceptional Child*. Vintage, 1998.

Donna Haraway, "A Cyborg Manifesto: Science, Technology, and Socialist-Feminism in the Late Twentieth Century," in *Simians, Cyborgs and Women: The Reinvention of Nature* (New York; Routledge, 1991), pp.149-181.

Kittay, Eva Feder, and Licia Carlson, editors. *Cognitive Disability and Its Challenge to Moral Philosophy*. Wiley-Blackwell, 2013. Metaphilosophy, 18.

Carlson, Licia, and Eva Feder Kittay. 'Introduction: Rethinking Philosophical Presumptions in Light of Cognitive Disability'. *Cognitive Disability and Its Challenge to Moral Philosophy*, Wiley-Blackwell, 2010, pp. 1–25, https://doi.org10.1002/9781444322781.ch1.

Hay, William. *Deformity: an Essay*. 3. Dodsley, 1755.

Humanities

The emergence of Disability Studies as a distinct field of inquiry within the Humanities represents a relatively recent phenomenon, catalyzed by seminal texts such as Erving Goffman's *Stigma* (1968), Georges Canguilhem's *The Norma and the Pathological* (1966), and Michel Foucault's *The Birth of the Clinic* (1963). These works laid crucial foundations for understanding disability beyond the confines of medical discourse, challenging the dominant paradigm that pathologized disability until the 1980s. Prior to this shift, disability was predominantly viewed through a medical lens, characterized by a narrow focus on pathology within the medical field. However, with the advent of Cultural studies, a broader understanding of disability began to emerge, reframing it as a complex issue intertwined with identity and societal attitudes. Scholars began to explore disability in relation to other forms of minority identity, such as race, ethnicity, sexuality, and gender, recognizing commonalities and intersecting experiences.

This shift in perspective led to the establishment of various academic journals dedicated solely to Disability Studies, providing a platform for rigorous scholarly inquiry and discourse within the field. Additionally, interdisciplinary programs and departments focusing on Disability Studies began to emerge within universities, facilitating collaboration and furthering research in this burgeoning area. Through interdisciplinary engagement and critical examination, Disability Studies has expanded our understanding of disability beyond mere medical pathology, recognizing it as a multifaceted social construct shaped by historical, cultural, and political factors. By foregrounding issues of identity, representation, and social justice, Disability Studies has become an integral part of the broader humanities landscape, contributing to a more inclusive and nuanced understanding of human diversity. The exploration of disabled figures in literature initially revealed pervasive negative stereotypes, portraying them as morally corrupt, physically incapable, and mentally twisted. Scholars identified various forms of artistic expression, including novels, autobiographies, films, poems, and paintings, where disability featured prominently. These representations highlighted a cultural bias that perpetuated stigmatization and marginalization of disabled people.

Subsequently, a significant shift occurred with the emergence of the activist disability movement, which advocated for the recognition of a collective identity among disabled people. This movement challenged the conventional definitions of disability put forth by medical and psychoanalytic fields, asserting the importance of firsthand experiences of disabled people in shaping understanding and discourse. Scholars like Nancy Mairs, Audre Lorde, Paul Monette, Robert Murphy, John Hockenberry, and Susan Sontag emerged as influential voices, sharing their perspectives and insights derived from lived experiences. Prior to this phase, discussions surrounding disability were predominantly framed by medical professionals and scientists, often resulting in derivative and incomplete narratives. The elevation of disabled people as experts in their own right brought authenticity and depth to the discourse, shedding light on the diverse and nuanced realities of disability.

By centering the narratives and perspectives of disabled people, this phase of intellectual inquiry and activism challenged prevailing societal norms and advocated for greater inclusivity and representation. It underscored the importance of recognizing the agency and autonomy of disabled people in shaping their own narratives and driving social change.

In the evolution of Disability Studies, the second wave marked a pivotal shift towards amplifying the voices of disabled people, empowering them to narrate their own experiences. However, it was in the 1990s that the movement entered its third wave, heavily influenced by deconstruction theory. This wave prompted a deeper interrogation into the processes by which societal stigmatization of impairment occurs. Key scholars within this phase directed their focus towards critiquing the normative model, which deemed any deviation from typical human physiology as abnormal, consequently leading to exclusion from mainstream society. This shift in perspective redirected attention from the individual towards the broader societal structures that perpetuate marginalization and discrimination.

Central to this transition was the ascendancy of the social model of disability, which supplanted the traditional medical model. Scholars like Rosemarie Garland Thomson and Robert Bogdan explored how societies categorized people based on their physical and intellectual capacities. They unveiled the mechanisms through which so-called "normal" bodies were privileged, while those deemed "abnormal" or "deviant" were relegated to the margins. One prominent example examined was the phenomenon of freak shows, where people with unusual physical characteristics were put on display to satisfy the voyeuristic curiosity of the audience. Such displays reinforced the essentialism of the "normal" human body, positioning it as the ideal while reducing those with differences to objects of spectacle. Moreover, these exhibitions served to reinforce power dynamics, with the "normal-bodied" audience assuming positions of authority and superiority over the exhibited people. This analysis shed light on how societal constructions of normalcy and deviance are not inherent but rather socially constructed, perpetuating systems of oppression and marginalization.

Thus, the third wave of Disability Studies ushered in a broader understanding of disability as a social construct, challenging entrenched notions of normalcy and deviance while advocating for greater inclusivity and recognition of diverse human experiences. In his work *Bending Over Backwards* (2002), Lennard J. Davis brings to light the profound impact of societal norms, particularly those centered around achieving the status of white, middle-class males, on people' concepts of identity. Davis argues that in this framework, identity is often subordinated to the pursuit of normality, with the disabled body positioned as the antithesis of this ideal, thereby denying people with disabilities a valid identity. To articulate the complexities of this dynamic, Davis introduces the concept of 'dismodernism.' This term encapsulates the intersection of disability and modernity, highlighting how the prevalence of eugenics and the medical model has contributed to an identity crisis among disabled people. Within this paradigm, disability is perceived as a deviation from the norm, leading to the marginalization and erasure of disabled identities.

The third stage of Disability Studies builds upon Davis's insights, drawing parallels between disability and other marginalized identities such as queer, colonial, and racialized identities. Instead of viewing disability as a metaphor for physical deficiency, scholars in this stage assert the constitutive nature of disabled identities. They emphasize the valuable contributions of disabled people to literary and cultural discourse, challenging prevailing norms and advocating for greater representation and inclusivity. By reframing disability as a vital aspect of identity, third-stage Disability Studies reject the notion of disability as a deficit to be overcome. Instead, they celebrate the diversity and richness of disabled experiences, recognizing their inherent value within broader social and cultural contexts. This shift in perspective not only challenges societal perceptions of disability but also underscores the importance of embracing difference and promoting inclusivity in all aspects of human experience.

David Mitchell and Sharon Snyder illuminate the portrayal of disabled bodies in literary narratives, framing them as symbolic prosthetics within the storytelling framework. They argue that disabled characters often serve as conduits for eliciting pathos and contributing depth to the narrative fabric. However, this portrayal raises critical questions, particularly when considering that literature is predominantly crafted by able-bodied writers. The representation of disabled characters in these narratives invites scrutiny into the authenticity and sensitivity of their depiction. Moreover, the integration of disabled students into humanities classrooms has been significantly improved by legislative measures such as the Americans with Disabilities Act and advancements in technological accommodations. These advancements have facilitated better access to educational environments. However, with the introduction of Disability Studies within the Humanities, disabled students are empowered to critically interrogate the assumed categories of aesthetic and epistemological inquiry.

By engaging with Disability Studies, students can challenge entrenched notions of normativity and privilege within literary and academic discourse. They can explore how disability intersects with broader themes of identity, representation, and power dynamics within literary narratives and academic frameworks. This critical inquiry enables a deeper understanding of the complexities of disability and its portrayal in literature, while also fostering inclusivity and diversity within the humanities.

Suggested Readings:

Couser, G. Thomas. *Recovering bodies: Illness, disability, and life writing*. Univ of Wisconsin Press, 1997.

Davis, Lennard J., *Enforcing Normalcy: Disability, Deafness, and the Body*. London ; New York :Verso, 1995.

Mitchell, David T., and Sharon L. Snyder. *Narrative Prosthesis: Disability and the Dependencies of Discourse*. University of Michigan Press, 2000.

Siebers, T. 'Disability in Theory: From Social Constructionism to the New Realism of the Body'. *American Literary History*, vol. 13, no. 4, Oxford University Press (OUP), Apr. 2001, pp. 737–754, https://doi.org10.1093/alh/13.4.737.

Snyder, Sharon L., and Jo Brenda. *Disability Studies: Enabling the Humanities*. Edited by Rosemarie Garland Brueggemann, Modern Language Association, 2002.

Impairement

The term "impairment" is frequently utilized inter-changeably with "disability" in everyday language, often seen as a more appropriate and respectful way to describe certain conditions. For instance, referring to someone as "hearing impaired" may seem less stigmatizing compared to terms like "handicapped" or "deformed." However, both within Disability Studies and medical discourse, there exists a clear distinction between "impairment" and "disability." Within the British "social model" of disability, "impairment" denotes a physical or biological limitation, while "disability" refers to the societal processes that transform such impairments into obstacles. This distinction was elucidated by the Union of the Physically Impaired against Segregation (UPIAS) in 1975, asserting that disability is a construct imposed upon people with impairments by societal structures, resulting in unnecessary isolation and exclusion from full participation in society. Clinicians, scholars, activists, and the general public often view impairment as more scientific and objective compared to disability. This perception stems from the belief that impairments are tangible and measurable physical conditions, lending them an aura of reliability and precision. However, this perspective fails to account for the social, cultural, and environmental factors that shape experiences of disability, overlooking the ways in which societal attitudes and structures contribute to marginalization and exclusion.

By recognizing the distinction between impairment and disability, and acknowledging the social construction of disability, we can better understand the complex interplay between individual physical limitations and societal barriers. This nuanced understanding is essential for fostering inclusivity and promoting social justice for people with disabilities.The concept of impairment has intriguing origins, tracing back not to the medical profession or disability activism, but rather to the US life insurance industry, particularly during the era following the formal abolition of slavery. In the 19th century, as the institution of slavery waned and former slaves gained their freedom, the life insurance industry played a significant role in insuring against potential losses associated with human cargo.

However, with the abolition of slavery, the focus shifted, and registrars and underwriters within the life insurance industry began employing the notion of "impairment" as a tool to perpetuate a differential hierarchy in the valuation of human life. Around 1847, renowned scientist Josiah C. Nott raised concerns about regional biases within insurance companies. As the 1880s unfolded, overt discrimination became increasingly untenable as a standard practice. At this juncture, insurers pivoted towards utilizing the concept of impairment as a proxy for people with weaker vital statistics, effectively legitimizing discriminatory practices. As states began enacting legislation in the 1890s to prohibit discrimination based on race, underwriters adapted by reclassifying marginalized groups as low-income wage workers or labeling them as mentally impaired, thus circumventing legal barriers while perpetuating systemic inequalities. This historical context underscores the instrumental role of the life insurance industry in shaping societal attitudes towards impairment and perpetuating systemic discrimination. By examining the evolution of the concept of impairment within this context, we gain insight into the intersections of economics, social policy, and racial oppression in shaping perceptions of human worth and value.

The concept of "impairment" originated from scientific

assessments conducted by medical experts, actuaries, and underwriters, who sought to quantify and assign monetary value to social differences and debilities. Scientists utilized impairment as a basis for distinguishing between people, employing measures such as family medical histories and analyses of blood and urine samples to establish criteria for differentiation. However, the disability rights movement, particularly in Great Britain, challenged the primacy of impairment and instead advocated for a focus on disability. This shift was driven by the recognition that impairment, with its associations of limitation, lack, and deficiency, perpetuated the fantasy of a normative human body. Scholars have extensively explored the historical, institutional, and cultural dimensions of impairment, revealing its constructed nature and highlighting its role in reinforcing societal norms and hierarchies.

Despite critiques of impairment as a stigmatizing concept, scholars like Tom Shakespeare and Davis argue for its preservation. They contend that impairment serves as a valuable descriptor for aspects of disability that cannot solely be attributed to social and environmental factors. By acknowledging the complex interplay between impairment and disability, these scholars advocate for a more nuanced understanding of disability that encompasses both social and biological dimensions.

The term "impairment" is inherently complex, characterized by its multifaceted definitions and significance within the realm of bodily experiences. Its conceptualization has evolved over time, shaped by both chronological developments and ideological debates. A pivotal moment in defining impairment occurred in 1976 when the Union of the Physically Impaired Against Segregation (UPIAS) put forth its own definitions, notably omitting the term "handicap" and establishing a clear distinction between impairment and disability.

According to UPIAS, impairment refers to the physical condition of lacking part or all of a limb, or having a defective limb, organ, or bodily mechanism. It is inherently rooted in the body itself, representing a tangible manifestation of physical difference or limitation. On the other hand, disability encompasses the social oppression experienced by people with impairments, whether through societal stigma or the imposition of restrictions on their participation and inclusion. Disability, in this framework, is not inherent to the individual's bodily condition but is rather situated within society or cultural contexts.

This delineation between impairment and disability highlights the complex interplay between individual bodily experiences and broader social structures. While impairment is rooted in the physical body, disability is fundamentally shaped by societal attitudes, norms, and practices. Understanding this distinction is crucial for addressing the systemic inequalities and barriers faced by people with impairments, as it underscores the importance of addressing both the physical and social dimensions of disability. By recognizing the social construction of disability, efforts can be made to dismantle discriminatory practices and promote inclusivity and accessibility for all people, regardless of their bodily differences.

Criticism of the World Health Organization's (WHO) definition of disability emerged from scholars and professionals worldwide, who found it to be overly rigid and lacking in its representation of the complex intersections among various categories. Additionally, many viewed the definitions as devoid of social consciousness or analysis. This dissatisfaction with the prevailing conceptualization of disability sparked a body of scholarship, spearheaded by figures such as Michael Oliver and Tom Shakespeare, which sought to delineate between the "medical and social model of disability."

In this framework, impairment came to be associated with the medical model of disability. This model focuses on identifying problems within the individual's body and typically prescribes solutions such as cures, charity, or viewing disability through the lens of personal tragedy and pain and suffering. As a result, impairment, once considered a neutral term, became laden with negative connotations within the binary framework of social versus medical models of disability. Critics argued that the medical model pathologizes disability by framing it solely as an individual problem to be fixed or alleviated, rather than acknowledging the role of societal barriers and discrimination in shaping disabled people' experiences. This critique underscores the need for a more holistic and socially conscious approach to understanding disability, one that acknowledges the interplay between individual impairments and broader social structures.

By shifting focus towards the social model of disability, scholars like Oliver and Shakespeare aimed to challenge traditional notions of impairment and disability, emphasizing the importance of addressing systemic barriers and promoting inclusivity and accessibility for all people. This reconceptualization of disability not only critiques the medical model but also advocates for a more nuanced understanding that recognizes the complex interactions between individual bodies and social contexts. Feminist disability scholars, including prominent figures such as Susan Wendell, Sharon Stone, Jenny Morris, and Liz Crow, offered significant critiques of the impairment/

disability binary and the corresponding medical and social model rhetoric. These scholars aimed to deconstruct the binary framework, which often contained masculinist assumptions and neglected the nuanced experiences of people living with impairments or disabilities.

Central to their critique was the recognition of the devaluation of pain and suffering within the lived experiences of people with impairments or disabilities. They argued that traditional discourses tended to prioritize certain aspects of disability, such as physical limitations, while overlooking the profound impact of pain and suffering on people' lives. Moreover, these feminist disability scholars highlighted the neglect of bodies affected by invisible or less-visible impairments in Disability Studies discourse. Importantly, many of the impairments that were marginalized in discussions disproportionately affected women. Conditions such as chronic fatigue syndrome and depression, which are often overlooked or dismissed, were brought to the forefront by these scholars. They called attention to the intersectional nature of disability, emphasizing the importance of recognizing how gender intersects with disability experiences.

In response, these theorists advocated for a return of lived experience to the discourse of Disability Studies. They urged for a more inclusive and comprehensive theorizing and representation of impairment that accounts for the diverse experiences of people living with disabilities. By centering lived experiences and amplifying voices that have been marginalized within the Disability Studies discourse, these feminist scholars aimed to create a more nuanced and inclusive understanding of disability that acknowledges the complexity and diversity of disability experiences.

Suggested Readings:

Hughes, Bill, and Kevin Paterson. 'The Social Model of Disability and the Disappearing Body: Towards a Sociology of Impairment'. *Disability & Society*, vol. 12, no. 3, Informa UK Limited, June 1997, pp. 325–340, https://doi.org10.1080/09687599727209.

Morris, Jenny. *Encounters With Strangers: Feminism and Disability*. Women's Press (UK), 1996.

Michael, Oliver. *The Politics of Disablement*. London: Macmillan. 1990.

Wendell, Susan. *The Rejected Body: Feminist Philosophical Reflections on Disability*. Psychology Press, 1996.

Illness

In the discourse of Disability Studies, it is crucial to differentiate between two closely related terms: "disease" and "illness." While these terms are often used interchangeably, they carry distinct meanings that are significant in understanding the lived experiences of people. "Disease" typically refers to a pathological condition or entity, often viewed as disembodied and abstract within academic contexts. It is understood as a medical diagnosis, such as cancer or polio, characterized by specific physiological or pathological changes in the body. From this perspective, disease is conceptualized as a clinical entity that can be objectively identified and diagnosed by medical professionals. In contrast, "illness" encompasses an individual's subjective experience of living with a disease and the broader repercussions it has on their identity and existence. It encompasses the emotional, psychological, social, and cultural dimensions of living with a health condition. Illness involves the personal narratives, emotions, and lived experiences of people as they navigate the challenges posed by their health conditions.

Progressive medical approaches recognize the importance of acknowledging and addressing illness alongside disease. While disease-focused treatments aim to target the pathological aspects of a condition, illness-focused approaches prioritize the holistic well-being of people by considering the broader impact of the disease on their lives. This may involve providing support for coping with emotional distress, managing social implications, and maintaining a sense of identity and dignity in the face of illness.

By distinguishing between disease and illness, Disability Studies emphasizes the importance of recognizing and validating people' subjective experiences and narratives. This nuanced understanding helps foster a more holistic approach to healthcare and support services, ensuring that people receive comprehensive care that addresses not only the physiological aspects of their conditions but also the emotional and social dimensions of their illness experiences. Arthur Kleinman, a pioneering medical anthropologist and psychiatrist, introduced an approach that revolutionized the understanding of illness experiences. Notably, this approach is not limited to medical practitioners; significant figures like sociologist Arthur Frank and literary critic/internist Rita Charon have also contributed to this field. Their work has been instrumental in shaping the discourse of 'Narrative Medicine'.

In Narrative Medicine, clinicians engage deeply with patients' narratives to gain insight into their experiences of illness. The focus is on understanding the patient's subjective perspective, particularly how they perceive and experience their own bodies. This approach has shown promising results in enhancing understanding of illness and disability, as highlighted by Couser (1997). However, it is essential to acknowledge that Narrative Medicine primarily operates within the medical realm and may not fully transcend its medical counterpart. In the context of Disability Studies, terms such as "patient" and "illness" can be problematic. They often imply a passive recipient of medical care and reinforce the medicalization of disability, overlooking the broader social, cultural, and political dimensions of disability experiences.

The use of these terms can also obscure the agency and autonomy of people with disabilities, reducing them to mere subjects of medical treatment rather than active participants in shaping their own narratives and experiences. Therefore, while Narrative Medicine offers valuable insights into illness experiences, it is essential to critically examine and expand its application within the context of Disability Studies, ensuring a more inclusive and comprehensive understanding of disability that incorporates diverse perspectives and experiences. The intersection of disease and disability presents a complex challenge within the field of Disability Studies. While disease is often associated with contagion and carries negative connotations, disability also faces stigma and is subject to "person-first" terminology, which aims to prioritize the individual over their bodily condition. However, Disability Studies conceptualizes sickness and disability as distinct phenomena.

The term "illness" is problematic within the framework of Disability Studies as it tends to conflate disability with a medical model of disability. This model categorizes disabled people as "sick" and in need of medical intervention for a cure. This perception obscures the nuanced distinction between impairment and disability.

Impairment refers to a dysfunction within the body, which may potentially be amenable to medical treatment or prosthetic modification. Disability, on the other hand, encompasses the environmental barriers and societal attitudes that exclude or impede people with impairments. Addressing disability requires not only medical interventions but also structural changes in legal, social, and architectural contexts to create inclusive environments. The blurring of boundaries between impairment and disability perpetuates a narrow understanding of disability that solely focuses on medical interventions, overlooking the broader social and environmental factors that shape disability experiences. Disability Studies advocates for a more holistic approach that acknowledges the complex interplay between individual impairments and societal barriers, emphasizing the importance of addressing both aspects to achieve true inclusion and accessibility for all people.The social model of disability is paramount in emphasizing the distinction between disability and illness, thereby highlighting the unique experiences and needs of disabled people. This model underscores that disability is not solely an individual health condition but is heavily influenced by social, cultural, and environmental factors. By centering on the societal barriers and attitudes that impede the full participation of disabled people, the social model of disability challenges the notion of equating disability with illness.

Confusing disabled people with those who are ill undermines the principles of the social model of disability and fails to recognize the diverse needs and experiences of disabled people. It overlooks the structural inequalities and systemic barriers that contribute to disability and perpetuates a narrow understanding of disability solely as a medical condition requiring treatment or cure. In contrast, Narrative Medicine, while a variant of the medical model, seeks to understand the multifaceted experiences of people living with health conditions, including disability. It acknowledges the importance of listening to patients' narratives and understanding their subjective experiences of illness, which may encompass physical, emotional, social, and existential dimensions. However, narrative medicine operates within the framework of the medical model, focusing primarily on individual experiences and medical interventions.

While Narrative Medicine offers valuable insights into the personal narratives and subjective experiences of illness, it is essential to complement this approach with the principles of the social model of disability. By integrating a social model perspective into healthcare practices, practitioners can better understand and address the structural barriers and systemic inequalities that impact disabled people' lives. This holistic approach ensures that the needs and experiences of disabled people are fully recognized and accommodated, fostering greater inclusivity and equity in healthcare and society as a whole.In contrast to the social model of disability, which emphasizes the societal aspects of disability and the need for structural changes to promote inclusivity, the medical model primarily focuses on treating the individual's health condition without considering broader social factors. However, it is essential to recognize that the distinction between disability and illness is not always clear-cut and that people may experience both simultaneously.

Indeed, disability and illness often intersect and coexist within an individual's lived experience. While they are distinct concepts, they can overlap, with disability sometimes leading to illness and vice versa. For instance, certain disabling conditions may result from various diseases, such as deafness, blindness, or paralysis. Similarly, disabilities can contribute to the development of secondary health issues; for example, paralysis may lead to bedsores or urinary tract infections. Moreover, some chronic or terminal illnesses carry societal taboos and stigmas similar to those associated with disabilities. This further blurs the boundary between disability and illness, highlighting the interconnectedness of these concepts and their shared impact on people' lives.

From a legal perspective, many diseases, including HIV/AIDS, cancer, mental illnesses, and diabetes, are considered disabilities due to their significant impact on people' daily functioning and quality of life. This recognition underscores the complex relationship between health conditions and disability status, acknowledging that people with certain diseases may face similar barriers and discrimination as those with disabilities.The American Disabilities Act (ADA) of 1990, reinforced by the ADA Amendments Act of 2008, marked a significant milestone in granting rights to people with disabilities and illnesses. The ADA's definition of disability was intentionally broad and comprehensive, reflecting the diverse range of conditions and experiences encountered by people with disabilities. However, recent developments within the field of Disability Studies have called into question the traditional distinction between illness and disability.

Tom Shakespeare, a prominent British scholar and activist, challenges the prevailing social model of disability, which posits that societal barriers and attitudes are the primary sources of disability. In his work *Disability Rights and Wrongs* (2006), Shakespeare critiques the social model for its limitations and inherent flaws. He argues that the social model can be restrictive and fails to fully capture the complexities of disability experiences. Shakespeare contends that the social model's emphasis on societal barriers may overlook the unique challenges faced by people with specific impairments and disabilities. Moreover, he suggests that the social model's rejection of medical research and development may hinder advancements in understanding and treating various health conditions. Furthermore, Shakespeare warns against the potential consequences of solely relying on the social model for political organization within the disability rights movement. He highlights the importance of recognizing the diverse needs and experiences of people with disabilities and illnesses, advocating for a more inclusive and nuanced approach to disability rights advocacy. Initially, scholars in Disability Studies advanced the argument that disability is a socially constructed concept similar to gender and race. However, as the field has evolved, scholars are now grappling with the limitations of this analogy. Unlike gender and race, impairment carries inherent limitations that cannot be fully addressed through social reform alone.

Impairment encompasses various physical or cognitive limitations that people may experience, which can include chronic pain, progressive degeneration, and even premature death. Unlike social constructs like gender and race, which are primarily shaped by societal norms and structures, impairment is rooted in bodily dysfunctions that may have biological or genetic origins. While disability and impairment are distinct from disease and illness, they share commonalities in terms of being associated with bodily dysfunctions. Disability Studies scholars recognize the complexity of these concepts and the interplay between individual experiences and broader social structures.

Acknowledging the limitations of the gender and race analogy, scholars in Disability Studies are exploring new frameworks and perspectives to understand disability more comprehensively. By recognizing the unique challenges and experiences faced by people with impairments, Disability Studies aims to promote inclusivity, accessibility, and equity for all people, regardless of their physical or cognitive differences. Disability scholars' oversight of bodily dysfunctions has primarily benefited academic discourse rather than people living with these conditions. However, Tom Shakespeare advocates for a nuanced approach that acknowledges the limitations of the social model of disability while also recognizing the importance of accommodation. Shakespeare does not advocate for the complete abandonment of accommodation but rather highlights the inadequacies of solely relying on the social model, which often disregards biological and medical factors. He argues that disabled people require more support and intervention from society to achieve true social inclusion. Merely creating a level playing field is insufficient; there is a need for redistribution to address the economic disparities faced by people with disabilities.

In addressing the economic needs of disability, new approaches and remedies are necessary. One such approach is to acknowledge and accept the overlap between two populations: the disabled and the ill. By recognizing the shared experiences and challenges faced by people with disabilities and illnesses, society can develop more comprehensive strategies for promoting inclusivity, accessibility, and equity. Shakespeare's perspective underscores the importance of moving beyond theoretical frameworks and academic debates to address the practical needs and concerns of people living with disabilities and illnesses. It emphasizes the necessity of adopting holistic approaches that integrate both social and medical perspectives to foster genuine social inclusion and support for all people, regardless of their health conditions.

Suggested Readings:

Charon, Rita. *Narrative Medicine: Honoring the Stories of Illness*. New York: Oxford University Press, 2006.

Couser, G. Thomas. *Recovering Bodies: Illness, Disability, and Life Writing*. Madison: University of Wisconsin Press, 1997.

Kleinman, Arthur. *The Illness Narratives: Suffering, Healing, and the Human Condition*. New York: Basic Books, 1988.

Institutions

The theory of Disability Studies works towards eliminating negative stereotypes and stigma attached to disability, which devalues disability. Disability theorists also try to promote a positive approach towards people with disabilities, enhancing their self-esteem. Thus, it works in a two-fold way. Disabled people have long been discriminated against and marginalised because they deviate from the prescribed norms of society. Disability theorists endeavour to expose the practices of institutionalisation and devaluation of certain groups. According to the Oxford English Dictionary, an 'institution' is "an establishment, organization, or association instituted for the promotion of some object, especially one of public or general utility, religious, charitable, educational etc.". However, in the field of Disability Studies, institutions have double meaning; it can be defined as the physical abode established to shelter the disabled population and provide them with the daily means to survive. However, it can also mean various public organisations that have significant contributions to improving the condition of disabled people, such as hospitals, almshouses, schools, and prisons. While the ableist majority seeks to institutionalise physically disabled people by excluding them from the mainstream society, and constant attempts have been made by Disability theorists to erase such barriers and integrate disabled people into the cultural reality by disclosing the latent ideological, cultural, economic and political forces which reinforce such initialisation. Initially, people with disabilities were not given much attention, and society did not care about providing any assistive means to them; they were segregated and even sterilised; however, it was much later that various residential institutions were built to shelter them and sustain their living in death existence. However, before asylum, training schools, and rehabilitation centres came into existence, many such institutions were built where disabled people were forced to live a solitary life, for instance, Bethlehem Hospital, institutions for leprosy containment, etc. Eighteenth-century Europe saw the rise of various institutions built for separating the others of society, the poor, the orphan, the disabled, and the criminal, which Foucault termed as 'Great Confinement '. The increasing emphasis on reason and logic during the Enlightenment era significantly contributed to the othering of mentally unstable and cognitively deficient persons, which further created the necessity for building residential institutions for disabled people, who were considered a threat to thriving humanity. The establishment of such institutions significantly flourished during the nineteenth century with the upcoming surge of 'Modernity' which emphasised the need for disabled people to become active working members of society and thus contribute to a country's economy. Critics like Dorothea Dix argued against the wrong confinement of disabled people with the morally degraded abusers of society. Although institutionalisation seemed to be a well-built and positive approach of society to enhance the living conditions of disabled people, it however further marginalised them and promoted more oppressive and abusive treatment towards them. Eugenics prohibited the disabled from copulating to end the passing of defective genes in future races, requiring an institution to segregate them in an enclosed space. By the middle of the twentieth century, these were attacked by Disability Studies activists and scholars and called for the deinstitutionalisation movement in the 1970s. However, this did not secure the social inhabitation of disabled persons since most of them were unemployed and therefore had to live with meagre substance and scarcity. The Disability Rights movement propagated the need for the independent existence of disabled people, legal amendments and necessary policies and measures implementations. Unfortunately, the deinstitutionalisation movement could not put an end to the institutional lives of disabled people since even though they could live independently still, many of them couldn't avail the necessary social support or personal caretakers or attendants due to which confinement within the four walls of a hospital remained the only option left. Moreover, there still occur instances of physical or psychologically abusive treatment towards the disabled in relatively smaller community settings due to a lack of awareness and social consciousness. According to Ervin Goffman, 'total institutions' refer to the places where' a large number of like situated people, cut off from the wider society for an appreciable period of time, together lead an enclosed formally administered round of life". He found out the possible causes for the identity crisis and inhuman status of disabled persons by analysing their situation and treatment towards them in the total institutions. The contribution of Michael Foucault has been very influential in the field of Disability Studies; his concepts of "biopower", "discourse", and "asylum" all leave remarkable traces on the production of various disability concepts on the basis of power relations. As Foucault defined, institution is the centre of disciplinary practices, and it works by power relation, where relatively less abled and weaker subjects are objectified and defined by the powerful authorities, and this is somewhat similar in the cases of institutions for the 'feebleminded', who have no power over themselves, the definition of themselves was provided by others. Disability Studies expose such hidden agendas of the ableist majority behind the segregation and marginalisation of the disabled, the intended attempt of charity or providing them with a better life, to provide them with shelter and protection, and also the Eugenics propaganda that these impotent people are a threat to a society's progress therefore, must be erased. Disability scholars expose certain ableist beliefs, such as

1. Disability is an individual burden and personal tragedy which must be defined and cured by medical professionals to bring them back as close as possible to the normal stature of human beings.
2. The justification for making decisions for the disabled populations on their behalf that they are considered feeble and weak-minded, being unable to decide for themselves.
3. That disabled people are different from the normal majority and must be treated accordingly.
4. Lastly, professional experts of higher authorities are

better capable of managing their lives than them; thus, they should be given the power over disabled people to implement policies and measures without even taking their opinions.

Thus emerges the slogan that "nothing about us without us". Disability Studies thus take consideration of the voices of the disabled people "from below" and value the first-person narratives of disabled people regarding institutionalisation or deinstitutionalisation. However, if one looks at the history of disability, disabled people cannot be seen as merely passive victims of an oppressive discourse since there are many instances of their rebellion and self-advocacy, through which they challenged the institutionalisation and called for an independent living movement. Institutionalisation and Disability are further studied in the context of leprosy, which largely affected colonial South India. Although leprosy in today's time is no more an incurable disease, initially, it left many people disabled and even segregated from society because it disfigured the body and affected the limbs, causing them to be numb and ineffective. With the advancement of medical science, the effects of leprosy can be minimised and managed to some extent. Like disabled people, leprosy-affected people are also subjected to society's stigmatised notions and stereotypical attitudes. The physical deformity, visible disfigurement, and loss of limbs or sight make them abnormal before society's eyes, so they are not considered fit to live in mainstream society. This is why, during the nineteenth century, the fear of being contaminated by the disease caused the isolation and segregation of the affected persons and forming institutions. However, the indigenous population affected by leprosy were treated differently than the settler communities affected by the same. The colonial ruler's fear of being infected by the disease and its result of horrific appearance justified the segregation of the affected people in remote islands. Colonial authorities also built separate institutions to provide care and treatment to leprosy sufferers. An attempt at institutionalisation was also made in fifteenth-century Europe to contain the devastating plague. Later, in the nineteenth century, prisons, workhouses, asylums, and almshouses were built to broaden the institutional framework, which was seen to be the apparent solution to both the social problems of crime and disorder and the demands of charity. Although several professionals such as Phillippe Pinel in Paris or Quakers in England considered supportive care to be better meant to manage feebleminded or mentally unstable people than incarceration still, confining them within an institutional setting was thought to be a better option to control those who deviated from the norms. The rise of institutions during the nineteenth century implied a more dependency on the government's laws and regulations to resolve any social issues which were previously solved by religious or social organisations. Those with a visible disability and the ones who have been the victim of leprosy. In the nineteenth century, the British occupied India, and the definition of infirmity included both. Both of them were subject to institutionalisation. However, not all types of physical abnormalities require confinement within rigid boundaries of institutional buildings. However, the principal target of segregation after the Lepers Act of 1898 was leprosy-affected persons; other forms of prominent disability such as deafness, lame, and blindness were not similarly targeted since they were not contagious or that much grotesque to our vision. They were confined because of the social perception of disability. Even the confinement of the leprosy sufferers was executed based on their socio-economic status; those who were supported by their families and were still able to earn their living were not subject to compulsory confinement. The poverty-stricken victim of the disease was institutionalised. However, since leprosy left the outside appearance of the affected person maimed and grotesque, they were better kept hidden from the public view to maintain the decorum of society. Thus the value of a leprosy sufferer disabled person depended both on his capacity to earn as well as on his aesthetic appearance. Leprosy was also seen to be the effect of one's karma or past deed in Hindu philosophy; thus, the affected victim was considered to be a sinner suffering his punishment. However, government institutions designed to provide care to leprosy sufferers didn't fulfil the criteria of total institutions as defined by Erving Goffman because, unlike Goffman's concept, these institutions did not separate the inmates completely from their families or the outside world; they were still allowed to keep contact with them. Thus, it left them in an ambivalent position; it was hard to figure out whether they were patients or prisoners. Until 1898, there was no law in India which justified the incarceration of leprosy victims. In the last decades of the twentieth century, institutionalisation lost its importance in managing a disease or controlling law violators because of its high maintenance cost and less effective results. Disabled people are endowed with support and government facilities in today's world than institutional care. In today's world, disability is more to be seen as an experience which does not need isolation or segregation from a normal society.

Suggested Readings:

Foucault, Michel. *The Birth of the Clinic: An Archaeology of Medical Perception*. Vintage, 1994.

Foucault, Michel. *Madness and Civilization: A History of Insanity in the Age of Reason.* Psychology Press, 2001.

Goffman, Erving. *Asylums: Essays on the Social Situation of Mental Patients and Other Inmates.* Routledge, 2017.

Rothman, David J. *The Discovery of the Asylum: Social Order and Disorder in the New Republic.* Routledge, 2017.

Invalid Women

The term "invalid" has undergone a significant shift in meaning over time, transitioning from its original medical usage to now signify someone who is incapable of performing certain tasks. During the 19th century, femininity was often pathologized and associated with illness, portraying women as fragile and weak in various forms of art, literature, and medical writings of that era. However, modern feminist critics have deconstructed this portrayal of femininity in several ways:

(1) Patriarchal Control: Feminist critics view the representation of femininity as an illness as a manifestation of patriarchal attempts to control women's bodies. Patriarchal societies sought to maintain power and dominance over women by imposing societal norms and expectations upon them.

(2) Resistance to Cultural Conditioning: Feminist analysis also recognizes the portrayal of femininity as an illness as a form of resistance to societal norms and cultural conditioning. Women who challenge traditional gender roles and expectations may be labeled as "sick" or "invalid" by patriarchal societies in an attempt to marginalize and suppress their voices.

(3) Male Power Dynamics: Some feminist critics interpret the depiction of femininity as an illness as a reflection of power dynamics within male-dominated

societies. Men, who historically held positions of authority and privilege, exerted control over women's bodies and identities, reinforcing notions of female weakness and dependency.

(4) Cultural Privilege and Power: Feminist analysis further highlights how the portrayal of femininity as an illness serves to perpetuate cultural privilege and power dynamics. Those who hold authority within patriarchal structures use femininity, constructed as weak and vulnerable, as a source of power to exert control over women's lives while reinforcing their own dominance.

The historical treatment of women as "invalid" not only perpetuated gender inequalities but also deprived them of equal rights and opportunities as citizens. This belief stemmed from the notion that women, particularly those from middle and upper-class backgrounds, were inherently weak and fragile, incapable of fulfilling the responsibilities of citizenship such as voting or participating in the workforce effectively. Certain roles, particularly those perceived as demanding or traditionally associated with masculinity, were viewed as unsuitable or even harmful for women due to their supposed fragility, according to society. The association of femininity with invalidism reflects how society perceived and treated disability. Disabled people and women were both marginalized and restricted from fully participating in social, political, and economic spheres. Cultural norms and societal expectations erased any distinction between disabled people and "invalid" women, conflating their identities and reinforcing their exclusion from societal norms and opportunities.

As a result, women were denied agency and autonomy, and were relegated to roles deemed more suitable for their perceived weaknesses. This perpetuated a cycle of discrimination and oppression, further entrenching gender inequalities and reinforcing patriarchal power structures. The intersectionality of gender and disability compounded these injustices, as disabled women faced double marginalization and discrimination based on both their gender and disability status.

Throughout history, women writers with chronic diseases have highlighted the interconnectedness of disability and illness, shedding light on the influence of gender roles in shaping perceptions of disability. In the mid-19th century, Edgar Allan Poe famously declared that the death of a beautiful woman was the most poetic topic, reflecting prevalent societal attitudes that romanticized female frailty and vulnerability.

Literature from this era frequently depicted women as frail and delicate, embodying the archetype of the tubercular heroine or the fainting damsel on a couch. Paintings such as those depicting Albine and Ophelia further perpetuated this imagery of mad, dead, or dying women. These representations extended into contemporary films and fictional works, maintaining the portrayal of women as inherently vulnerable and prone to illness. However, behind these depictions lies the social and cultural conditioning of patriarchal societies, which systematically oppressed and suppressed women. Women were denied agency over their career choices, financial management, and participation in government. Additionally, they were expected to fulfill traditional roles as wives and mothers, often bearing numerous children without regard for their physical or emotional well-being.

The immense pressure placed on women to conform to societal expectations, combined with the lack of autonomy and support, undoubtedly contributed to mental and emotional strain. Many women experienced chronic stress, anxiety, and depression as a result of their restricted roles and the demands placed upon them by patriarchal norms.Thus, while women may have appeared physically healthy on the surface, the societal pressures and gender-based expectations imposed upon them led to a myriad of mental and emotional health issues. Women's experiences of illness were often intertwined with their marginalized status within society, highlighting the complex relationship between gender, disability, and societal power dynamics.

In the 19th century, female bodily experiences such as menstruation, pregnancy, and menopause were often pathologized and medicalized by societal norms and medical interventions. Elaine Showalter, a prominent feminist scholar, suggests that female illness during this period was not merely a result of physiological factors but also a response to oppressive power structures. Showalter posits that illnesses like hysteria were modes of protest for women, serving as expressions of resistance against patriarchal dominance.

According to Showalter, women who were labeled as ill may have been perceived as rebellious or politically resistant, using their supposed ailments as a means of challenging societal norms and asserting their agency. In this view, illness becomes a form of empowerment and a tool for subverting oppressive systems of power.

However, Showalter also acknowledges that not all uses of illness as a form of power are positive or progressive. She points to instances where women feigned illness or exaggerated their symptoms to manipulate and control others, as depicted in Harriet Beecher Stowe's "*Uncle Tom's Cabin.*" In the novel, characters such as Topsy exploit their perceived vulnerabilities to garner attention and sympathy, highlighting the potential for illness to be wielded as a tool of manipulation and domination.

Rosemarie Garland Thomson draws parallels between societal assumptions about women's bodies and those of disabled people, tracing the historical roots of disability discourse back to Aristotle's writings. According to Thomson, Aristotle categorized the absence of a penis as a deformity, positioning both femininity and disability as forms of deficiency. Through this lens, she suggests that oppression is not rooted in concrete bodily differences but rather in societal norms and expectations.

During the feminist struggle for equality, women contested notions of invalidity, advocating for their right to vote and hold office by contrasting themselves with physically, emotionally, and intellectually disabled men. This intersectional approach to activism highlighted the interconnectedness of gender and disability issues, challenging traditional notions of power and authority.In more recent scholarship, writers like Nancy Mairs have explored the complex relationship between femininity and disability, shedding light on the shared experiences and challenges faced by women with disabilities. Similarly, Lucy Gosaly and Anne Finger have examined the overlapping experiences of illness and disability, blurring the boundaries between these categories.

Susan Wendell, in her work *The Rejected Body (1996)*, further explores the intersection of feminism, disability, and illness, emphasizing the importance of recognizing the social and cultural factors that contribute to disability experiences. Today, representations of ill women have evolved, moving away from portrayals of weakness and invalidity to more nuanced depictions that acknowledge the diverse realities of women's health. Contemporary writers challenge cultural norms and advocate for more inclusive and holistic approaches to healing that address the societal roots of disability for women. By interrogating cultural attitudes and promoting diverse narratives, they seek to create spaces where women with disabilities can thrive and be celebrated for their strength and resilience.

Suggested Readings:

Wendell, Susan. "Old Women Out of Control: Some Thoughts on Aging, Ethics, and Psychosomatic Medicine." *In Mother Time: Women, Aging, and Ethics,* edited by Margaret Urban Walker, 133–150. Lanham, MD: Rowman and Littlefield, 1999.

——.*The Rejected Body: Feminist Philosophical Reflections on Disability.* London: Routledge, 1996.

Infertility

Infertility, defined as the inability to conceive after a year of unprotected intercourse, is recognized as a significant medical condition by nonprofit organizations such as the American Society for Reproductive Medicine (ASRM) and the National Infertility Association. Both organizations classify infertility as a "disease" that interferes with the body's fundamental reproductive function. In both women and men, infertility can arise from a variety of underlying conditions and factors. In women, common causes include disorders such as endometriosis and polycystic ovarian syndrome, as well as issues like premature ovarian failure. Certain infections, such as mumps contracted after puberty, can also impact female reproductive health. Hormonal imbalances in the hypothalamus can disrupt the production of eggs and affect fertility.

Similarly, male infertility can stem from a range of factors, including testicular injuries, chromosomal abnormalities, and conditions like cryptorchidism (undescended testicles). Certain medical treatments, such as cancer therapies, can also impair sperm production and fertility in men. Additionally, direct physical trauma to the testicles can contribute to male infertility. In its early usage, sterilization surgery served as a tool for social control, distinct from infertility which has a natural and biological origin. Sterility refers to the inability to conceive due to the absence of fertilization, while infertility encompasses a broader range of factors that can impede conception. However, in contemporary times, sterilization procedures are often chosen voluntarily, particularly in countries like the USA.

Historically, during the seventeenth and eighteenth centuries, American colonists commonly used the term "barrenness" to describe the inability to bear children, a concept predominantly associated with women. Men were typically presumed fertile if they were capable of engaging in sexual intercourse. This gendered perception of fertility contributed to societal prejudices and stigmatization, particularly directed towards women who were unable to conceive. It wasn't until the nineteenth century, with advancements in gynecology, that the treatment of infertility expanded to include the term "sterility." This terminology shift helped to dismantle the prevailing notion that infertility was solely a female issue. Gynecologists of this era recognized that both men and women could be affected by factors contributing to infertility.

By broadening the understanding of infertility to include sterility, medical professionals challenged gender biases and acknowledged the complex interplay of biological, physiological, and environmental factors that can impact fertility. This shift in terminology paved the way for more inclusive approaches to diagnosing and treating infertility, recognizing that both men and women may require medical intervention to address reproductive challenges. During the 1860s, some physicians proposed the use of microscopic tests to examine semen, a diagnostic technique that required husbands to participate in the process alongside their wives. This approach aimed to assess male fertility directly but also inadvertently challenged traditional notions of masculinity, as men were now expected to engage in a diagnostic process traditionally associated with women. This shift in expectations may have unsettled some men, leading to resistance or discomfort with the new approach.To address these concerns and secure cooperation, medical professionals of the time reverted to using the term "sterility" instead of "infertility" in their discussions and diagnoses. Sterility, an older term dating back to the 1940s and 1960s, was perceived as less emasculating and more conducive to garnering male participation in treatment.

In contemporary reproductive medicine, fertility specialists recognize that both partners in a couple may be affected by infertility issues. This acknowledgment reflects a more inclusive understanding of reproductive health, recognizing that infertility can stem from various factors affecting either or both partners. From a clinical perspective, infertility is categorized into two main types. Primary infertility occurs when a couple has never been able to conceive naturally or achieve a full-term pregnancy. This form of infertility may be attributed to factors such as reproductive health issues, hormonal imbalances, or genetic factors.

On the other hand, secondary infertility refers to the inability to conceive again after successfully having a child. Despite having previously conceived and given birth, couples experiencing secondary infertility may encounter difficulties when attempting to conceive again. This form of infertility can be caused by a variety of factors, including age-related declines in fertility, changes in reproductive health, or underlying medical conditions. By distinguishing between primary and secondary infertility, clinicians can tailor treatment approaches to address the specific needs and challenges faced by each individual or couple, facilitating more effective management and support for those struggling with fertility issues.

Contemporary medical interventions offer a range of treatments for infertility, drawing upon conventional techniques such as surgery, artificial insemination (which has been practiced since the nineteenth century), ovulation-inducing therapies, and advanced assisted reproductive technologies like in vitro fertilization (IVF) with intracytoplasmic sperm injection (ICSI). These treatments have revolutionized the management of infertility, providing hope and options for couples struggling to conceive. However, infertility is not solely a biological condition; it also carries significant social, cultural, and psychological implications for affected people and couples. Society often attaches stigma and shame to infertility, particularly for women, who may face societal pressure and expectations regarding motherhood and reproductive capabilities. Women who are unable to conceive or carry a child to term may experience feelings of inadequacy, isolation, and a sense of loss, as they grapple with the perceived failure to fulfill societal expectations of womanhood and motherhood.

The inability to reproduce can lead to profound psychological distress and strain on relationships, as couples navigate the emotional rollercoaster of fertility treatments, pregnancy losses, and the uncertainty of outcomes. Additionally, societal norms and attitudes towards infertility can exacerbate these challenges, perpetuating stereotypes and misconceptions that further marginalize people experiencing infertility. In response to these societal pressures and personal struggles, some couples may explore alternative paths to parenthood, such as surrogacy or adoption. These options offer viable alternatives to biological parenthood and can provide fulfilling avenues for building a family. However, the decision to pursue alternative paths to parenthood can also be complex and emotionally fraught, requiring careful consideration and support.

Ultimately, infertility is a multifaceted issue that extends beyond the realm of biology, encompassing social, cultural, and psychological dimensions. By fostering greater understanding, empathy, and support for people and couples facing infertility, society can help to alleviate the stigma and challenges associated with this condition, promoting inclusivity, compassion, and acceptance for all paths to parenthood. Social scientists have noted a striking difference in the way infertility affects men compared to women. While both genders may experience disappointment and frustration, men often approach infertility with a sense of resignation rather than profound emotional distress. This observation has led researchers to suggest that men may lack the same depth of emotional investment or attachment to the idea of child-rearing as women do. Such findings challenge traditional notions of masculinity, which often emphasize stoicism and emotional detachment.

This disparity in emotional response raises important questions about the social construction of gender roles and expectations. If we view society as structured primarily around binary notions of male and female, the differing reactions to infertility highlight the limitations of such rigid categorizations. Men's relatively muted emotional response to infertility challenges conventional stereotypes about masculinity and calls into question the assumption that men are inherently less nurturing or emotionally connected to the idea of parenthood. In light of these observations, some social scientists argue that infertility should be recognized as more than just a medical condition; it should also be understood as a disability with significant social and psychological implications. By framing infertility as a disability, researchers highlight the complex interplay of biological, social, and psychological factors that contribute to the experience of infertility. This perspective underscores the importance of addressing not only the medical aspects of infertility but also the social and emotional needs of people and couples affected by this condition.

By acknowledging infertility as a disability, society can better understand and address the multifaceted challenges faced by those struggling to conceive. This includes providing support services, fostering open dialogue, and challenging harmful stereotypes and stigmas associated with infertility. Ultimately, a more inclusive and compassionate approach to infertility can help to alleviate the burden and isolation experienced by people and couples navigating this complex and often emotionally fraught journey.

Suggested Readings:

Balen, Rachel, and Marilyn Crawshaw. *Sexuality and*

fertility issues in ill health and disability: From early adolescence to adulthood. Jessica Kingsley Publishers, 2006.

Shigley, Sally Bishop. "Great Expectations: Infertility, Disability, and Possibility." *The Palgrave Handbook of Infertility in History: Approaches, Contexts and Perspectives* (2017): 37-55.

Invisibility

Invisibility, in its broadest sense, refers to the condition of being unseen or overlooked, where people' presence, rights, and needs are disregarded, relegating them to the margins of society. This unfortunate reality characterizes the experience of many disabled people in mainstream discourse. Throughout history, literature has often been regarded as a reflection of societal norms and values. Yet, despite the prevalence of disabled characters in literary works spanning ancient to modern times, their representation remains largely sidelined and their narratives neglected. Disabled characters populate the pages of literature across genres and epochs, embodying a diverse array of experiences and identities. However, their stories frequently languish in the shadows, relegated to secondary roles or dismissed entirely. This relegation mirrors the broader societal tendency to marginalize and overlook the needs and perspectives of disabled people.

Despite their ubiquity in literature, disabled characters often fail to receive the attention and exploration they warrant. Their presence is acknowledged, yet their experiences are not granted the depth and nuance afforded to other characters. Instead, they are relegated to tokenistic roles or used merely as plot devices, their narratives devoid of meaningful exploration or consideration.This pattern of invisibility perpetuates harmful stereotypes and reinforces societal attitudes that devalue the lives and voices of disabled people. By failing to engage with the realities of disability in literature, society misses out on opportunities for empathy, understanding, and meaningful dialogue. The absence of nuanced portrayals of disabled characters not only diminishes the richness and diversity of literary representation but also perpetuates the erasure of disabled experiences from the cultural consciousness.

In order to combat this pervasive invisibility, it is imperative that literature and broader societal discourse actively engage with the diverse experiences and perspectives of disabled people. By centering their voices and experiences, literature can serve as a powerful tool for challenging ableism, fostering empathy, and promoting social change. Only through meaningful representation and inclusion can we begin to dismantle the barriers that perpetuate the invisibility of disabled people in both literature and society at large.

In the realm of Disability Studies, the term "invisibility" encapsulates the pervasive phenomenon wherein people with disabilities find themselves consistently overlooked or disregarded within societal structures. Their lived experiences and unique needs often go unrecognized or inadequately addressed. This invisible status manifests in myriad ways in everyday life, ranging from physical obstacles that impede access to buildings and public spaces to social and cultural barriers that ostracize or stigmatize them. Inaccessible environments, whether due to architectural limitations or a lack of accommodations, serve as tangible manifestations of this invisibility. For many people with disabilities, navigating public spaces becomes a constant struggle against physical barriers that impede their mobility and autonomy. Moreover, the marginalization and stigma they encounter in social interactions underscore the deeper, more insidious forms of invisibility they face.

Compounding these challenges is the systemic neglect within the public sector, where policies and practices often fall short in meeting the needs of disabled people or ensuring equitable opportunities. The dearth of inclusive policies and accommodations perpetuates the cycle of invisibility, further marginalizing an already vulnerable population. Additionally, the notion of "overcoming" prevalent in societal discourse surrounding disability exacerbates this marginalization. The burden is placed squarely on the individual with a disability to surmount the barriers imposed by society, effectively negating the responsibility of broader societal structures to foster inclusivity and accessibility. This emphasis on individual triumph serves to absolve society of its failure to create an environment that is truly welcoming and inclusive for all. Beyond its broader connotations, the notion of "invisibility" extends to encompass the realm of "Invisible Disability," referring to conditions or disabilities that are not immediately apparent externally. In a society where identity often hinges on visible attributes, the invisibility of such disabilities can engender a profound identity crisis for those affected. Without overt markers of their condition, people may find themselves grappling with the need to assert their identity through political and social engagement, striving to validate their experiences and needs in a world that may overlook or dismiss them. Conversely, the pursuit of visibility in the context of disability introduces its own complexities. In Disability Studies, the act of "staring" is recognized as a negative phenomenon, indicative of objectification and dehumanization. The scrutiny and attention directed towards people with disabilities can serve to reduce them to mere objects of curiosity or pity, eroding their sense of agency and dignity. The psychological toll of being constantly subjected to the gaze of others can have profound and deleterious effects on a disabled person's psyche, exacerbating feelings of alienation and otherness.

In response to these dynamics, Disability Studies seeks to illuminate and address the multifaceted forms of invisibility experienced by people with disabilities. By amplifying the voices and experiences of those affected, Disability Studies endeavors to challenge societal norms and prejudices, advocating for a more inclusive and equitable society that recognizes and respects the full spectrum of human diversity. Through education, advocacy, and policy reform, Disability Studies aims to dismantle barriers to visibility and promote the rights and dignity of people with disabilities, fostering a culture of acceptance and belonging where all people are valued for their inherent worth and contributions.

Suggested Readings:

Baynton, Douglas C. "Disability and the Justification of Inequality in American History." *The New Disability History: American Perspectives*, edited by Paul K. Longmore and Lauri Umansky, 33–57. New York: NYU Press, 2001.

— — —. *Forbidden Signs: American Culture and the Campaign against Sign Language*. Chicago: University of Chicago Press, 1996.

— — —. "A Silent Exile on This Earth." *The Disability Studies Reader*, edited by Lennard J. Davis, 33–48. New York: Routledge, 2006a.

Medicalisation

The term "medicalisation," popularized by Ivan Illich in his seminal work "Limits to Medicine: Medical Nemesis" (1975), sheds light on the complex interplay between medicine and society. Illich's critique centers on the unintended consequences of medical intervention, arguing that in some instances, medical practices exacerbate rather than ameliorate social and biological conditions. Building on Illich's framework, Peter Conrad defines medicalisation as the process whereby non-medical issues are redefined and addressed through a medical lens, often framing them as illnesses or disorders. This phenomenon occurs when societal problems are pathologized and medical solutions are sought as the primary means of addressing them.

Within the context of Disability Studies, the medicalisation of disability serves to reframe disability solely as a medical issue, effectively reducing the multifaceted experiences of disabled people to a set of medical symptoms and diagnoses. This narrow perspective implies that disability can be remedied through medical interventions, such as surgeries or treatments, with the aim of restoring the individual to a state of "normalcy" or "health." In this paradigm, disabled people are cast as inherently flawed or diseased, perpetuating stigmatizing stereotypes and reinforcing notions of their vulnerability and dependency on medical intervention. By pathologizing disability, the medical model overlooks the social, cultural, and environmental factors that contribute to disablement, thereby neglecting the broader systemic barriers that hinder full participation and inclusion. Moreover, the medicalisation of disability can lead to the marginalization of disabled voices and experiences, as their narratives are subsumed within the biomedical framework and overshadowed by medical professionals' expertise and authority. This erasure of disabled agency further perpetuates their disenfranchisement and reinforces the power dynamics that privilege medical professionals as the arbiters of disability discourse.

With the ascent of capitalism, a transformation occurred in the perception of human bodies. Rather than being regarded as inherently valuable living entities, people became increasingly viewed as mere cogs in the machinery of production, valued primarily for their efficiency in driving economic growth. This shift toward the commodification of human beings had profound implications, particularly for those deemed less capable within the framework of market capitalism.

Within this capitalist paradigm, certain people were marginalized and stigmatized as being less productive or economically viable. Their perceived diminished value within the capitalist system rendered them disposable or in need of remediation to enhance their capacity to contribute to the workforce. Consequently, the imperative arose to either eradicate these perceived deficiencies through medical intervention or to increase their productivity through various means.

Historically, perceptions of disability were often intertwined with notions of moral failing or divine punishment. However, in pre-capitalist societies, people with disabilities were not systematically segregated or ostracized from the broader community. Instead, they often remained integrated within their social fabric, albeit with varying levels of accommodation and support.

The advent of capitalism, however, ushered in a new era where people with disabilities were increasingly marked as "others" – outsiders whose differences rendered them unfit for full participation in society. This categorization spurred efforts to either "correct" their disabilities through medical means or to marginalize and exclude them altogether. In this capitalist framework, disabled people became objects of medical scrutiny and intervention, with their worth measured against their ability to contribute to economic productivity. Those deemed unable to meet this standard were often relegated to the margins of society or subjected to coercive measures aimed at assimilating them into the workforce. During the Victorian era, a period marked by its emphasis on refinement and societal norms, a series of laws known as "ugly laws" were enacted. These laws mandated that people with physical deformities or abnormalities should be kept out of public view and confined within designated spaces with strict boundaries. This legislative action served to reinforce the marginalization of disabled people, casting them as unfit for public exposure or social interaction. Consequently, institutionalization emerged as the preferred method of control and management for people with disabilities.

The implementation of these laws effectively rendered disabled people invisible within society, relegating them to the confines of institutions where they were isolated from the broader community. This enforced invisibility perpetuated the marginalization and stigmatization of disabled people, further reinforcing their status as outsiders deemed unworthy of inclusion in public life. Paradoxically, while disabled people were marginalized and hidden from public view, there existed a pervasive societal curiosity surrounding the unknown and the unusual. This fascination with the rare and the extraordinary led to the rise of freak shows, where people with physical abnormalities were exhibited for public entertainment. In these exhibitions, disabled people were labeled as "freaks" and presented as spectacles of deviation from normative bodily standards. Their differences were exaggerated and sensationalized to captivate audiences and generate profit for showmen. Rather than being recognized as people with inherent dignity and humanity, disabled bodies were objectified and commodified for public consumption, perpetuating harmful stereotypes and reinforcing societal attitudes of otherness and exoticism.

The term "freak" became synonymous with disabled people, further distancing them from the societal mainstream and solidifying their status as objects of curiosity rather than people deserving of respect and inclusion. This commodification of disabled bodies within freak shows served to reinforce societal perceptions of disability as something abnormal and inherently inferior, perpetuating a cycle of marginalization and exploitation. Medicalization played a significant role in facilitating government policies, particularly in the implementation of eugenic measures that targeted disabled people. Under the guise of medical intervention, government officials mandated the forced sterilization of disabled people, justified by the principles of eugenics, which had been legitimized through legal channels. These coercive practices aimed to control and manipulate the genetic composition of populations, perpetuating ableist ideologies and reinforcing systemic discrimination against disabled people. In response to the shortcomings of the medical model of disability, which pathologized impairment and emphasized individual deficits requiring medical intervention, emerged the social model of disability. This paradigm shift reconceptualized disability as a social construct rather than a medical condition, asserting that people become disabled not solely due to their physical impairments, but primarily as a result of the societal barriers and inaccessible environments they encounter.

According to the social model, disability is not an inherent flaw residing within the individual, but rather a consequence of an unwelcoming and inaccessible environment. It highlights the role of societal attitudes, infrastructural barriers, and discriminatory practices in perpetuating disability exclusion and marginalization. Unlike the medical model, which posits disability as a personal deficiency necessitating medical treatment or cure, the social model emphasizes the need for systemic change to dismantle barriers and promote inclusion. Central to the social model is the recognition that disability is shaped by social, cultural, and environmental factors, rather than being solely determined by an individual's impairment. By reframing disability as a matter of social justice and human rights, the social model advocates for the creation of an inclusive society that accommodates and respects the diverse needs and experiences of all people, regardless of ability. The social model of disability presents a fundamental shift in understanding disability, emphasizing that it is not solely an individual burden or personal tragedy but rather a consequence of societal attitudes, oppression, and discrimination faced by disabled people due to their non-normative bodies. This perspective underscores the importance of addressing systemic barriers and societal prejudices that contribute to the marginalization of disabled people.

Despite the advocacy of the social model, the medicalization of disability persists as an ongoing phenomenon. Medicalization compels people to rely on medical interventions, often under pressure to access benefits, insurance coverage, therapies, workplace accommodations, or mobility aids. This reliance on medical solutions perpetuates the notion that disability is primarily a medical issue, reinforcing the dominance of the medical model within society. However, contemporary discourse challenges the dichotomy between the social and medical models of disability, as articulated by Susan Wendell. Wendell argues that there exists a close relationship between chronic illness and disability, blurring the boundaries between the two conceptual frameworks. She contends that disabled people may benefit from both the social model, which focuses on societal barriers, and the medical model, which emphasizes individual health and impairment.

Wendell's perspective challenges the assumption that all disabled people can thrive without medical assistance, highlighting the diverse experiences and needs within the disabled community. By acknowledging the complexities of disability and chronic illness, Wendell advocates for a more nuanced approach that recognizes the intersecting influences of social, environmental, and medical factors on individual well-being.

Suggested Readings:

Nagi, S. Z. 'Some Conceptual Issues in Disability and Rehabilitation'. *Sociology and Rehabilitation*, edited by M. Sussman, American Sociological Association, 1965.

Nagi, S. Z. 'The Disabled and Rehabilitation Services: A National Overview'. *American Rehabilitation*, vol. 2, no. 5, pp. 26–33,1977.

Oliver, Michael. *The Politics of Disablement: A Sociological Approach*. Palgrave Macmillan, 1997.

Thomas, C. *Female Forms: Experiencing and Understanding Disability*. Open University Press, 1999.

Thomas, C. 'Disability Theory: Key Ideas, Issues and

Thinkers'. *Disability Studies Today*, edited by C. Barnes et al., Polity Press, 2002, pp. 38–57.

Modernity

Modernity, characterized by the emergence of new ideas, beliefs, and practices that challenged traditional norms and conventions, significantly influenced the conceptualization of disability. This period witnessed the proliferation of key features such as capitalism, the industrial revolution, scientific advancements, religious skepticism, and technological innovations, all of which played pivotal roles in shaping perceptions and responses to disability. In the early stages of modernity, people with disabilities were often marginalized and segregated, particularly within government hospitals and asylums, where they were confined on the basis of poverty and perceived social deviance. However, as modernity progressed, disability began to be perceived as a societal problem necessitating intervention and resolution. Initially, attempts to address disability were rooted in charitable endeavors, reflecting a humanitarian impulse to alleviate the suffering of those deemed less fortunate. However, with the advent of the Enlightenment era, there emerged a growing emphasis on the expansion of scientific knowledge and the systematic study of organic existence and life forms.

Despite these advancements, the categorization of disability remained a formidable challenge. The diverse manifestations of disability defied easy classification, complicating efforts to develop comprehensive approaches to addressing the needs of disabled people. This complexity fueled ongoing debates and discussions surrounding the nature, causes, and implications of disability within the broader context of modern society. During the era of modernity, the medical model of disability gained prominence, reshaping perceptions by framing disability as a personal tragedy and individual burden requiring a cure. This perspective positioned disabled people as subjects in need of medical intervention to rectify their impairments and assimilate them into mainstream society. While modern medicine and technology presented newfound opportunities for people with disabilities to lead more independent and fulfilling lives, the advent of modernity also ushered in a host of ableist attitudes and practices that perpetuated exclusion and discrimination.

Within the framework of the medical model, disability became an object of scientific scrutiny, measurement, treatment, and control. As science and modernity progressed, questions arose regarding the degree of disability and how it should be assessed. Disabled bodies were subjected to scientific analysis, with efforts directed toward understanding, quantifying, and ameliorating impairments. Furthermore, the twentieth century witnessed the entanglement of disability with notions of masculinity. People with disabilities were often deemed less masculine, as societal norms equated masculinity with physical strength, vigor, and autonomy. This association between disability and masculinity reinforced stereotypes and prejudices, further marginalizing disabled people and undermining their sense of identity and self-worth.

Suggested Readings:

Bauman, Zygmunt. *Modernity and the Holocaust*. Wiley-Blackwell, 1989.

Foucault, Michel. *Abnormal: Lectures at the Collége de France 1974-1975*. edited by Valerio Marchetti and Antonella Salomoni, Picador, 2003.

Mitchell, David T. and Sharon L. Snyder. *Cultural

Locations of Disability. University of Chicago Press, 2006.

Pernick, Martin S. *The Black Stork: Eugenics and the Death of "Defective" Babies in American Medicine and Motion Pictures Since 1915.* Oxford UP, 1996.

Minority

The term "minority" traditionally denotes a group of people constituting a smaller portion of a larger community, distinguished by factors such as nationality, ethnicity, origin, language, or culture. Minority groups often experience discrimination and marginalization across various aspects of society, including education, employment, and political representation. Within the realm of Disability Studies, the concept of minority extends to people with physical deformities or impairments, who represent a relatively smaller segment of the population. However, contemporary scholarship within Disability Studies challenges traditional notions of disability by emphasizing the transient nature of ability. According to this perspective, no individual remains permanently non-disabled throughout their lifespan, as anyone can potentially experience disability at any point in their life due to injury, illness, or aging.

This concept is encapsulated by the term "temporarily-abled bodies" (TAB), which underscores the idea that able-bodiedness is not a fixed state but rather a temporary condition that may be subject to change. From this viewpoint, disability is not an inherent characteristic of certain people but rather a dynamic and fluid aspect of human experience that can manifest at different stages of life. By highlighting the temporality of ability and disability, Disability Studies challenges prevailing assumptions about the fixed nature of bodily function and underscores the importance of recognizing the diversity and variability of human embodiment. This perspective encourages a more inclusive understanding of disability that acknowledges the potential for all people to experience impairment or disability at some point in their lives, emphasizing the need for greater societal awareness, accommodation, and support for people with disabilities.

The term "minority" historically denotes groups of people who constitute a smaller portion of the population and are often marginalized or excluded from mainstream societal structures. Originally, the term was primarily associated with stigmatized groups such as African Americans, women, and racial minorities, who sought civil rights recognition and social and political acknowledgment. However, early Disability Studies scholars did not initially identify disabled people as part of a minority group; instead, they occupied a presumed majority status as non-disabled people. In recent years, Disability Studies scholars have begun to recognize parallels between the Disability Rights Movement and other marginalized minority groups based on race and gender. By adopting the terminology of "minority" to describe the disabled population, scholars aimed to highlight the systemic marginalization and exclusion experienced by disabled people within society. Framing disability as a minority status allowed the disability rights movement to draw upon the strategies and frameworks developed by other minority groups, providing a foundation for advocacy and activism within academic and political spheres.

Embracing the identity of a minority group has enabled disabled people to assert pride in their identity and challenge societal perceptions of disability as a deficit or aberration. By claiming their status as a minority, disabled people have taken steps to overcome feelings of inferiority and the burden of societal stigma. Acceptance of oneself as disabled is a crucial first step in the struggle for recognition and equality, empowering people to assert their rights and demand societal acknowledgment and accommodation.

Suggested Readings:

Barnes, Elizabeth. *The minority body: A theory of disability.* Oxford University Press, 2016.

Gliedman, John, and William Roth. *The Unexpected Minority: Handicapped Children in America.* New York: Harcourt Brace Jovanovich, 1980

Normality

In the realm of Disability Studies, the concept of 'Normality' serves as a benchmark, a perceived standard or accepted norm against which all human forms are measured. It encompasses a socially constructed ideal of what is deemed 'normal' or 'typical' in terms of physical, cognitive, or sensory abilities. While this notion of 'normality' holds significance within Disability Studies, it also carries implications of labeling and categorizing people, often resulting in discrimination and marginalization for those whose abilities fall outside this narrow construct. The concept of 'normality' is deeply entrenched within the medical model of disability, which views any deviation from this norm as a deviation to be 'cured' or remedied through medical intervention. Within this framework, the focus is on restoring the individual as closely as possible to the perceived 'normal' state, often disregarding the societal barriers that contribute to the individual's experience of disability. This approach absolves society of its responsibility to create an inclusive environment that accommodates the diverse needs of all people.

In contrast, the social model of disability challenges

the notion of 'normality' by highlighting the role of societal barriers in creating disability. According to this model, it is not the individual's impairment that renders them disabled, but rather the barriers imposed by society that restrict their full participation in social activities and opportunities. By shifting the focus from the individual to the environment, the social model emphasizes the importance of creating a more accessible and inclusive society that enables disabled people to fully engage in all aspects of life. Central to the social model is the recognition of disabled people' inherent rights to participate in society on an equal footing with their non-disabled peers. It underscores the need to dismantle physical, attitudinal, and systemic barriers that impede access and inclusion, advocating for changes that promote equality and autonomy for all people, regardless of ability.

Offer and Sabshin present multiple perspectives on the concept of normality, each offering insights into its complexities and implications.

Firstly, they discuss normality in terms of health, presenting a binary perspective where people are categorized as either healthy or ill. This perspective oversimplifies the spectrum of health and illness, disregarding the nuances of in-between conditions and variations in the degree of illness. By defining normality solely in opposition to disease, this model fails to adequately address early disease prevention or detection.

Secondly, Offer and Sabshin explore the notion of normality as a utopian concept, associated with idealized beings or states. In this view, normality represents an aspirational ideal, beyond the reach of most people. This perspective highlights the inherent idealism and unattainability of the concept of normality, which may lead to feelings of inadequacy or failure for those who do not conform to societal norms.

The third perspective presented by Offer and Sabshin is commonly found in the medical field, emphasizing normality as an average factor. This perspective posits that normality is determined by the statistical mean or average of a given population, with deviations from this central point considered abnormal or deviant. For example, people falling within the average range of height are deemed normal, while those above or below this average are seen as deviations from the norm.

Finally, Offer and Sabshin highlight the cultural value of normality, underscoring how the concept is deeply embedded within cultural and contextual frameworks. Norms and expectations surrounding normality vary across cultures and historical contexts, shaping perceptions of what is considered normal or abnormal within a given society.

The concept of the 'normal body' is inherently intertwined with cultural factors such as nationality, ethnicity, and origin. It recognizes that human beings are products of their cultural contexts, and thus, the notion of normality is shaped by cultural representations and perceptions. Normality cannot be understood in isolation from culture; rather, it is deeply embedded within cultural frameworks and varies across different societies and historical periods.

In this context, the social model of disability places responsibility on society for the discrimination and marginalization experienced by disabled people. According to this perspective, it is not the individual's impairment that renders them disabled, but rather the societal barriers and attitudes that restrict their full participation in social life. Disability is framed as a social construct, with society's norms, values, and structures creating conditions of disablement.

Throughout history and across cultures, the interpretation of disability has varied significantly. In some cultures, visually disabled people have been revered as healers, prophets, or saviors, with their impairment viewed as a mark of divine favor or spiritual insight. However, in other cultural contexts, disabled people have been stigmatized and perceived as dangerous or burdensome to society, leading to their marginalization and exclusion.

This variability underscores the dynamic and context-dependent nature of disability perceptions and experiences. It highlights the importance of understanding disability within its cultural and historical context, recognizing that societal attitudes and beliefs play a crucial role in shaping perceptions of disability and determining the degree of inclusion or exclusion experienced by disabled people. Disability in people is often assessed across three key dimensions: physical appearance, intellectual ability, and behavior. The significance attributed to these aspects varies across cultures, shaping perceptions of normalcy and deviation.

Physical appearance plays a significant role in how disability is perceived, with weight serving as a notable factor. In Western societies, obesity is often viewed as a form of disability due to its potential to restrict mobility and impact overall health. However, in other cultures like China, heavyweight may be associated with fertility and considered desirable rather than disabling.

Intellectual ability is another dimension through which disability is evaluated. High IQ levels are typically celebrated as a positive attribute, with people deemed geniuses for their exceptional intelligence. Conversely, low IQ levels may lead to negative labels such as "idiot." Interestingly, deviations from the normative range of intelligence, even if higher than average, are not typically considered abnormal.

Behavior also influences perceptions of disability, with people whose behavior diverges from accepted norms often facing exclusion from mainstream society. Attitudes towards behaviors such as homosexuality vary widely across different cultures and historical periods. While the ancient Greeks viewed homosexuality positively, associating it with artistic and intellectual prowess, Christian societies historically condemned it as a criminal offense.

One approach to fostering acceptance of disability is to recognize deviations from the norm as variations within the spectrum of human diversity, rather than labeling them as deviant or abnormal. By creating a more inclusive and welcoming environment for people with diverse characteristics and abilities, societies can promote greater acceptance and understanding of disability. This involves challenging societal norms and prejudices, embracing diversity, and promoting equality and inclusion for all people, regardless of their physical appearance, intellectual ability, or behavior.

Suggested Readings:

Harrington, Gordon M. "Psychological testing, IQ, and evolutionary fitness." *Genetica* 99 (1997): 113-123.

Houston, Robert Allan. «Class, gender and madness in eighteenth-century Scotland.» *Sex and Seclusion, Class and Custody*. Brill, 2003. 45-68.

Kaplan, Abraham. "A philosophical discussion of normality." *Archives of general psychiatry* 17.3 (1967): 325-330.

Pain

Disability and 'pain' are inherently connected, whether physical or psychological. Generally, the image of a disabled person ingrained in our minds is that of a helpless victim or sufferer. Etymologically, the word pain means penalty, punishment and revenge; however, in the fourth century, the meaning of pain evolved to signify suffering and affliction. According to Adam Smith, one can never realise the pain of others unless and until it happens to themself. Pain is an entirely intimate phenomenon; one must first go through a similar experience to empathise with another individual's pain. For example, Sophocles's character Philoctetes is left to die by Odysseus and his fellow men since he is unable to manage his tremendous pain resulting from a snake bite. A wounded soldier would be nothing less than a burden, and it would only hinder them from their way to victory in the Trojan War. Thus, pain is a personal tragedy and individual burden, to which society always steer clear of its responsibility. Such a view ignores society's failure to provide access to disabled people, and above that, society restricts their movement and causes them further pain through its policy of exclusion. The association of pain with a disability has, for ages, justified the suicidal tendency of disabled persons and doctors' withdrawal from life-sustaining treatment to disabled patients. Ironically, society finds the death of a disabled person a more valid and legitimate option than trying to eradicate their pain and provide them equal access and rights. They generally do not have any first-hand experience with pain, poverty or disability. The law also justifies the legislature of 'assisted suicide' in the name of freeing disabled people from their lifelong exposure to pain, however as Carol Gill argues, in this process, no opinions of disabled people were sought, and the ableist majority decided the rules and regulations of their life.

There is the presumption that medical treatment is capable of eliminating the pain, and so it is cunningly ignored in the verdict given by the court. Physical pain is also considered most difficult to express in words, which is why the clinical setting offers the Wong-Baker-faces pain scale, where the victim can communicate the degree of his pain through measuring scales. According to Elaine Scarry, disabled people in pain are seen as helpless victims or cunning pretenders, trying to avail undue advantage for their disability and get their necessary accommodation and resources at the expense of faking exaggerated pain. However, physical pain is a common cause that can restrict people's mobility and eventually disables them. Chronic pain is something that one has to deal with for a prolonged period of time, and it can recur at any time in future. Chronic pain, no matter which body part it affects, makes the sufferer's life unbearable, and all his endeavours to live a normal life turn out to be futile. Their prolonged suffering from pain and medical treatment's inability to cure it increases their depression and mental anxiety. Numerous physicians and experts have given theories on different kinds of pain, such as S.weir Mitchell, the American neurologist who defined the severity of pain caused by nerve injury, or Johannes Müller's concept of 'Gemeingefihl' or 'Canestgesis' which refers to the inability of a person to perceive the internal sensations correctly. Even though there were no evident symptoms, people who complained about pains were regarded as delusional, stupid or even criminal.

In the 1980s, Goldscheider publicly approved Sheerington's observation that the human body's central nervous system responds to the sensations it receives from the outside and the brain's recognition of spatial and temporal patterns of sensation results in physical pain. Livingston, after a detailed case study of patients with industrial injuries, discovered a vicious circle due to which constant and prolonged pain changes the organic structure of the nervous system itself, producing chronic pain. Henry K.Beecher found out the surprising fact that the patients who had undergone a clinical surgery felt much more intense pain than the soldiers who were badly injured on the battlefield, and the possible reason for this, he assumed, was that this wound of the soldiers was a means of freedom from the battlefield, it was considered to be an end of their life-threatening experience and constant fear of death. In contrast, on the other hand, it was the fear of the unknown and disruption of their normal life for the surgery patients. Thus, physical pain has a strong connection to one's psychological status.

This experience of pain is different for different people due to its association with diverse emotions. In the book *The Management of Pain*, Bonica also agreed with Beecher, stating that every pain has psychological and physiological components. Wall and Melzack established the International Association for the Study of Pain (IASP) along with John Bonica, which was dedicated to studying the intricate science behind pain. The American Pain Society (APS) was founded in 1977. As a result, professional research on pain saw more improvement, and many new theories emerged. The two most groundbreaking theories are that long-standing acute pain can change the organic form of the central nervous system and make it more sensitive, leading to chronic pain. To elaborate, this theory was dramatically represented by Gary Bennett and

XieYukuan at the National Institute of Health in 1989. And another observation is that the enduring capacity of pain and reaction to it largely depends on one's race, gender, ethnicity and experience. While women are more vulnerable to pain, they can tolerate chronic pain better. Again, African Americans are more prone to disability due to pain than people of white race. After analysing these observations, one can conclude that pain experiences vary from person to person. The origin of pain is the brain and central nervous system. Better treatments for pain are available today than in the 1900s due to the innovation in science, technology and medicine. Several campaigns have supported using opiate drugs in severe pain related to cancer. Still, drug regulatory authorities restrict the sale of opiates. There is a constant search for an alternative to opiate drugs. There is a psychological invention in the treatment of chronic pain employing learning and behavioural theory. According to Richard Sternbach, an individual's response and reaction to pain are based on his past experience, and it can be relearned. Despite many such relevant attempts to theorise pain, little attention is paid to eliminating the patient's pain; the topmost priority is to cure the disease, while the patient can suffer unbearable pain.

Suggested Readings:

Baszanger, Isabelle. *Inventing Pain Medicine: From the Laboratory to the Clinic*. Rutgers University Press, 1998.

Morris, David. *The Culture of Pain*. University of California Press, 1991.

Scarry, Elaine. *The Body in Pain: The Making and Unmaking of the World*. Oxford University Press, 1985.

Siebold, Cathy. *The Hospice Movement: Easing Death's Pains*. Twayne, 1992.

Performance

The concept of 'performance' extends beyond theatrical stages to encompass the everyday actions and behaviors through which people represent themselves to others. As famously articulated by Shakespeare, life itself can be seen as a stage, with each person assuming various roles and personas in their interactions with the world. In this context, all people, disabled or not, engage in performative acts as they navigate their daily lives. For people with disabilities, who are often subjected to heightened visibility and scrutiny due to their differences, the notion of performance takes on added significance. Their actions and movements, whether consciously or unconsciously, are imbued with a sense of performance as they negotiate physical and social environments that may not always be accommodating or inclusive.

Simple tasks such as walking with a wheelchair, using crutches, or navigating spaces while limping become performative acts through which disability is made visible to others. These actions not only serve practical purposes but also communicate aspects of identity, agency, and embodiment to observers. Moreover, the performative aspect of disability extends beyond physical movements to encompass broader social interactions and identity expressions. For example, people may engage in performative acts of self-advocacy, challenging stereotypes and advocating for their rights and dignity. On occasion, people with disabilities may exaggerate the extent of their disability to gain access to advantages or resources that would otherwise be unavailable to them. This exaggeration, or performance, of disability can be seen as a strategic means to overcome barriers and secure necessary support. Similarly, disability performance is often employed by beggars as a means of eliciting pity and sympathy from others, thereby facilitating their means of livelihood.

Disability performance encompasses a range of actions and behaviors undertaken by people with disabilities, whether consciously or unconsciously. This performance serves a dual purpose: outwardly, it may be aimed at eliciting a specific response or reaction from others, such as gaining access to resources or support; inwardly, it may serve as a means of affirming one's identity and agency in the face of societal stigma and discrimination. For some people, disability performance may involve exaggerating certain aspects of their disability in order to navigate social and physical environments that are not always accommodating or inclusive. This may include emphasizing mobility limitations or visible impairments to gain preferential treatment or accommodations.

At the same time, disability performance may also be a means of self-expression and empowerment for people with disabilities, allowing them to assert their identity and agency in a world that often marginalizes or overlooks their experiences. By outwardly performing their disability, people may challenge societal norms and expectations, asserting their right to access resources and participate fully in society.

On one hand, stage performances serve as a powerful medium through which people with disabilities can challenge and reshape societal perceptions of disability. By showcasing their talents and abilities on stage, disabled performers have the opportunity to confront stereotypes and misconceptions, presenting themselves as strong, independent, and proud of their disabled identity. Through improvisation and modification, they can subvert the prevailing image of disabled people as pitied or helpless, asserting their agency and autonomy in the process. Moreover, stage performances offer a platform for disabled people to explore and define their identities and roles. By participating in theatrical productions or other forms of performance art, they can actively engage in the process of self-discovery and expression. This allows them to assert control over their narratives and representation, deciding for themselves how they wish to be seen and heard by audiences.

In addition to individual empowerment, stage performances also have broader societal implications. By showcasing the talents and perspectives of disabled people, these performances challenge societal norms and promote greater inclusion and acceptance. Through their creative endeavors, disabled performers make their voices heard and their demands known, contributing to a more diverse and equitable cultural landscape.

The Paralympics serve as a notable example of disability performance on a global scale. Here, disabled athletes have the opportunity to showcase their skills and abilities, challenging stereotypes and preconceived notions about disability in sports. Through their participation, they assert their equal involvement in societal performances, demonstrating that disability does not limit one's potential for achievement and excellence. The identity of people with disabilities is often visually represented through specific performances that highlight their experiences and challenges. Utilizing various aids such as crutches, glasses, wheelchairs, and other adaptive devices, people with disabilities make their impairments visible to the public, setting them apart from the able-bodied majority. However, questions arise regarding the historical and contextual nature of these disability performances. Do they evolve over time, and are they influenced by different cultural, ethnic, and racial backgrounds? Moreover, can individual performances by disabled people challenge societal perceptions of disability and potentially destabilize entrenched beliefs?

Disability performances can vary across historical periods, contexts, and cultural settings. These performances may reflect evolving attitudes towards disability and changing societal norms. Different cultures, ethnicities, and races may prescribe distinct performances for disabled populations, influenced by cultural beliefs, traditions, and values surrounding disability. Individual performances by disabled people have the potential to challenge societal perceptions of disability and disrupt established narratives. By asserting their agency and autonomy, disabled people can challenge ableist assumptions and advocate for greater inclusivity and acceptance. This process of destabilization can extend beyond personal interactions to influence broader societal attitudes and policies, including those within the political arena. However, disability stage performances also face various challenges and ethical considerations. In literary and theatrical productions, non-disabled actors are often given preference over disabled actors to portray disabled characters, perpetuating a lack of authentic representation. Additionally, accessibility issues may arise, such as the need for stages to be made more inclusive and accommodating for wheelchair users or people using crutches. Ethical considerations surrounding disability performance, including the potential for segregation of different types of disabilities, further complicate the issue.

Throughout history, disability stage performances have been influenced by the phenomenon of the freak show, reflecting society's fascination with people who deviate from typical physical norms. Across cultures, there has been a longstanding curiosity surrounding deformed or distorted beings, which has contributed to the popularity of disability stage shows. Despite this historical association, many countries today boast thriving disability performance scenes, festivals, and artists, demonstrating a shift towards more inclusive and diverse representations.

Disability performance encompasses a wide range of artistic expressions, with performers who have disabilities creating and showcasing work that challenges ableist assumptions and celebrates diversity. This form of expression promotes disability pride and empowerment by providing a platform for people to assert their identities and talents on their own terms. By integrating disability culture, history, and politics into their artistic endeavors, performers can amplify their voices and advocate for social justice and equality.

At its core, disability performance serves as a powerful tool for raising awareness about disability issues and advocating for change. Through creative expression, performers can shed light on the lived experiences of people with disabilities, highlighting both the challenges they face and the resilience they embody. Disability performance also serves as a means of reclaiming narratives and challenging stereotypes, fostering a greater sense of inclusivity and representation within the arts and broader society. Furthermore, disability performance can serve as a catalyst for broader social and political change. By addressing systemic barriers and advocating for greater accessibility and inclusion, performers can inspire meaningful dialogue and action on issues of disability rights and equality. Through their artistic endeavors, they can challenge societal norms and promote a more inclusive and equitable world for people of all abilities.

Suggested Readings:

Auslander, Philip, and Carrie Sandahl. *Bodies in Commotion: Disability and Performance*. Ann Arbor: University of Michigan Press, 2004.

Fox, Ann M. "How to Crip the Undergraduate Classroom: Lessons from Performance,Pedagogy, and Possibility." *Journal of Postsecondary Education and Disability*, vol. 23, no. 1, 2010, pp 38–47.

Hadley, Bree. "(Dia) logics of Difference Disability, performance and spectatorship in Liz Crow's Resistance on the Plinth." *Performance Research* 16.2 (2011): 124-131.

Henderson, Bruce, and Noam Ostrander. *Understanding Disability Studies and Performance Studies*. London: Routledge, 2010.

Kuppers, Petra. *Disability and Contemporary Performance: Bodies on Edge. New York*:Routledge, 2003.

— — —. *Disability and Performance*. London: Haworth Press, 2001.

Prosthetics

Prosthetics serve as artificial devices designed to replace specific body parts lost due to surgical amputation, accidents, or other traumatic events. These devices play a crucial role in aiding people to maintain everyday functionality and mobility following the loss of a limb. The human body is susceptible to a myriad of conditions, ranging from diseases to accidents, which can result in limb loss, thereby hindering an individual's ability to actively participate in societal activities. In the realm of medical science, continuous advancements and technological innovations have led to the development of sophisticated prosthetic devices that can seamlessly integrate with the body. These advancements aim to enhance the quality of life for people with limb loss by providing them with functional and lifelike replacements for their missing body parts. From mechanical limbs to bionic prosthetics, the field of prosthetics offers a wide range of options tailored to meet the diverse needs of people with limb loss.

It is important to note that prosthetics aren't limited to just limb replacements. Medical science also addresses various other types of disabilities, such as hearing impairment, visual disability, and locomotor disability, by providing appropriate mechanical devices. These assistive devices are designed to mitigate the challenges faced by people with disabilities, enabling them to navigate daily life more easily. However, the distinction between prosthetics and assistive devices lies in their integration into the body's daily routine. A prosthetic device is considered truly prosthetic when it becomes seamlessly integrated into the individual's bodily functions and activities, effectively mimicking the lost limb's functionality. In contrast, assistive devices may offer support or assistance but aren't directly integrated into the body's functioning.

Prosthetic devices encompass a diverse range of custom-designed tools aimed at replicating the appearance and functionality of missing limbs or body parts. These devices can be attached to the body through various means, offering people with limb loss the opportunity to regain mobility and functionality in their daily lives. Examples of prosthetic devices include wooden legs, split-hook hands, myoelectric limbs, replaced hip joints, hearing aids, eyeglasses, and reconstructed bones. Customization of prosthetics is essential to meet the unique needs of each individual. Given the intricacies of the human body and the specific requirements of different users, prosthetic devices are tailored to fit seamlessly into the user's lifestyle and provide optimal support and functionality. Whether used as decorative accessories or implanted biologically into the body, prosthetics are designed to enhance the user's quality of life and restore a sense of normalcy.

The field of prosthetic science continues to evolve and expand, driven by various factors such as warfare, natural disasters, technological advancements, and the prevalence of fatal diseases. Instances such as world wars and battlefield injuries have historically led to an increased demand for prosthetic devices, as many soldiers and civilians alike are left with disabilities that affect their ability to live independently. However, advancements in prosthetic technology offer hope for people facing limb loss, providing them with the means to regain mobility and engage in everyday activities.

The need to study and develop prosthetic science is more pressing than ever, given the growing number of people in need of prosthetic devices worldwide. Technological innovations and ongoing research efforts hold the promise of further enhancing the functionality and effectiveness of prosthetic devices, ultimately improving the lives of people with limb loss and other disabilities. Through continued advancements in prosthetic science, people can aspire to reclaim their independence and lead fulfilling lives despite physical challenges. During historical periods when medical science was less advanced, injuries sustained by war soldiers often led to severe infections that necessitated amputation as a life-saving measure. In such circumstances, prosthetics emerged as a crucial innovation, offering hope and mobility to people who had lost limbs. However, societal attitudes toward amputees with prosthetics were often influenced by the theory of social Darwinism, which propagated the notion of "survival of the fittest." As a result, people with prosthetics were sometimes stigmatized as being less human or imperfect, leading to their exclusion from mainstream society.

Many people who relied on prosthetic devices faced societal prejudices and discrimination. Some preferred to conceal their prosthetics, opting for empty sleeves or pant legs to avoid drawing attention to their disability. Others, unable to find gainful employment due to societal biases, resorted to begging as a means of livelihood. Despite these challenges, the emergence of World War II sparked renewed interest and demand for prosthetic devices, particularly to support the countless soldiers returning home with war-related injuries.

In response to this growing demand, efforts were made to advance prosthetic technology and rehabilitation programs. In 1945, the National Academy of Science initiated a research program focused on the rehabilitation of injured people, including the development of prosthetic devices. Through interdisciplinary approaches incorporating robotics, ergonomics, kinesiology, and human engineering, prosthetic devices underwent significant modifications and innovations. These advancements not only improved the functionality and effectiveness of prosthetics but also contributed to the overall rehabilitation and reintegration of people with limb loss into society.

Prosthetics serve as a means to address physical deficiencies in the human body, whether congenital or resulting from surgical procedures or traumatic injuries. The emergence of prosthetics can be traced to various historical contexts, including wartime conflicts, industrialization, advancements in medicine, accidents, and injuries.

Historians often analyze the development of prosthetics within the broader socio-cultural and technological frameworks of these contexts.

From a mechanical and engineering perspective, prosthetics entail the design and implementation of hardware systems that mimic or replace missing or impaired body parts. Engineers and mechanics focus on the functionality and usability of prosthetic devices, ensuring they meet the specific needs and requirements of people.

In the realm of rehabilitation, prosthetics not only aim to restore physical function but also address the psychological and emotional aspects of adapting to life with a prosthetic limb. Rehabilitation professionals work with people to integrate prosthetic use into their daily lives and overcome any psychological barriers or challenges associated with their condition. Beyond its practical function, a prosthetic can symbolize various meanings, including patriotism and sacrifice in the context of war-related injuries. It may serve as a symbol of modernity, representing advancements in technology and medicine. For people with disabilities, particularly those perceived as less masculine or incomplete, the use of prosthetics can be a means of asserting their manhood and reclaiming agency over their bodies.

Modernist thinkers have explored the concept of prosthetics in relation to human enhancement, viewing prosthetic devices as extensions of the human body that transcend conventional physical limitations, effectively turning the individual into a cyborg. However, media and cultural representations often prioritize the technological aspects of prosthetics over the lived experiences of disabled people, relegating the disabled body to a secondary status. There is ongoing debate regarding the use of prosthetics to "pass" as non-disabled, as well as concerns about the suitability of certain devices for specific groups within the disabled community. While some may view prosthetics as a means of achieving superhuman abilities, the majority of disabled people rely on such devices primarily to regain functionality and access to social resources rather than for the enhancement of abilities. Ultimately, the use of prosthetics reflects complex intersections of technology, culture, identity, and social norms within society.

Suggested Readings:

Mitchell, David T., and Sharon Snyder. *Narrative Prosthesis: Disability and the Dependencies of Discourse.* University of Michigan Press, 2000.

Snyder, Sharon L., and David T. Mitchell. "Re-engaging the body: Disability studies and the resistance to embodiment." *Public culture* 13.3 (2001): 367-389.

Ott, Katherine. «The sum of its parts.» *Artificial parts, practical lives: Mod-ern histories of prosthetics* (2002): 1-42.

Panchasi, Roxanne. «Reconstructions: prosthetics and the rehabilitation of the male body in world wariFrance.» *Differences: A Journal of Feminist Cultural Studies* 7.3 (1995): 109-141.

Race

Race studies is a multifaceted discipline that delves into the intricate dynamics surrounding racial and ethnic groups, encompassing their social, cultural, political, and economic experiences. This interdisciplinary field scrutinizes how race and ethnicity shape both individual and collective identities, while also exploring the intersections of race with other social categories like gender, class, sexuality, and disability. By examining historical legacies and contemporary manifestations of racism, discrimination, and inequality, race studies aims to illuminate the systemic barriers faced by racial and ethnic minorities and advocates for strategies to foster social justice and equality.

In parallel, Disability Studies constitutes a distinct academic domain focused on understanding the experiences of people with disabilities within society. Scholars within this field analyze the social, cultural, and structural factors that contribute to the marginalization and discrimination of disabled people. They also explore issues related to identity, access, inclusion, and empowerment, seeking to challenge ableist norms and promote the rights and agency of people with disabilities. While race studies and Disability Studies are distinct fields of inquiry, there exists a notable convergence in their focus on marginalized and discriminated minority groups. Scholars such as Rosemarie Garland Thomson and Lennard J Davis have highlighted the parallels between these two domains. In their pursuit of civil rights protection and identity, Disability Studies scholars often align themselves with the minority model, drawing connections between the experiences of disabled people and those of racial and ethnic minorities. This intersectional perspective underscores the interconnected nature of oppression and marginalization, emphasizing the importance of solidarity and advocacy across diverse social movements.

The association between Disability Studies and Race studies as minority fields allows for a historical examination that reveals significant parallels between these two domains. Both disability and race have been intertwined in systems of oppression and marginalization throughout history. Scholars like Douglas Baynton have drawn attention to the fact that both disabled people and non-white people were viewed as deviations from an idealized norm, which served to justify their marginalization within society.

One notable manifestation of this marginalization was the emergence of eugenics, a movement that sought to improve the human race by eliminating perceived defects through selective breeding. Eugenicists advocated for the sterilization of people deemed mentally unstable or disabled, as well as non-white racial minorities, in order to prevent the propagation of what they considered to be undesirable traits. This discriminatory ideology extended beyond race and disability to include lower-class white women, whom eugenicists also deemed biologically inferior. Consequently, eugenicists sought to control the reproductive capacity of these people to prevent the perceived degradation of the superior white society.

The ideology of eugenics served as a powerful tool for justifying the oppression and elimination of marginalized groups such as non-white races, lower classes, and disabled people. According to eugenicists, these groups were believed to possess various pathological defects that rendered them inferior and unworthy of equal treatment within society. This discriminatory ideology was not only employed to justify domestic policies but also served as a rationale for the colonization of third-world countries inhabited by non-white races by purportedly superior white colonizers.

Despite being excluded and marginalized, these imperfect bodies were paradoxically exploited by the ableist majority for economic gain. They were often put on display as "freaks" to satisfy the voyeuristic curiosity of the so-called superior human race. Throughout history, numerous instances exist of people with racial and disability differences becoming objects of fascination and spectacle, drawing crowds and generating profits for their exploiters. Consequently, these racialized and disabled bodies were perceived as either repulsive anomalies or intriguing curiosities, depending on the perspective of the observer.

The intertwined histories of race and disability highlight the complex and interconnected nature of oppression and marginalization. For critical race scholars, studying race without considering disability is challenging due to the inherent similarities and intersections between these two dimensions of identity. By examining these shared experiences, scholars can gain deeper insights into the mechanisms of power and privilege that have shaped societal attitudes towards marginalized communities and work towards dismantling systems of oppression that perpetuate inequality.Stuart Hall and other scholars in race studies have elucidated the daily experiences of racialized people as profoundly "crippling" and "deforming." In doing so, they inadvertently reinforce the same ideology of normativity and biological perfection that historically served to marginalize certain groups, thereby justifying their oppression and exclusion. By implicitly positioning disability as a condition from which one should seek escape rather than embracing it, they perpetuate societal norms that privilege able-bodiedness and perpetuate inequality.

Blanchett, Klingner, and Harry have delved into the intersectional impact of race, class, and disability, particularly on economically disadvantaged students. They demonstrate how these intersecting identities contribute to mental instability and emotional vulnerability, hindering access to compensatory services that could mitigate these challenges. Moreover, they reveal how the privilege afforded to white people further exacerbates disparities in access and support.

The connection between poverty and disability is undeniable, with financial constraints often exacerbating health issues and limiting access to necessary resources and support systems. For Black people with disabilities, this intersectionality results in double marginalization, as they contend with both racial discrimination and the challenges of disability. Factors such as inadequate housing, nutritional deficiencies, and limited access to healthcare increase their susceptibility to disability at any point in their lives. Rather than viewing race and disability as interchangeable concepts, it is essential to recognize their interdependency and how they mutually constitute each other within social, political, economic, and cultural contexts. Understanding the intricate intersections of these identities is crucial for addressing systemic inequalities and advocating for more inclusive and equitable policies and practices.

Suggested Readings:

Stone, Dan. *Breeding Superman: Nietzsche, Race and Eugenics in Edwardian and Interwar Britain.* Liverpool University Press, 2002.

Stubblefield, Anna. ""Beyond the pale": Tainted whiteness, cognitive disability, and eugenic sterilization." *Hypatia* 22.2 (2007): 162-181.

Stubblefield, Anna. "The entanglement of race and cognitivedisability." *Metaphilosophy* 40.3-4 (2009): 531-551.

Walker, Lisa. *Looking like what you are: Sexual style, race, and lesbian identity.* NYU Press, 2001.

Rehabilitation

Rehabilitation refers to the process of restoring or enhancing an individual's ability to perform daily activities, participate in social life, and achieve their goals, despite the limitation caused by their disability. It can involve a range of intervention strategies such as physical therapy, occupational therapy, speech therapy, assistive technology, psychological counselling etc. The ultimate goal of rehabilitation is to help people with disabilities achieve their maximum potential and live a fulfilling life. However, there are various nuances to the term due to the existence of different models and meanings of disability. For example, the medical model of disability perceives disability as an individual phenomenon, a personal tragedy, and this disability can be objectively diagnosed to offer a treatment or cure; it tries to bring the disabled person as close as possible to the normal human form. To 'fix' the deficiency or 'cure' is the ultimate goal of the medical model. The social model of disability, on the contrary, believes that disability is not an individual's burden; it attacks society based on its inability to create a more welcoming environment, and its physical barriers which hinder the disabled person's growth and mobility. According to this model, it is not the impairment which makes the person disabled; rather, it is the society which is disabling. Thus the focus of rehabilitation shifts from an individual's problem towards a more community-based approach. It attempts to alter society's views and preconceived notions to lessen the discrimination that excludes disabled people from mainstream society. As a result, various policies, societal changes, and architectural modifications happened to smoothen the journey of disabled people's a life. However, most of the persons in laws and legislation did not have enough idea about various nuances and problems of disability, so there was the slogan "Nothing about us, without us".

Disabled people claimed equal participation in decision-making since only they had first-hand experience with disability. Their opinions should be considered while making policies and decisions about their life. It rejected the old medical model, which imposed decisions and treatment on disabled people by objectifying their disability. One advantage of providing disabled people with the power to make their own life decisions is that, in this process of recognising their limitations, they gain a better perception of their disability. They learn how to cope with it or manage its problems. As a result, they become more self-reliant and physically and emotionally independent. This can be achieved by asking disabled people for their opinions regarding the changes and measures that should be implemented in their lives. Secondly, the scope of rehabilitation should be broadened, moving it beyond the limited area of hospitals and clinics and incorporating it into the abode of disabled people. Community-based rehabilitation (CBR) is gaining widespread importance through its organization of local community-based programs, often with the help of government agencies, NGOs etc., to meet the basic needs of disabled people and integrate them into societal activities and employment. The World Health Organization encourages community-based rehabilitation through the organisation of local communities, providing guidelines and measures on how to cater to this issue of disability. During the 1980s, disability came to be seen as variations in human existence rather than as the pre-existing concept of 'deviant' from the 'norm'. They saw disability as the result of the interaction between impaired people and their environment.

Functional Index Measure (FMI) Functional Independence Measure (FIM) measures the degree of impairment of a person by evaluating one's daily activities. FMI is used globally in rehabilitation settings to assess the individual's progress and decide on the other measures that should be taken to get the expected outcome. This helps in evaluating the institution's or the individual's achievement. There have also been technological modifications in rehabilitation settings have further enhance the desired outcome of implementing such rehabilitation therapies. Advancements in medical fields, clinical surgery, biology, genetics, all significantly contributed to the betterment of rehabilitation.Modification in both the inside and external worlds are necessary for a disabled person to live a more independent and free life. Diet, nutrition, social inclusion, architectural modifications, and the use of assistive devices are all essential. Unfortunately, despite various technological improvements in recent rehabilitation, very few disabled people can benefit from such devices. Their issues should receive more attention, and these policies and technologies should be made more accessible to all sections of society.

Suggested Readings:

Harsløf, Ivan, Ingrid Poulsen, and Kristian Larsen, eds. *New dynamics of disability and rehabilitation: Interdisciplinary perspectives*. Springer, 2019.

Ganvir, Shyam D. *Disability and Rehabilitation*. Jaypee Brothers Medical Publishers Pvt Limited, 2023.

Representation

Representation in Disability Studies refers to the portrayal of disability and disabled people in various forms of media, including literature, film, television, art, and other cultural expressions. It also includes how disabled people are depicted in public discourse, policies, and social attitudes. Representation is a crucial area of inquiry in Disability Studies because it shapes how society views and treats disabled people. Historically, disabled people have been marginalised and excluded from mainstream society, and their representations in media and culture have often reinforced negative stereotypes and harmful attitudes.

It involves examining how disability is represented in cultural texts and analysing how disabled people are represented in society more broadly. It seeks to promote greater understanding and acceptance of disability and disabled people in all aspects of society.

Representation has different perspectives in different aspects; in the political sense, representation can be summed up through the slogan, "Nothing about us without us", which denied the voice to the disabled subjects; they were rendered as incapable, inferior, who could have no say or opinion in the discussion about themselves. It was the non-disabled majority who laid down the policies and regulations regarding disabled people's lives on their behalf of them. Society linked their bodily deformity with cognitive inefficiency in discussing their needs and demands. Even now, we hardly find any disabled people occupying a political position in society. So, they were denied self-representation in the political arena. Douglas Baynton, in his essay, "Disability and the Justification of Inequality in American History" (2001), depicted how disability was inherently linked to race and gender and how their marginalisation and exclusion were justified on the basis of disability. As a result of which, women and black people, for the sake of gaining independence and civil rights, performed certain self-representative roles to disassociate themselves from the disabled minority, which further justified the society's policy of exclusion of people with disabilities.

The Americans with Disabilities Act passed in 1990, called for equal civil rights and citizenship for disabled populations. Under the leadership of Ed Roberts and Rolling Quads, the Disability Rights movement of the 1960s was chiefly concerned with the political self-representation of disabled people. However, the possible rationale for negating the representation of people with disabilities may be rooted in the social contract theory of the West in the eighteenth century since theorists of social contract deliberately ignored intellectually disabled people and refused to represent them in popular culture. John Locke believed in the "free, equal, and independent" nature of humans who, in social contract philosophy, would mutually benefit one another; Rawls also relied on the same notions of fullness and active participation of human beings in society. Naturally, they both excluded the otherwise passive, weaker, dependent human beings as before being unable to represent themselves and who must be represented through another's voice. Thus, the focus of Disability Studies is to emphasise the necessity of giving disabled people the right, the voice, and the power to represent themselves in both aesthetic and political fields, coming out from the margins to the centre.

In an aesthetic sense, disabled people are represented in the literary and media culture as evil, negative and villainous, perpetuating their images as crooked and always satanic in the popular imagination. Such portrayals of disabled persons are responsible for the negative stereotypes and stigma that exist against disabled persons. There are numerous examples where Oedipus's sin is associated with his swollen ankle; in the Indian epic, Ramayana KujiManthara twists the entire plot with her conspiracy; her crooked body is linked with her dubious mind. In Western countries during Renaissance, there was a fascination and stigma towards people with disabilities, which Shakespeare also made use of by associating Richard the Third's villainy with his deformed body, even though, in reality, he was not so. Blindness is associated with one's moral or intellectual lack. Disability Studies analyse and seek to revert such representations in literature, where one's disability is linked to his sins from the past life since such negative images of the disabled are responsible for their discrimination and vicious stereotypes, which have been ingrained in people's minds for ages. Just like gender discrimination, Disability Studies also possess the ideology of 'separate spheres', where disabled people are very naturally imagined as short-tempered, indignant, and having a bitter outlook towards life in general through their ruthless representation in literature.

For Rosemarie Garland Thomson, the 'realistic representation' does not only designate a representation which is the most exact copy of reality; rather, it should be the least stigmatising mode of representation. However, there lies a subtle difference between the representation of 'images of women' and 'images of disabled'; since it is beyond the binary representation of positive and negative, it goes much beyond that since 'disability' is most often used as a metaphor, for instance, one is referred to as blind or dead(though he is not literally so) if he ignores the prominent injustices happening around him. In theology, disability is seen as a result of either God's punishment or reward. Disability as representation serves a range of functions in narrative films and literature, as AtoQuayson has listed nine such functions, which he termed as "a typology of disability" are disability as a null set/ or moral test, disability as the interface with otherness, disability as an articulation of disjuncture between thematic and narrative vectors, disability as moral deficit or evil, disability as an epiphany, disability as signifies of ritual insight, etc. Thus analysis of several representations of disability is very crucial in Disability Studies to perceive how different disabilities are understood throughout the ages and their impacts on disabled people's psyche. It claims a different mode of seeing and interpreting images by breaking out of the existing mode of reading literary representations.

Suggested Readings:

Frontera, Walter R., et al. *DeLisa's physical medicine and rehabilitation: principles and practice*. Lippincott Williams & Wilkins, 2019.

Linker, Beth. *War's waste: rehabilitation in World War I America*. University of Chicago Press, 2019.

Reproduction

The reproduction of physically impaired children has long been a concern for parents and society, prompting various ideologies and practices aimed at preventing their existence. In the era of eugenics, which advocated for the improvement of the human race through selective breeding, the prohibition of disabled people from engaging in sexual relationships was seen as a means to prevent future generations from inheriting disabilities. Similarly, Michel Foucault justified the sterilization of disabled people as a way to enhance the overall quality of the human population and protect it from perceived degradation.

The concept of reproduction extends beyond the mere biological act to encompass the life experiences of disabled children and their impact on families and society as a whole. For disabled children, life presents unique challenges that differ significantly from those faced by their non-disabled peers. Their experiences in school, on the playground, and within their own homes are shaped by their disabilities, which influence their psyche and overall well-being.hese experiences highlight the need for greater awareness and understanding of the lived realities of disabled children and their families. Addressing the challenges they face requires not only societal acceptance and support but also policies and practices that promote inclusivity and accommodate their diverse needs. By recognizing and embracing the unique perspectives and contributions of disabled people, society can move towards a more equitable and compassionate future for all. The challenges faced by families with disabled children extend beyond the immediate concerns of caregiving to encompass broader societal attitudes and policies regarding disability. Parents of disabled children often grapple with the emotional and practical complexities of raising a child with unique needs, navigating a landscape that may be ill-equipped to support their family unit adequately.

Scholars and policymakers have raised various questions about the implications of disability within the family unit. One key concern is whether disabled people, as parents, may transmit their condition to future generations, prompting debates about reproductive rights and genetic testing. Additionally, there is interest in understanding how disabled parents navigate the complexities of raising non-disabled children and the potential effects of disabled families on broader societal dynamics.

Historically, there has been a stigma surrounding the reproductive capabilities of disabled people, with some advocating for measures to restrict their ability to marry and reproduce in an effort to prevent the transmission of perceived genetic defects. These attitudes persisted into the late nineteenth and early twentieth centuries, with limited opposition to biased ideas that sought to control the reproduction of disabled people.

Critics of such measures have highlighted several concerns. Firstly, they argue that despite efforts to prevent the birth of disabled children through selective abortion and genetic testing, societal barriers to inclusion and accessibility persist, perpetuating the experience of disability. Secondly, they contend that improving access to societal institutions and public services for disabled people could significantly alleviate the hardships they face and facilitate their integration into mainstream society.

There exists a widespread belief that disability inherently diminishes one's quality of life, contributing to the stigma and discrimination faced by disabled people. However, it is crucial to challenge this notion and instead recognize disability as one of the many characteristics that make up a person's identity. Disability should not be equated with an individual's ability or potential, and parents should be encouraged to embrace their physically impaired child as capable of leading a fulfilling and meaningful life, just like any other non-disabled child.

In the context of Disability Studies, the concept of reproduction extends beyond biological procreation to encompass the perpetuation and reinforcement of disability within society. This includes both physical reproduction, such as the passing on of disabilities genetically, and social and cultural reproduction, which involves the perpetuation of ableist attitudes and practices that marginalize and discriminate against disabled people. By acknowledging the multifaceted nature of reproduction in Disability Studies, scholars and activists seek to challenge and dismantle the systemic barriers and prejudices that contribute to the marginalization of disabled people. This entails promoting social and cultural shifts that prioritize inclusion, accessibility, and the celebration of diverse abilities, ultimately fostering a more equitable and inclusive society for all people, regardless of disability status.

In the realm of Disability Studies, the concept of reproduction encompasses both physical and social/cultural dimensions, shedding light on the intricate mechanisms through which disability is perpetuated and experienced within society. Physical reproduction pertains to the transmission of genetic conditions or disabilities from one generation to the next, highlighting the intergenerational impact of hereditary factors. Conversely, social and cultural reproduction delves into the portrayal and representation of disability in various spheres, including media depictions, societal attitudes, and everyday interactions. Often, these representations reinforce negative stereotypes, contribute to systemic discrimination, and shape perceptions of disability within society.

By examining reproduction within the context of Disability Studies, scholars and activists gain insight into the multifaceted nature of disability and its pervasive influence across different domains of life. This holistic approach allows for a deeper understanding of how disability is experienced, perpetuated, and challenged within various social, cultural, and institutional contexts. Moreover, it underscores the importance of advocating for a more inclusive and accessible society that prioritizes the rights and well-being of disabled people.

Empowering parents of disabled children with knowledge and resources is crucial in fostering an environment where these children can thrive and lead fulfilling lives. Providing support and guidance to parents helps dispel misconceptions and prejudices surrounding disability, reducing the perception of disabled children as burdensome and instead emphasizing their inherent value and potential. Ultimately, promoting informed and supportive parenting practices contributes to the creation of a more inclusive and accepting society for people of all abilities.

The Prenatally and Postnatally Diagnosed Conditions Awareness Act of 2008 stands as a pivotal legislation that upholds the freedom of parents to make informed decisions regarding the upbringing of a child with a disability. It acknowledges the complex considerations parents face, including mental, financial, and physical preparedness, and affirms their right to choose whether to proceed with the pregnancy of a child with a diagnosed disability. This legislation ensures that parents have the autonomy to act according to their personal circumstances and values. In instances where parents may feel unequipped to navigate the challenges associated with raising a disabled child, it is essential that their decisions are respected without judgment or coercion. However, it is crucial to recognize that discouragement from adoption agencies, social service workers, or medical professionals may stem from ingrained biases and misconceptions about disability rather than a genuine assessment of parental capability. Such attitudes can perpetuate stigmatization and undermine the rights of people with disabilities and their families.

The underlying principle of parental choice extends beyond the decision to continue or terminate a pregnancy to encompass the ability of people with disabilities to pursue parenthood if they so desire. Despite prevailing societal norms that may question their capacity for parenthood, people with disabilities should have equal opportunities to raise children and experience the joys and challenges of parenting.Upholding their right to choose parenthood fosters inclusivity and recognizes their inherent value and capabilities as parents.

Suggested Readings:

Fine, Michelle, and Adrienne Asch. "The question of disability: no easy answers for the women's movement." *Reproductive Rights Newsletter* 4.3 (1982): 19-20.

Finger, Anne. "Claiming All of Our Bodies: Reproductive Rights and Disabilities." *Test Tube Women: What Future for Motherhood*, edited by Rita Arditti, Renate Duelli-Klein, and Shelley Minden, Boston: Pandora Press, 1984, pp. 281–297.

Saxton, Marsha. "Born and Unborn: The Implications of Reproductive Technologies for People with Disabilities." *Test-Tube Women: What Future for Motherhood*, edited by Rita Arditti, Renate Duelli-Klein, and Shelley Minden, Boston: Pandora Press, 1984, pp.298–312.

Sex

The intersection of sexuality and disability sheds light on complex dynamics that influence perceptions and experiences of sex among people with disabilities. Despite advancements in societal attitudes, people with disabilities are still often subjected to stereotypes regarding their sexuality, ranging from being perceived as asexual to being viewed as having uncontrollable sexual urges. These misconceptions can lead to feelings of unease, humiliation, and stigmatization, perpetuating negative effects both within "normal" society and among people with disabilities themselves.

Sexuality is deeply intertwined with human identity and social interactions, serving as a fundamental aspect of self-identity and self-esteem. For people with disabilities, navigating sexuality-related challenges may involve grappling with issues of self-perception, societal expectations, and interpersonal relationships. These challenges extend beyond mere physicality and encompass broader dimensions such as interdependence and social integration. Furthermore, sex is commonly understood not only in its biological context but also in its relational and emotional dimensions. It encompasses notions of intimacy, connection, and fulfillment, all of which contribute to holistic understandings of human sexuality. For people with disabilities, navigating these aspects of sex may involve overcoming barriers related to accessibility, communication, and societal attitudes. In addition to addressing physical barriers, promoting sexual health and well-being for people with disabilities requires challenging societal norms and fostering inclusive environments that recognize and respect diverse expressions of sexuality. This involves promoting positive attitudes, providing education and resources, and advocating for policies and practices that uphold the rights and dignity of all people, regardless of ability.

Sexuality has long been entrenched within a gendered framework, perpetuating notions of binary roles where one partner is seen as active (typically male) and the other as passive (typically female). Furthermore, traditional views of sexuality often prioritize procreation over amusement, emphasizing the reproductive aspect of sexual activity. While such beliefs may be considered historical artifacts by some, they continue to influence attitudes and values, even in the most progressive Western cultures. Within the context of disability, the association between sex and reproduction can be particularly harmful. This presumed relationship often leads to misconceptions and stigmatization surrounding the sexual expression of people with disabilities. Despite the atrocities of eugenics movements in the 20th century, discussions around sterilization for people with disabilities persist, reflecting deep-seated societal biases and ableism.

Young people with disabilities frequently encounter barriers to comprehensive sex education, as their needs are often overlooked or marginalized within educational institutions and healthcare systems. Additionally, families, institutions, and group homes may actively work to restrict the sexuality of children and adults with disabilities, further perpetuating feelings of shame, isolation, and denial of autonomy.

These restrictive attitudes and practices not only infringe upon the sexual rights of people with disabilities but also perpetuate harmful stereotypes and reinforce societal prejudices. Addressing these issues requires a multifaceted approach that includes comprehensive sex education, destigmatization of disability and sexuality, and the promotion of inclusive and affirming environments that respect the autonomy and agency of all people, regardless of their abilities. By challenging ingrained beliefs and advocating for systemic change, we can work towards creating a society that values and supports the sexual health and well-being of all people.

In their seminal work *The Sexual Politics of Disability* (1996), Shakespeare, Gillespie-Sells, and Davies provided a platform for people with disabilities to openly discuss their sexual desires and needs, challenging prevailing beliefs of sexual indifference among disabled people. Rather than adhering to societal norms that promote asexual perceptions of disability, the authors advocated for a more inclusive approach to sex education that fosters individual autonomy and exploration.

It is argued that offering comprehensive sex education tailored to the specific needs of people with disabilities would be more beneficial than attempting to suppress or redirect sexual urges into "safe" outlets. Such an approach would empower people to make informed choices about their sexual health and relationships, while also encouraging a positive and affirming attitude towards sexuality. However, despite the importance of addressing the sexual needs of people with disabilities, there persists a condescending attitude towards the sexuality of those with cognitive and developmental disabilities. This attitude stems from societal perceptions that equate disability with a lack of sexual agency or autonomy, perpetuating harmful stereotypes and barriers to sexual expression. Moreover, discussions of impaired sexuality have historically been dominated by the medical model of disability, which views disability primarily as a medical problem to be treated or controlled. This has led to actions such as eugenic sterilization and the implementation of social workers' schemes aimed at regulating the sexual behavior of people with disabilities.

It is important to recognize that people with disabilities may also internalize negative attitudes towards sex, reflecting societal norms and expectations. This underscores the need for comprehensive sex education that addresses not only physical impairments but also the social and psychological aspects of sexuality, promoting a positive and inclusive understanding of sexual health and well-being for all people, regardless of ability. By challenging outdated beliefs and advocating for a more inclusive approach to sexuality, society can work towards creating environments that respect and affirm the sexual rights and autonomy of people with disabilities. The discussion surrounding laws and rights for people with disabilities has often overshadowed more nuanced aspects of their lived experiences, particularly concerning practical, affective, and emotional dimensions. Until recently, topics related to sexuality, self-identity, self-esteem, interdependence, and social connections received limited attention in both academic and activist circles. However, there is a growing recognition of the need for sexual citizenship within disability activism. Although this discourse often restricts sexuality to measurable and categorizable forms, it neglects the diverse and complex ways in which people with disabilities experience and express their sexuality.

Despite advancements in societal attitudes, misconceptions persist regarding the sexuality of people with disabilities, with many still viewed as either asexual or driven by irrational sexual urges. This binary perception overlooks the rich diversity of sexual experiences and desires within the disability community, reinforcing harmful stereotypes and limiting opportunities for self-expression and fulfillment.

The perceived link between sex and reproduction, particularly concerning people with disabilities, has further perpetuated stigmatization and marginalization. Discussions around sex education for young people with disabilities are uncommon, with institutions, group homes, and families often imposing restrictions on sexual expression, denying young people with disabilities the opportunity to explore and understand their sexuality in a safe and supportive environment.

However, the broader discourse on laws and rights for people with disabilities has often overlooked the complexities of sexuality and intimacy, highlighting the need for a more holistic and inclusive approach that addresses the multifaceted dimensions of disability and sexuality. The book's title suggests that addressing sexuality within the context of Disability Studies requires more than simply acknowledging and discussing certain sexual practices, as previously done by feminist and gay liberation movements. Empirical research, such as the extensive study conducted by Nosek et al., (2001) on the sexuality of physically disabled women and Russell Shuttleworth's (2002) examination of male sexuality in cerebral palsy patients highlight both the diversity of sexual experiences among people with disabilities and the barriers that inhibit their sexual expression.

Despite the growing recognition of the importance of addressing sexuality within Disability Studies and rights advocacy, the subject has struggled to gain prominence compared to other more widely acknowledged political and disciplinary concerns. This may be attributed to various factors, including societal taboos surrounding sexuality and disability, as well as the historical marginalization of disabled voices within academic and activist circles. Furthermore, people with physical impairments often hold condescending attitudes toward the sexuality of those with cognitive and developmental disabilities, perpetuating negative stereotypes and inhibiting open discussions about sex within the disability community. As a result, people with disabilities may internalize these negative attitudes, further hindering discussions around sexuality and perpetuating societal stigma.

While the introduction of the social model of disability in the early 1990s was seen as a significant improvement over the pre-existing medical paradigm, the dominating rhetoric concerning laws and rights for people with impairments has often drowned out appropriate assessments of more ambiguous topics, including sexuality. Despite the growing demand for sexual citizenship within activist circles, discussions around sexuality are frequently limited to measurable and categorizable aspects, neglecting the practical, affective, and emotional dimensions of life with a disability.

In recent years, there has been a greater acknowledgment of the need to address the practical, affective, and emotional aspects of life with a handicap, as well as the importance of promoting sexual citizenship and autonomy for people with disabilities. However, there is still much work to be done to ensure that sexuality is fully integrated into Disability Studies and rights advocacy, and that the diverse experiences and needs of people with disabilities are adequately recognized and addressed. According to the Deleuzian perspective articulated by Deleuze and Guattari in their work *A Thousand Plateaus* (1987), bodies are not viewed as complete, unique, or autonomous entities. Instead, they are seen as interconnected components within vast assemblages that encompass human beings, along with various animal and mechanical elements. Within this framework, desire is not limited to sexual activity between autonomous bodies; rather, it extends to the diverse aspects of these assemblages, without fixating on any specific sexual goal or object.

The Deleuzian concept of sexuality for people with disabilities represents a departure from traditional notions, emphasizing a shift away from the negativity of mutual becoming towards the satisfaction of internal urges. Embodiment, according to this perspective, operates within an intracorporeal "plane" that is inclusive and hospitable to disabled people, rather than implying distinct and self-contained creatures. This challenges conventional understandings of disability by recognizing the fluid and interconnected nature of bodily experiences.

In this view, it is less surprising that many disabled people may rely on assistive or prosthetic technologies, as well as the assistance of other human bodies, to facilitate sexual interactions. These technologies and support systems are not seen as external aids but rather as integral components of the embodied experience, enabling people with disabilities to engage in fulfilling and meaningful sexual expression.

Many people within the LGBT community who also have disabilities often identify as non-heterosexual and encounter similar challenges in navigating societal norms and expectations. However, the term "queer" encompasses a broader scope, as it explicitly rejects all forms of normativity, not solely limited to sexual norms.

It is crucial to engage in a process of demystification concerning the cultural and political origins of terms such as "normal," "healthy," and "whole." This involves not only understanding the historical context and power dynamics behind these concepts but also working to destigmatize the conceptual differences they imply. As Serlin (2006) suggests, this dual approach seeks to unveil the underlying ideologies that perpetuate notions of normalcy and health, while also challenging and dismantling the stigma associated with deviations from these norms. By interrogating and deconstructing societal constructs of normalcy and health, people can begin to recognize and embrace the diversity of human experiences and identities, including those related to sexuality and disability. This process of demystification and destigmatization is essential for fostering a more inclusive and affirming society that celebrates the full spectrum of human diversity.

Suggested Readings:

Barry, Kathleen L. *The Prostitution of Sexuality.* NYU Press, 1996.

Shrage, Laurie. *Moral dilemmas of feminism: Prostitution, adultery, and abortion*. Routledge, 2013.

Shakespeare, Tom. *"Disabled sexuality: Toward rights and recognition." Sexuality and disability* 18 (2000): 159-166.

Shakespeare, Tom., et al. *The Sexual Politics of Disability: Untold Desires*. Burns and Oates, 1996.

Silverberg, Cory, and Miriam Kaufman. *The ultimate guide to sex and disability: For all of us who live with disabilities, chronic pain, and illness*. Cleis Press, 2016.

Sipski, Marca L., and Craig J. Alexander. *Sexual function in people with disability and chronic illness: A health professional's guide*. Aspen Publishers, 1997.

Sexuality

The phrases "sexuality", "freakish," "innocent," "normal", and "abnormal" are only a few of the disability-related terms whose histories are intricately entwined with one another. The eighteenth century saw the emergence and growth of systems of observation, supervision, intervention, imprisonment, correction, or "cure" carried out by authorities deemed to have "expert opinion" Michel Foucault stated in *The History of Sexuality* (1978) that by the late nineteenth century, the idea that sexuality was just "repressed" and required "liberation" had become pervasive. The same may be said of "ability" and "disability," which, like "sexuality," appeared as apparently knowable realities in Foucault's *The History of Sexuality*. Both are products of unending debate. Sexuality and ability were positioned as culturally and historically distinct forms of experience as well as cross-temporal and universal components of what it means to be a human being as a result of the formation and naturalisation of these discourses. What subsequently came to be characterised as "able-bodiedness" and "heterosexuality" was favoured and related by the naturalisation of sexuality and ability.

For instance, sexologists and professional psychologists pathologised homosexuality and other perversions by connecting them to various mental and physical disorders or infirmities. Since the 1970s, historians of sexuality have more clearly shown how the processes of incorporating sexuality into discourse developed a binary system of interpreting human sexuality that, in the end, prioritised heterosexuality and devalued homosexuality. These historians include John D'Emilio. In his article "Capitalism and Gay Identity" from 1983, D'Emilio makes the case that when labour started to be linked with a "public" setting away from the family, certain people who met in "homosexual" settings were able to adopt a homosexual or gay identity (bars, clubs, bathhouses). The house was now largely seen as an ideological (private and increasingly "heterosexual" location rather than a place where residents collaborated for survival. According to D'Emilio, a "new species" of humans was identified by Foucault's discourses on homosexuality. Over the course of the late nineteenth century and the beginning of the twentieth century, the state began to govern this new "species" more and more. For example, between 1870 and 1915, institutionalisation rates (removal from private home settings) soared by more than 1500 per cent.

The evolution of "sexuality" in the West has always been implicitly, if not openly, intertwined with disability in its contemporary form. Disabled persons were stigmatised and normalised, much as "homosexuals" in general. As a result, heterosexuality became established as the identity of the dominant, healthy group. The institutionalisation of the "feeble-minded" implies that throughout this time of expanding state control, there was also a strong emphasis on disability regulation and intervention. This connection gives rise to the long-held notion that certain handicapped persons have "excessive" sexual impulses and, consequently, an excessive libido. The commonly recognised (and frequently causally constructed) connection between these two alleged manifestations of pathological excess occasionally involved brutal and irreparably harmful methods of "rehabilitation," such as shock treatment, sterilisation, or castration.

The notion that people with disabilities have excessive sexuality dates back to the early 20th century. It can be found in several cultural contexts, such as freak shows where visitors may be tickled by exhibits that represent both bodily difference and excessive sexuality, and literary representations like William Faulkner's The Sound and the Fury (1929), in which a cognitively disabled character named Benjy is castrated because he is viewed as a threat. The belief that people with disabilities are entirely outside the system of sexuality is an apparently incongruous second way that sexuality and disability intertwined during the 20th century rather than one of pathological excess. People with disabilities are commonly discursively constructed as being unable to have sexual impulses or a sexual identity because of their purported "innocence," People from lower socioeconomic classes or people of colour, like Carrie Buck, were more likely to be perceived as excessive and dangerous than their white, middle-class, and disabled counterparts, so caricatures of race and class were frequently used to draw distinctions between "excessive" and "innocent," A specific handicapped individual (like Benjy from Faulkner's novels) may readily pass from one side to the other, albeit the line between innocent and excessive behaviour was sometimes fairly thin.

Alternative sexual experiences and subjectivities that might exist outside the heterosexual/homosexual dichotomy have been made possible by newer understandings of sexuality and disability. Sometimes being excluded from normality allowed for handicapped joys and ways of knowing that could not be explained by the predominating heterosexual systems. Some sexologists in the middle of the 20th century who worked with and interviewed handicapped women about their bodies and pleasures found forms of closeness, touch, and autoeroticism confusing. Disabled persons consciously engaged with conceptions of excessive, innocent, or alternative sexuality when they started to speak or sign back to the structures that traditionally had controlled them. This occasionally required claiming that persons with disabilities also had "normal" (heterosexual) sexualities, not excessive or unique ones. Additionally, activists promoted "liberation" from "repressive" concepts. Disabled activists worked with and through concepts of disability in order to discover or construct unique (and usually queer) pleasures and sexualities. Many authors, performers, artists, and activists who reflect the possibilities inherent in this third interwoven areas of sexuality and disability have emerged from the disability culture that exploded in the early twenty-first century. They include Mark O'Brien, Loree Erickson, Terry Galloway, Mat Fraser, Eli Clare, Greg Walloch, and Bethany Stevens, an "uppity crip scholar-activist and sexologist," among others. Stevens uses vocabulary that intentionally borrows from the denigrating history of sexology, joining other disabled activists and artists in doing so.

An important turning point in developing this third approach is the article "On Seeing a Sex Surrogate" by Mark O'Brien, which served as the basis for the 2012 film

The Sessions. According to Anne Finger in 1992, "Sexuality is often the source of our deepest oppression; it is also often the source of our deepest pain," For us, talking about being excluded from sexuality and reproduction is more challenging than addressing racism in the workplace, in schools, and housing (9). As the twenty-first century got underway, Finger's assertion—which could be used as a gloss to all three strategies for addressing the hampered history of sexuality—had become well-known and had been extensively discussed in both Disability Studies and rights movements (Siebers 2008b; Mollow and McRuer 2012). Even though sexuality continues to be a "source of oppression" for people with disabilities, it has developed into a very productive area for invention, experimentation, and transformation during the past 20 years. Health and social services frequently disregard the sexuality of persons with impairments. The United States paid much more attention to men's physical health and sexual function post-Vietnam War. The importance of sexuality to both men and women with disabilities is now widely acknowledged.

Physiological issues and sexual function:

Varying disabilities have different effects on sexual responsiveness, while the majority have no impact on sexual functioning. People with sensory pathway disabilities frequently experience difficulties with sexual function. It can be challenging for males to get and keep an erection, and for women, vaginal sensation, lubrication, and orgasm can be uncomfortable.

Physical disability and sexual functioning:

Spinal cord damage is likely to have long-lasting effects on sexual responsiveness. Many men with SCI can erect, although it depends on how severe and comprehensive the damage is. More people are likely to be able to erect themselves if they have partial upper motor neuron injuries. About 45% of people report having orgasms on their own. Due to the frequent occurrence of retrograde ejaculation, ejaculation is less likely than erection. In women with incomplete spinal injuries at all levels, vaginal lubrication may still be present. There is often no psychogenic or reflexogenic lubrication in women with full injuries between T10 and T12 levels. Nearly 50% of men with multiple sclerosis (MS) may ultimately have trouble getting an erection, and lesions of the thoracic spine and autonomic nerves are believed to be the source of this. Along with numbness, spasms, lethargy, and painful erections, MS frequently affects women. People with disabilities who are unable to engage in sexual activities may experience despair and low self-esteem due to their decreased sexual response. In Western society, where there is a great focus on sexual performance, some people may believe they are unsuitable as sexual partners due to their poor sexual functioning.

Intellectual disability and sexual functioning:

Sexual functioning is often not a problem for people with intellectual limitations. There are a few noteworthy cases where genetic aetiology influences the operation of the person's reproductive system and sexual development. Due to their extremely low fertility rate, men with Down Syndrome may need assistance to reproduce children. Men with Prader-Willi Syndrome may develop hypogonadism and cryptorchidism.

While certain disabilities are associated with sexual dysfunction, other obstacles to sexual expression are probably present across the spectrum of impairments. These limitations include physical restrictions such as limited movement, speech difficulty, reliance on others for care, and social prejudices. People with physical limitations are sometimes stereotyped as dependent and helpless. Particularly those with intellectual impairments who are seen to be oversexed and hazardous due to an underlying lack of self-awareness. Or they are said to be asexual, always act like children, and lack adult sexual impulses. The hidden taboo around sexuality and disability draws attention to how seldom the sexual and emotional needs of persons with disabilities are met in popular culture. The eugenics philosophy has harmed and still affects people with disabilities. In the past, there has been a worry that persons with impairments may have disabled children, and it has been thought that this should be prevented. According to Robert Murphy, those who are able-bodied dislike and find handicapped people repugnant. Like any other member of society, people with disabilities are susceptible to sexually transmitted diseases. There is proof that the rate of sexual abuse among people with disabilities is higher than that of the general population. If people are not educated about the hazards and preventive measures, their risk of exposure is increased .

Informational hurdles must be taken into account in sex education and HIV/AIDS education. In all physical limitations, restricted mobility may obstruct sexual expression. Nonheterosexual forms of sexuality may be valued in a more accepting sexual philosophy. It could encourage a more creative and adventurous attitude toward sexual behaviour and expression. Social isolation can restrict a person with a disability's options for social interaction and sex because of overly protective parents and reliance on others for care. Large-scale external forces that affect people's sexualities can be applied to those with impairments. Their sexuality is impacted by the environments they reside in, including institutions, nursing homes, boarding houses, hospitals, and group homes. Sadly, people with intellectual impairments who have lived in community group homes and institutions have noted decreased possibilities for sexual interaction. The ability to experience intimacy and express sexuality is also impacted by more pervasive prejudice against persons with disabilities. College and the workplace are common places for people to establish friends or find relationships, but if a person is removed from either setting, their social life may suffer.

There are some transgender, intersex, gay, lesbian, and bisexual persons with impairments. When they are combined with a handicap, these sexual minorities confront particular difficulties. The investigation of a person's sexuality is made more challenging by reliance on others for care. There may be a concern associated with asking to wear the clothes of their choosing for transgendered persons who need help getting dressed. The widespread belief that people should only be in monogamous relationships impacts the sexualities of persons with disabilities. In order to learn, people with disabilities need to be free to take risks. Thus, they shouldn't be overprotected out of fear of suffering mental or bodily injury. People need a secure environment that allows privacy, personal control, and choice to promote healthy and positive sexuality. According to American handicapped feminist Ann Finger, our deepest oppression is frequently rooted in our sexuality. Relationships between heterosexual, gay, monogamous, and polyamorous people with disabilities are common. They are discovering and imparting practical methods for enhancing sexual satisfaction and self-esteem. By putting disabled people's sexual rights first, we can ensure that most people will experience these success stories as the norm in the future.

Suggested Readings:

McRuer, Robert, and Anna Mollow, eds. *Sex and disability*. Duke University Press, 2012.

Cooper, Elaine, and John Guillebaud. *Sexuality and disability: a guide for everyday practice*. CRC Press, 2017.

Space

Every individual inhabits a unique position within the fabric of society, traversing through life's journey within the confines of physical space. Space serves as the backdrop against which human existence unfolds, shaping and reflecting one's interactions with the world around them. It is within these spatial dimensions that people navigate their daily lives, encountering and engaging with various elements, both tangible and intangible. Paterson and Hughes delineate the concept of "non-impaired carnality," underscoring the idea that spatial environments are predominantly designed with able-bodied people in mind. The infrastructure and layout of spaces often cater to the needs and abilities of those without physical impairments, perpetuating a societal norm that implicitly excludes people with disabilities. This exclusion becomes palpable when people with disabilities encounter barriers to access and participation, serving as a stark reminder of their perceived difference and marginalization within society.

Despite advancements in accessibility awareness, many public spaces continue to present formidable challenges for people with disabilities. Architectural features such as stairs, narrow doorways, and inaccessible restrooms render these spaces virtually inaccessible to wheelchair users and people with mobility impairments. Moreover, the oversight of disability-inclusive design principles in the planning and construction of roads, educational institutions, and government buildings further exacerbates the systemic barriers faced by people with disabilities. The lack of equal access to public spaces not only impedes the physical mobility of people with disabilities but also reinforces social and psychological barriers, perpetuating feelings of exclusion and alienation. The failure to prioritize accessibility reflects a broader societal disregard for the diverse needs and experiences of people with disabilities, underscoring the imperative for systemic change and inclusive design practices. The oversight of accessibility issues within public spaces has persisted largely unchecked for years, leaving the needs and inconveniences of people with disabilities unaddressed. In understanding the dynamics of space, scholars delineate three distinct categories: absolute space, relative space, and relational space, each offering unique insights into the interplay between physical environments and human experience.

Isaac Newton's concept of absolute space characterizes it as devoid of external relations, perpetually uniform and immovable. Within this framework, structures such as buildings and towers serve as tangible manifestations of absolute space, occupying fixed and stable positions within the physical landscape. Absolute space provides a foundational framework for understanding spatial configurations and delineating boundaries within the built environment. Relative space, in contrast, is defined by the spatial positioning of objects in relation to one another. The location of an object within relative space is contingent upon its relationship with surrounding entities, highlighting the contextual nature of spatial perception. Relative space acknowledges the dynamic interplay between objects and their spatial context, emphasizing the importance of spatial relationships in shaping human experience and interaction.

Relational space encompasses the relational dynamics between objects and their spatial environment. Unlike absolute and relative space, relational space transcends mere physical positioning, focusing instead on the symbiotic relationships that define spatial existence. In relational space, the absence of relational connections between objects can render space devoid of meaning or significance, underscoring the intrinsic link between spatial relationships and human existence.

Space, in its various manifestations, serves as the backdrop for human existence, providing the canvas upon which life unfolds. It is within the confines of space that people occupy physical presence and interact with their surroundings, shaping and being shaped by the spatial context in which they exist. From the tangible structures of absolute space to the dynamic interplay of relational connections, space plays a fundamental role in shaping human perception, experience, and interaction with the world.

The human body's relationship with space is inherently intertwined with societal norms and perceptions, shaping the lived experiences of people, particularly those with physical deformities. Historically, the physically deformed body has been relegated to the margins of society, deemed incongruent, repulsive, and aberrant. Without designated spaces tailored to accommodate their needs, intellectually deficient people often found themselves confined to institutions such as asylums, hospitals, and prisons, perpetuating their exclusion from mainstream societal spaces.

These designated spaces not only reinforce the segregation between disabled and abled populations but also serve to normalize the marginalization of bodily differences. Michel de Certeau's conception of space as a "practiced place" elucidates how societal norms dictate the use and perception of space, effectively rendering physically deformed bodies as insignificant and unworthy. This normalization of bodily seclusion exacerbates the obstacles faced by disabled people in pursuing their life goals, amplifying the impact of disability on their daily lives.

The design of physical space and the objects within it wield significant influence over people's experiences and opportunities. The neglect of disabled people' needs and unequal treatment underscores broader issues of social injustice and unequal access, hindering their mobility and impeding their progress. By acknowledging and addressing these disparities, society can work towards creating more inclusive and equitable environments that afford all people the opportunity to thrive and participate fully in societal life.

In the narrative of modern disability history, the pursuit of spatial equality stands as a pivotal battleground against social injustices ingrained in the production of space. Disability rights organizations, epitomized by the American Disabled for Accessible Public Transit (ADAPT), have spearheaded campaigns advocating for spatial accommodations to alleviate the challenges faced by wheelchair users. A notable example of such advocacy is the push for bus lifts, which enable wheelchair users to access public transportation with greater ease and autonomy. Similarly, in the United Kingdom, visually impaired people have mobilized to challenge urban design practices that fail to prioritize their safety and accessibility. Protest movements have emerged to condemn the absence of designated spaces for visually impaired pedestrians, compelling them to navigate shared spaces alongside motor vehicles and other pedestrians. This lack of spatial consideration not only undermines the safety and independence of visually impaired people but also reinforces their marginalization within public spaces.

For Disability Studies scholars, these spatial injustices are emblematic of broader societal attitudes and structures that perpetuate the exclusion of disabled people. By addressing spatial inequalities and advocating for inclusive design practices, Disability Studies scholars aim to facilitate the integration of disabled minorities into mainstream society and foster environments that enable them to lead fulfilling and dignified lives. This intersectional approach recognizes the interconnectedness of spatial arrangements, social dynamics, and individual experiences, emphasizing the importance of collective action in dismantling barriers and advancing disability rights and accessibility.

Suggested Readings:

Titchkosky, Tanya. *The question of access: Disability, space, meaning.* University of Toronto Press, 2011.

Harvey, David. *David Harvey: A critical reader.* Blackwell Pub, 2006.

Imrie, Rob. "Auto-disabilities: The case of shared space environments." *Environment and Planning A* 44.9 (2012): 2260-2277.

Stigma

Stigma represents the collective negative perceptions, biases, and stereotypes harbored by society towards people with disabilities. These ingrained attitudes can materialize as overt discrimination, subtle prejudice, and systemic marginalization, profoundly impacting the lives of disabled people across various domains, including education, employment, healthcare, and social engagement. The ramifications of stigma extend beyond societal barriers, permeating the internal landscape of people with disabilities, shaping their self-perception, and influencing their sense of self-worth and belonging. The pervasive nature of stigma can erode the self-esteem and confidence of disabled people, compelling them to internalize the degrading narratives and limiting beliefs imposed upon them by societal norms. Consequently, feelings of shame, guilt, and social isolation often plague disabled people, exacerbating their struggle for acceptance and inclusion in society. Disability Studies scholars underscore the imperative of dismantling stigma as a fundamental step towards fostering social justice and enhancing the quality of life for people with disabilities.

Addressing stigma entails a multifaceted approach that encompasses advocacy, policy reform, and public awareness initiatives. Disability rights advocates advocate for the implementation of inclusive policies and practices that prioritize accessibility, accommodation, and equal opportunities for people with disabilities in all spheres of life. Moreover, educational campaigns and awareness-raising efforts play a pivotal role in challenging negative stereotypes and dispelling misconceptions surrounding disability. By confronting and challenging stigma, society can move towards a more equitable and inclusive future, where people with disabilities are afforded the dignity, respect, and opportunities they deserve. This collective effort towards destigmatization holds the promise of creating a more compassionate and accepting society, where all people can thrive regardless of their physical or cognitive abilities.

Stigma operates as a powerful force that categorizes and ostracizes people with physical impairments, relegating them to the margins of society and perpetuating a pervasive sense of otherness. This societal branding, fueled by negative perceptions and stereotypes, erects barriers that hinder the full participation of disabled people in various aspects of life, including access to essential services and opportunities. Originating from the Greek term for "pricking" or "puncturing," stigma inflicts a metaphorical wound upon the social fabric, leaving those labeled with disabilities vulnerable to discrimination and exclusion.

Historically, stigma has been intertwined with notions of race, color, and moral standing, as evidenced by the dehumanizing treatment endured by enslaved people during the nineteenth century. However, within certain religious contexts, such as Christianity, stigma has been imbued with paradoxical connotations, representing both suffering and divine grace. The bleeding wounds of saints, revered as stigmata, were interpreted as manifestations of spiritual connection with Christ, offering a stark contrast to the prevailing societal stigma.

In the modern era, stigma has evolved into a collective phenomenon, transcending individual characteristics to encompass a broader array of perceived differences, including physical and cognitive disabilities, unconventional sexual orientations, and menial socio-economic status. This shift is underscored by the emergence of eugenics and population control movements, which pathologized and marginalized certain groups based on their perceived inferiority. As stigma continues to shape societal attitudes and behaviors, efforts to combat its pernicious effects remain imperative. By challenging stereotypes, advocating for inclusive policies, and promoting empathy and understanding, society can work towards dismantling the barriers imposed by stigma and fostering a more equitable and compassionate world for people with disabilities. Disability Studies scholars critique the pervasive reliance on statistics as a means of delineating between the norm and the deviant within society. This emphasis on achieving a "normal" human stature has created a rigid essentialism that marginalizes and stigmatizes bodies that diverge from this idealized standard. In this framework, deviations from the norm are often viewed as abnormal and unacceptable, perpetuating a cycle of discrimination and abuse against those with atypical bodies.

Drawing on the insights of French sociologist Emile Durkheim, Disability Studies scholars argue that deviance is an inherent feature of any society, serving as a catalyst for change and innovation. Even revered figures such as saints are not exempt from being labeled as deviant within certain social contexts. Deviance thus plays a crucial role in the process of categorizing human bodies according to their perceived degree of normativity.

Legislation such as the Americans with Disabilities Act (1990) acknowledges the role of stigma in determining who is eligible to access facilities and benefits within society. However, Disability Studies scholars caution that stigma itself is inherently disabling, exerting a profound psychological impact that erodes people' self-esteem and reinforces society's perception of them as inferior or "other." This insidious influence of stigma can profoundly shape people' experiences and opportunities, perpetuating inequalities and hindering their full participation in social life.

Erving Goffman's seminal work *Notes on the Management of Spoiled Identity* (1963) introduced the groundbreaking concept of stigma, shedding light on the subtle yet pervasive processes through which it operates in society's collective consciousness. Goffman delineates stigma as the consequence of people failing to meet societal norms and expectations, whether in terms of behavior or physical appearance, leading to their oppression and social exclusion. He underscores the significance of how society perceives and treats these deviant people, prioritizing societal reactions over the nature or cause of their deviance.

Goffman, along with Durkheim, views stigma as a relative concept that emerges within internal communities as a result of unequal power dynamics, rather than an absolute, static term. Normativity, according to their perspective, is not fixed but varies across cultures and societies. However, Goffman's portrayal of stigmatized people tends to cast them in a negative light, depicting them as weak and incapable. He identifies three categories of stigma: physical deformities ("abominations of the body"), moral transgressions (such as homosexuality, categorized as "blemishes of individual character"), and affiliations with marginalized groups based on race, nationality, or religion ("tribal stigma").

Goffman's focus primarily lies on the plight of people who deviate from societal norms, rather than on oppressed groups marginalized due to their origins or nationality. He places particular emphasis on moral deficiencies and how they stigmatize people. Goffman's central concern is the internalization of negative self-perceptions by stigmatized people, leading them to perceive themselves as inferior without questioning prevailing societal norms.

Lennard J. Davis builds upon Goffman's framework by highlighting the significance of physical appearance in constructing the disabled body. He emphasizes how society assigns stigma based on outward appearances, further contributing to the marginalization and exclusion of people with disabilities. Rosemarie Garland Thomson delves into the intricate power dynamics between the "starer" and the "staree," highlighting the complex relationship and the imbalance of power inherent in the act of staring. The act of staring reduces people with prominent deformities to objects of gaze, often categorizing them as "freaks" and stripping them of agency over their own bodies. While visible abnormalities are often associated with stigma, Thomson also emphasizes that invisible disabilities hold the same potential for stigmatization. Stigmatized people frequently feel compelled to conform to societal norms and present themselves as "normal" to avoid social shame and discrimination. However, this pressure to assimilate can have detrimental effects on their well-being.

Tobin Siebers explores the concept of "disability as masquerade," wherein people with disabilities may strategically portray or conceal their disability based on convenience, particularly to access basic necessities. This underscores the complex interplay between disability, identity, and social expectations. Stigma, in essence, is closely intertwined with societal norms and serves as a tool for categorizing people as either "normal" or "deviant" based on established social standards.

Disability Studies scholars advocate for recognizing and addressing the negative repercussions of stigma and emphasize the importance of ethical treatment and inclusivity towards people with disabilities. By challenging societal norms and fostering understanding and acceptance, they aim to create a more equitable and compassionate society for all people, regardless of ability or appearance.

Suggested Readings:

Goffman, Erving. Stigma: Notes on the Management of Spoiled Identity. New York: Simon and Schuster, 1963.

Phelan, Jo C. "Geneticization of Deviant Behavior and Consequences for Stigma: The Case of Mental Illness." *Journal of Health and Social Behavior*, vol. 46, no. 4, SAGE Publishing, Dec. 2005, pp. 307–22. https://doi.org/10.1177/002214650504600401.

Technology

Technology, despite facing criticism and controversy throughout history, has undeniably been a driving force behind the advancement of modern society. While figures like William Blake have condemned technology for its perceived role in eroding human innocence, its transformative impact on humanity and the environment cannot be overlooked. Technology encompasses the utilization of mechanical devices and engineered tools to achieve various objectives. Biotechnology, closely related to technology, harnesses biological systems, living organisms, and genetics to develop modified products, further contributing to human progress.

According to Stephen Kline, technology is characterized as a combination of hardware and human effort aimed at accomplishing goals beyond individual capacity. However, within Disability Studies, the concept of technology takes on additional nuances. Scholars in this field distinguish between impairment and disability, viewing impairment as existing bodily deformities or cognitive deficiencies that do not inherently render people disabled. Instead, it is societal attitudes and architectural barriers that create disabling environments, hindering the full participation and fulfillment of disabled people.

In this context, technology serves as a boon, offering assistive devices and solutions to enhance the lives of disabled people and mitigate the negative impact of their impairments. These technologies range from mobility aids like wheelchairs and prosthetics to communication devices and sensory aids, empowering disabled people to navigate their environments more independently and participate more fully in society. Thus, technology plays a crucial role in fostering inclusivity and accessibility for people with disabilities, enabling them to lead more fulfilling lives despite physical or cognitive challenges. The social model of disability places the responsibility on society for its failure to provide equal access to technological systems, thereby marginalizing disabled people and excluding them from full participation in mainstream society. Technology, with its capacity to enhance human abilities, holds particular promise for the disabled population, offering innovative solutions to overcome physical and cognitive barriers. Scholars argue that technological advancements are necessary to compensate for human limitations, as human capacity alone may not suffice to achieve remarkable feats. However, the widespread adoption of technology has also led to concerns about its potential negative impacts, such as increased unemployment due to automation. Tobin Siebers highlights how communication practices and modes are fundamentally altered for people with sensory disabilities, emphasizing that the disabled body reshapes the process of representation itself. For example, deaf people may rely on heightened visual acuity, while blind people may develop heightened senses of touch.

The exclusion of disabled people from mainstream society has spurred technological innovations aimed at fostering inclusion and accessibility. For instance, blind students can now access educational materials through audiobooks and text-to-speech scanning machines, enabling them to continue their studies more independently. However, it is essential to recognize the dual nature of technology, as it can both enable and disable people. While technology offers numerous benefits, such as cost-effectiveness, time-saving, and improved accuracy, its widespread adoption can also lead to job displacement and exacerbate socioeconomic inequalities. Thus, while technology holds tremendous potential to enhance the lives of disabled people, it is crucial to address its broader societal implications and ensure that technological advancements promote inclusivity and equity for all. Postmodern theorists caution against the potentially detrimental impacts of digital and networked technology on human embodiment and perception. According to Paul Virilio, the proliferation of computers and other technical devices risks transforming humans into mechanical entities, leading to solitary lives detached from reality. This technological immersion can result in a sense of detachment from physical reality, effectively "handicapping" people by limiting their movements and social interactions.

The duality of technology, described as a "double logic," offers both benefits and drawbacks to humanity. While technological advancements have the potential to enhance various aspects of human life, they also introduce new challenges and risks, particularly concerning issues of embodiment and socialization.

Disability Studies scholars critique the representation of disability in science and technology studies (STS) and media, accusing them of using disability as a metaphor or trope in discussions of cyborgs, prostheses, and posthumanism. This use of disability as a metaphor oversimplifies the complex experiences of disabled people and perpetuates stereotypes and misconceptions. Moreover, the representation of disability in literary and media culture encompasses multifaceted aspects aimed at challenging traditional notions of embodiment and perception. By interrogating societal norms and conventions regarding bodies, these representations seek to disrupt established power dynamics and promote inclusivity and diversity. Alison Kafer advocates for a disability consciousness that acknowledges the intersecting experiences of disabled people with cyborgs, highlighting both the potential benefits and catastrophes that technological advancements may bring for the disabled population. This perspective challenges the notion that the interaction between humans and machines always yields positive outcomes, recognizing the complexities and nuances involved, including issues such as global unemployment resulting from increased technology usage.

Media activists and disability scholars critically examine the visual representation of disabled people in films and media, emphasizing the role of visual rhetoric in shaping societal perceptions and attitudes towards disability. These representations are subject to subversion and reinterpretation, offering opportunities to challenge and disrupt prevailing stereotypes and stigmas.

The term "assistive technology," credited to John M. Williams in 1982, gained prominence in response to the devastating consequences of world wars, particularly in addressing the needs of disabled people. Assistive technology devices encompass a wide range of tools and appliances created or modified using technology to enable disabled people to lead fulfilling lives by overcoming physical limitations and accessing social opportunities.

However, Katherine Ott questions the use of the term "assistive technology device," arguing that it unnecessarily singles out certain devices for disabled people when all technical devices are ultimately created to fulfill human needs and enhance human capabilities. This labeling contributes to the further stigmatization of disability by implying a segregation between assistive and non-assistive technologies, reinforcing the notion of disability as an inherently negative characteristic.Richard Ladner critiques the term "assistive technology" for its implication that disabled people inherently lack independence and require assistance to function properly, perpetuating the stereotype of disabled people as dependent beings. This focus on technological solutions overlooks the broader social issues such as architectural barriers, negative stereotypes, and discriminatory attitudes that hinder the full participation of disabled people in society. Similarly, "adaptive technology" specifically refers to machinery designed for disabled people, particularly in the realm of computers. While these devices claim to promote independence for disabled people, they simultaneously foster dependence on technology and biomedicine. The complex designs of adaptive technologies may offer solutions to specific challenges faced by disabled people, but they also reinforce the narrative of disability as a problem to be fixed through technological intervention.

Biomedical technologies, which promise to alleviate disability and enhance functioning, can further marginalize disabled people by emphasizing the need for medicalization and technological intervention. By framing disability as a condition that requires treatment and correction, biomedical technologies contribute to the stigmatization of disability and reinforce societal norms regarding physical and cognitive abilities.Assistive and adaptive technologies, while invaluable for people with visible disabilities, also highlight and potentially stigmatize invisible disabilities that might otherwise go unnoticed, such as hearing impairment or speech deficiencies. By emphasizing the need for technological aids, they reinforce societal norms of normalcy and functionality. Martha Scheres delves into the complexity of the term "use," noting that the decision to utilize an assistive device is deeply personal and varies from individual to individual. Despite their widespread adoption in contemporary society, there are significant rates of abandonment of these devices. Sally Watt has categorized four types of users who resist using such devices, whether due to personal choice or the inaccessibility of the aids themselves.

In recent years, Disability Studies scholars have shifted their focus to terminologies surrounding the use of assistive devices. They advocate for terminology that promotes autonomy and agency, preferring terms like "wheelchair user" over "wheelchair-bound." This linguistic shift emphasizes the individual's ability to make choices and lead an independent life, rather than being defined solely by their reliance on assistive technology.

Suggested Readings:

Ladner, Richard. "Accessible Technology and Models of Disability." *Design and Use of Assistive Technology: Social, Technical, Ethical, and Economic Challenges*, edited by Meeko Mitsuko K. Oishi, Ian M. Mitchell, and H. F. Machiel Van der Loos, New York: Springer, 2010, pp. 25–33.

Scherer, Marcia. "The Change in Emphasis from People to Person: Introduction to the Special Issue on Assistive Technology." *Disability and Rehabilitation*, vol. 24, 2002, pp. 1–4.

Values

"Value" encompasses the intrinsic significance or merit attributed to specific principles, deeds, or attributes within our lives. It encompasses the process of discerning what is deemed beneficial or commendable, and what ought to be upheld in ethical deliberations. In the realm of morality, values are akin to foundational convictions or guiding precepts that inform our assessments of right and wrong, virtuous and reprehensible. They constitute the bedrock of moral reasoning, furnishing a framework for navigating ethical dilemmas. Values aid in gauging the moral import or significance of diverse actions, conducts, or consequences. They serve as benchmarks against which ethical choices are weighed and calibrated. Ultimately, value is a subjective construct, susceptible to variance across people, cultures, and societies. People may espouse divergent values and accord disparate moral considerations significance contingent upon their beliefs, cultural heritage, and life experiences. Thus, the landscape of values is dynamic and multifaceted, reflecting the complex interplay of individual and collective perspectives on morality and ethics.

Values play a pivotal role in shaping the treatment and perception of disabled people within society, as they underpin societal norms, attitudes, and behaviors towards those with disabilities. The manner in which disabled people are regarded and accommodated is contingent upon various factors, including the age at which their disability manifests, the underlying cause of their limitations, the visibility of their disability, and the extent to which it impacts their mobility and daily functioning.

Society's values are intricately intertwined with its treatment of disabled people, as societal norms and attitudes towards disability are often reflective of broader cultural values and beliefs. The adoption of inclusive measures and political initiatives by society can substantially impact the lives of disabled people, fostering greater accessibility, acceptance, and inclusion. The timing of disability onset also significantly influences the experience of people grappling with disabilities. Those who acquire disabilities later in life may grapple more acutely with the loss of physical mobility and independence, which can sometimes precipitate challenges to one's sense of self and identity. Conversely, people who experience disability during adolescence may undergo a process of adaptation and resilience-building, as they endeavor to navigate the obstacles posed by their disability. Disability can profoundly impact one's ability to fulfill social and familial roles, potentially leading to feelings of depression and inferiority. The formation of values, including moral principles, is often most influential during childhood, yet discussions about disability within families may be avoided, contributing to the stigmatization and exclusion of disabled people.

Parents' reluctance to address disability with their typically developing children can perpetuate negative attitudes towards disability, as disabled people may be viewed as undesirable or grotesque by their peers. This social ostracization can exacerbate the challenges faced by disabled children, as they may struggle to find acceptance and inclusion in social settings. While disability experienced during childhood may not initially elicit emotional distress for the affected child, as they mature, they may become increasingly aware of their differences and the discrimination they encounter. Moreover, the visibility of disability plays a significant role in how people are treated within society. Those with visible impairments often face heightened discrimination and social exclusion compared to people with invisible disabilities, as their differences are readily apparent and may attract negative attention and prejudice.People with invisible disabilities can indeed face discrimination and neglect from society due to the lack of apparent impairment. Without visible signs of disability, they may not receive the accommodations and support typically afforded to those with visible impairments. The value attributed to disability is highly dependent on various factors such as cultural norms, economic conditions, political climate, and social attitudes. These factors collectively shape how disability is perceived and treated within a given society.

Culture plays a significant role in determining the value assigned to disability and how people with disabilities are labeled and treated by the majority. Language also plays a crucial role in shaping discussions surrounding disability, as terminologies such as impairment, disability, and handicap carry distinct meanings and implications. According to the World Health Organization, impairment refers to a physical defect or intellectual deficiency that limits an individual's functional abilities and hinders their pursuit of life goals and societal opportunities. In contrast, disability encompasses the societal attitudes and barriers faced by people with impairments. It reflects the social conditions that fail to provide necessary accommodations and accessibility, thereby inhibiting the full participation of disabled people in society. This distinction underscores the importance of addressing not only the physical limitations of disability but also the societal factors that contribute to marginalization and exclusion. By fostering a more inclusive and accommodating environment, societies can strive towards eliminating barriers and promoting equal opportunities for people with disabilities, whether visible or invisible. Disability Studies scholars challenge the notion of disability as an individual burden or personal tragedy, instead viewing it as a social construct shaped by stigma and societal norms. According to this perspective, disability arises from the prejudices and biases directed towards people who deviate from society's accepted norms and standards. As a response to this understanding, the concept of Universal Design emerges, advocating for architectural modifications to create environments that are accessible to people of all abilities. This approach emphasizes the need for environmental change rather than expecting people to adapt to existing structures.

Language also plays a crucial role in shaping perceptions of disability and identity. Disability activists and scholars highlight the importance of using inclusive and respectful terminology when referring to disabled people. They argue that language constructs identity and can influence societal attitudes towards disability. The Disability Rights Movement promotes the use of "person-first" language, which prioritizes the individual's identity over their disability. By placing the person before the disability in linguistic terms, this approach emphasizes the autonomy and humanity of people with disabilities.

By adopting "person-first" language, disabled people are recognized as fully autonomous people whose disability is just one aspect of their identity, rather than defining their entire existence. This linguistic shift aims to enhance the value and dignity of disabled people in society, challenging stereotypes and promoting inclusivity. Ultimately, language serves as a powerful tool for driving social change and fostering a more inclusive and equitable society for people of all abilities.

In recent times, there has been a notable shift in the social values attributed to disability, which is evident in the policies and measures implemented by society. Historically, disabled people faced oppression and discrimination, often justified and even legally sanctioned by prevailing ideologies such as Eugenics. The negative values associated with disability within the majority culture perpetuated systemic inequalities and justified exclusionary practices. However, contemporary society has witnessed a significant change in attitudes towards disability, leading to a more positive perception of disabled people. As a result, public policies and measures are increasingly being formulated and implemented to support and accommodate the needs of disabled people. This shift reflects a broader recognition of the rights and dignity of people with disabilities within society.

The transformation in societal values regarding disability has paved the way for more inclusive and equitable policies that prioritize the well-being and empowerment of disabled people. Rather than being marginalized or stigmatized, disabled people are increasingly seen as valuable members of society who deserve equal opportunities and access to resources. This evolution in societal attitudes has led to the implementation of policies aimed at promoting accessibility, inclusion, and social justice for people with disabilities.

Suggested Readings:

Edwards, Steven D. *Disability: Definitions, Value and Identity*. Radcliffe Publishing Ltd, 2005.

Bickenbach, Jerome E., ed. *Disability and the good human life*. Cambridge University Press, 2014.

Violence

Violence, an innate aspect of human nature, has been intertwined with human history as a means to secure or enhance one's future. This propensity towards aggression is not exclusive to humans; even animals exhibit fierce behavior to assert dominance and ensure survival, adhering to the principle of "survival of the fittest." The World Health Organization (WHO) classifies violence into three primary models: self-directed violence, such as suicide; interpersonal violence; and collective violence, which involves large groups perpetrating violence against others to fulfill certain objectives.

The link between violence and disability is multifaceted. People may acquire disabilities as a result of violence, whether through participation in armed conflicts or as victims of street altercations. Additionally, people with disabilities are particularly vulnerable to experiencing violence in their personal lives. They face a higher risk of abuse both within their homes and in the broader community due to societal perceptions of their vulnerability and diminished capacity to defend themselves. In instances where people acquire disabilities due to violence, the consequences extend beyond physical impairment, often encompassing psychological and emotional trauma. Furthermore, the prevalence of violence against people with disabilities highlights the urgent need for comprehensive support systems and protective measures to safeguard their well-being and ensure their full participation in society. There is a prevailing belief in some circles that people with certain types of disabilities, particularly those related to intellectual impairment or cognitive dysfunction, are more prone to exhibiting aggressive behavior. Similarly, people struggling with depression and anxiety are often perceived to be at a heightened risk of suicidal tendencies. The contentious topic of physician-assisted suicide further complicates the discourse, as it involves providing terminally ill patients or those experiencing severe pain with the option to end their lives with medical assistance, ostensibly to relieve their suffering.

War stands out as one of the primary contributors to disability resulting from violence. Throughout history, armed conflicts, particularly large-scale conflicts like world wars, have resulted in countless people sustaining disabling injuries on the battlefield. However, war has also played a significant role in shaping societal attitudes toward people with disabilities. While disability was once viewed as a relatively rare occurrence, the aftermath of major conflicts saw a surge in the number of people living with disabilities. In many cases, veterans who had sacrificed their physical well-being in service to their country were regarded with reverence and admiration, shifting societal perceptions towards people with disabilities from disdain to respect and appreciation for their sacrifices. This evolution in attitudes highlights the transformative impact of war on the collective consciousness regarding disability. In response to the significant number of soldiers returning from war with disabilities, the United States enacted the Soldiers Rehabilitation Act and the Smith Fess Act. These legislative measures aimed to provide crucial support and assistance to the war-affected veterans. Through various provisions and programs, these acts sought to address the rehabilitation needs of soldiers who had sustained injuries or disabilities during their service. By offering access to medical care, vocational training, and other forms of support, these acts played a vital role in helping disabled veterans reintegrate into civilian life and regain a sense of independence and self-sufficiency.

Meanwhile, in third-world countries, political instability and civil unrest have also contributed to the prevalence of disability, often exacerbating the challenges faced by people living with disabilities. In addition to contending with their disabilities, these people often grapple with poverty, inadequate nutrition, and precarious financial circumstances. The lack of access to social services and rehabilitation measures further compounds their difficulties, as they are unable to avail themselves of the support systems and resources that are more readily available in developed countries. This creates a situation where people with disabilities in third-world countries face significant barriers to accessing essential services and opportunities for improvement, perpetuating cycles of marginalization and inequality.

Disabled people, particularly women, elderly persons, and children, are disproportionately subjected to abuse compared to their non-disabled counterparts. This vulnerability stems from various factors that intersect to create a conducive environment for abuse to occur. One significant challenge is that people with severe disabilities may be unable to recognize or comprehend that they are being abused, rendering them unable to report the abuse or seek help. This lack of awareness and communication ability empowers abusers, who may exploit the victim's inability to resist or report the abuse. Moreover, negative stereotypes and stigma surrounding disability contribute to justifying or rationalizing the mistreatment of disabled people. Society often perceives disabled people as inherently vulnerable or inferior, which can perpetuate attitudes that normalize or excuse abusive behavior towards them. Additionally, the nature of a person's disability may pose obstacles to reporting abuse; physical or cognitive impairments may hinder their ability to articulate their experiences or seek assistance effectively.

Furthermore, many disabled people may depend on their abusers for physical care, financial support, or other essential needs, creating a coercive dynamic that deters them from speaking out against mistreatment. This dependency can result in a reluctance to report abuse for fear of losing vital support systems or facing retaliation from the abuser. Inadequate responses to abuse against disabled people also stem from prejudice, ignorance, and institutional shortcomings. Authorities and service providers may lack the necessary training, awareness, or protocols to effectively address cases of abuse involving disabled victims. As a result, incidents of abuse may go unnoticed, unreported, or inadequately investigated, perpetuating cycles of victimization and impunity. Addressing the systemic barriers and biases that contribute to the abuse of disabled people requires comprehensive efforts to promote awareness, accessibility, and inclusivity within society and its institutions.In addition to facing challenges in reporting abuse, disabled people may encounter barriers within the legal system that impede their access to justice. Inaccessible infrastructure, communication barriers, and discriminatory attitudes can all hinder their ability to effectively navigate legal proceedings or communicate their complaints to legal advisors or authorities. This lack of accessibility within the justice system further exacerbates the vulnerability of disabled victims, as their grievances may go unrecognized or dismissed due to systemic barriers.

Furthermore, people with cognitive or psychiatric disabilities often face stigmatization and discrimination from society, with prevailing stereotypes portraying them as inherently dangerous or violent. This perception perpetuates fear and mistrust towards disabled people, particularly those with mental health conditions, and may influence societal responses to their behavior. However, it's essential to recognize that such stereotypes are unfounded and contribute to the marginalization and social exclusion of disabled people. Moreover, people with psychiatric disabilities who do not receive adequate treatment or support may be at a higher risk of engaging in violent behavior. Lack of access to appropriate mental health services, including medication and therapy, can exacerbate symptoms and lead to crises or conflicts that escalate into violence. Conversely, advancements in psychopharmacology and mental health treatment have contributed to reducing the incidence of violence among people with psychiatric disabilities by effectively managing symptoms and promoting stability.

Additionally, disability and violence are intertwined through the issue of suicide. Disabled people, particularly those facing significant physical or mental health challenges, may experience heightened feelings of despair, isolation, or hopelessness, increasing their risk of suicidal ideation or attempts. However, access to appropriate mental health care, supportive services, and community resources can mitigate these risks and provide avenues for support and intervention.

Suggested Readings:

Ternette, Emily. *Not a New Problem: Violence in the Lives of Disabled Women*. Fernwood Publishing, 2020.

Shah, Sonali, and C. Bradbury-Jones. Disability, *Gender and Violence over the Life Course*. Routledge, London, 2018.

Fitzsimons, Nancy M. *Combating violence & abuse of people with disabilities: A call to action*. Brookes Publishing, 2009.

Mason-Bish, Hannah. *"Conceptual issues in the construction of disability hate crime." Disability*, hate crime and violence. Routledge, 2012.

Visuality

The term "visuality" originated with Thomas Carlyle in 1841, referring to the mental process of picturing abstract ideas within one's mind. Hal Foster later expanded on this concept by drawing a distinction between "vision" and "visuality." Vision, according to Foster, pertains to the biological aspect of sight, rooted in human physiology and the functioning of the eyes. Visuality, on the other hand, encompasses the cultural practices and values that shape how people perceive and interpret visual stimuli. This differentiation between vision and visuality finds resonance in the social model of disability, a framework that distinguishes between a person's physical impairment and the societal construct of disability. In this model, impairment refers to the individual's personal bodily limitations, while disability arises from the social barriers and prejudices that restrict the disabled individual's participation and opportunities in society.

Disability Studies scholars have directed their focus towards examining how disabled people are visually depicted in culture and media, recognizing that these representations play a significant role in shaping societal perceptions and attitudes towards disability. These visual representations often emphasize the physical differences or abnormalities of disabled bodies, perpetuating stereotypes and stigmatizing attitudes. At the same time, there is a growing demand within Disability Studies to challenge and counteract these negative portrayals, advocating for more diverse and accurate representations of disability that reflect the lived experiences and capabilities of disabled people.

The scrutiny of visual representations of disability serves not only to critique existing stereotypes but also to advocate for the inclusion and empowerment of disabled people within society. By challenging narrow and stigmatizing depictions of disability, Disability Studies scholars aim to foster greater acceptance, understanding, and respect for disabled people, ultimately contributing to a more inclusive and equitable society.Disabledpeople have historically been objectified and exploited for entertainment, often presented on stage as spectacles to satisfy the curiosity of the public gaze. Laws and public policies have further perpetuated the exclusion of disabled bodies from mainstream visibility, ostensibly to uphold societal propriety and decorum. Although such practices have somewhat diminished over time, disabled people continue to be portrayed through a lens of pity and charity, failing to improve their social standing significantly.

To challenge this objectification, Disability Studies activists have highlighted the issue of social inaccessibility, which hinders disabled people's full participation in societal activities. Despite these efforts, the complexity of visuality becomes apparent as disabled people' needs and demands are frequently overlooked, while their physical differences often make them objects of curiosity or staring in society. This paradox underscores the disconnect between the visibility of disabled bodies and the acknowledgment of their rights and agency.

In examining the concept of blindness, Disability Studies scholars explore the dichotomy between vision and visuality. Blindness is often perceived as the antithesis of sight and light, yet human knowledge and understanding are largely shaped by visual perception. Consequently, people who are blind may face significant challenges in navigating and comprehending the world around them, as their access to information and essential activities is primarily through sight. This raises fundamental questions about how people who are blind or visually impaired can engage with and understand the intricacies of the world in the absence of visual stimuli. Disability Studies scholars have brought attention to the culturally constructed nature of blindness, particularly in the industrialized world, where a person's visual capability is often judged based on their performance in daily activities such as driving or reading. However, many people classified as blind may still retain some degree of vision, allowing them to perform visual tasks either through residual sight or their memory of prior visual experiences. This complexity gives rise to debates surrounding the terminology used to describe different levels of visual impairment.

Some argue that any deviation from the normative standard of visual acuity should be considered blindness, while others advocate for the term "visual impairment" to acknowledge the diverse range of visual experiences. The word "blind" itself is often used metaphorically to denote ignorance or bias, leading some scholars to prefer terms like "visually impaired" to avoid reinforcing negative stereotypes. Moreover, in efforts to provide access to disabled people, priority is often given to those with locomotive disabilities, such as wheelchair users, leading to the neglect of other disabled populations. This emphasis on physical mobility can result in people with other types of disabilities being marginalized or perceived as less disabled. Similarly, people with invisible disabilities face double stigma, as their impairments are not readily apparent and may be viewed with skepticism by others.

Therefore, Disability Studies scholars advocate for a deeper examination of the nuances of visuality and blindness to challenge existing norms and enhance the lives of disabled people. By interrogating societal perceptions and addressing the diverse experiences of disability, they aim to promote greater inclusivity and recognition of the needs of all disabled people.

Suggested Readings:

Wong, Alice, ed. *Disability visibility: First-person stories from the twenty-first century*. Vintage, 2020.

Foster, Hal. *Vision and visuality*. The New Press, (1999).

Black Eagle Books

www.blackeaglebooks.org
info@blackeaglebooks.org

Black Eagle Books, an independent publisher, was founded as a nonprofit organization in April, 2019. It is our mission to connect and engage the Indian diaspora and the world at large with the best of works of world literature published on a collaborative platform, with special emphasis on foregrounding Contemporary Classics and New Writing.